THE DA VINCI FRAUD

THE DA VINCI FRAUD

The True Story of Dan Brown and the
World's Greatest Literary Crime

Jack Dunn & Jonathan Coad

SILVERTAIL BOOKS • *London*

First published in Great Britain by Silvertail Books in 2021
www.silvertailbooks.com
Copyright © Jack Dunn and Jonathan Coad
The right of Jack Dunn and Jonathan Coad to be identified as the author
of this work has been asserted in accordance
with the Copyright, Design and Patents Act 1988
A catalogue record of this book is available from the British Library
978-1-913727-11-6

'For there is nothing hidden that will not be disclosed, and nothing concealed that will not be known or brought out into the open.'

Luke 8:17

Contents

Introduction

by Jonathan Coad

This is the extraordinary true story of how a novel written in 1996 was plagiarized to create the best-selling thriller of all time, a book which spawned a series of blockbuster movies and launched the career of one of the world's most successful authors.

That author is Dan Brown, and he began work on his career-defining book, *The Da Vinci Code*, barely three years after publication of a novel called *The Vatican Boys*, which was written by my client Jack Dunn. The two books share an astonishing number of similarities – far too many to be coincidental.

Since then Dan Brown has gone on to sell over 200 million books, including 80 million copies of *The Da Vinci Code*, and is worth around $160 million. He boasts on his website that his 'novels are published in 56 languages around the world with over 200 million copies in print'. His website also brags that in 2005 he was named one of the 100 Most Influential People in the World by *TIME* Magazine, whose editors credited him with 'keeping the publishing industry afloat; renewed interest in Leonardo Da Vinci and early Christian history; spiking tourism to Paris and Rome; a growing membership in secret societies; the ire of Cardinals in Rome; eight books denying the claims of the novel and seven guides to read along with it; a flood of historical thrillers; and a major motion picture franchise.'

But if Jack and I are right, Dan Brown is a charlatan, thief, liar and perjurer who has won court cases on both sides of the Atlantic under false pretences; and his publishers, Penguin Random House, have colluded with him and tried to prevent this book being published, despite having been provided with overwhelming evidence that Dan Brown is just as we characterise him.

This book – Jack and my blowing of the whistle on both of them – is called *The Da Vinci Fraud*, not because Dan Brown has committed a criminal offence of dishonesty, but because for all the reasons we record in this book I am certain that he has passed off my client's work as his own, just as his ex-wife Blythe claims he did with her work in her sworn evidence in their acrimonious divorce. I have acted for creatives for thirty years, and in my book stealing the work of a fellow author is a crime which any ethical publisher should call out rather than cover up.

We are not the only ones to make such allegations against Dan Brown and his publishers. In 2005 Michael Baigent and Richard Leigh filed suit in the High Court in London against Brown's publishers (who were also their own). They alleged that Dan Brown copied, to quote their lawyers, 'a substantial part of [their] work to produce an altered copy or a colourable imitation,' of their book *The Holy Blood and the Holy Grail*, thereby violating their copyright, which pretty well sums up Jack's claim.

They lost their case. But the judge did find that both copying and plagiarism had taken place, and consequently that Dan Brown's denial of this on oath was false. Dan Brown made no mention of *The Vatican Boys* in his evidence as being a key source, so if he did plagiarize that book in writing *The Da Vinci Code*, then he misled the court. None of this appears to matter to Penguin Random House whose support for him is unwavering and aggressive.

That same year Jack hired US attorneys and mounted his own well-founded copyright claim against Dan Brown and his publishers which he was confident that he would win based on the law and the facts. His cogent written evidence should leave any objective reader in no doubt of the rightness of his cause. But Jack was denied a jury and defeated by the brutal deployment of resources that were far greater than his. Firstly, by means of written submissions which were errant and misleading, and which included a denial by Dan Brown that he had even heard of *The Vatican Boys* before writing *The Da Vinci Code*; and secondly, a judge who refused to hear his oral submissions, and appears to have lacked the moral courage to make a finding against a mega-star author, a powerful publishing empire, and an entertainment giant (Sony Pictures). His judgment, as we will show, is replete with errors of law and fact.

Jack was then threatened by Dan Brown and his publishers with a huge costs order which they knew he could not afford if he did not sign away his right to appeal, which is what he was forced to do. It seems that despite the fact that in the United States the rights of authors to protect their work stem from its Constitution (specifically, Article I, Section 8, Clause 8 which secures 'for limited times to authors and inventors the exclusive right to their respective writings and discoveries'), in practice Jack's rights as an author enjoyed precious little protection in the face of immensely superior forces to his, which is another important issue addressed in this book.

Undeterred, he then instructed me, a London-based media lawyer. I was initially sceptical of what on the face of it appeared to be a thoroughly implausible claim. However, such was the weight of evidence that Jack sent over to me that I took up his cause. I advised him initially that although I too was satisfied that Dan

Brown had plagiarized his book, I was not sufficiently confident that a UK court would side with him in a claim for breach of copyright according to the strict rules that apply here – stricter than those that apply in the US, as I understand them. My advice was at least in part informed by the failure of the Leigh and Baigent claim.

The other problem was that Dan Brown and his publishers were evidently prepared to fight dirty when confronted with copyright claims against them, and could also afford a long legal fight, which Jack could not. That massively greater financial power had already been cynically wielded in the US by Dan Brown and the immense publishing empire that backs him, and I had no doubt the same ugly tactics would also be deployed on my side of the Atlantic.

So Jack decided to set down his story in a book, the one you are reading now, and to explain why he believes, as I do, that far from being an original work, *The Da Vinci Code* is in fact made up of a combination of other people's wayward and implausible historical ideas which Dan Brown took from *The Holy Blood and the Holy Grail*, and that he then spun into a thriller which in most other respects he stole from Jack's book, *The Vatican Boys*.

I have written the introduction to this book, which it has been my privilege to co-author, for a number of reasons. Firstly, because based on the comprehensive evidence that I have both seen and have helped compile, I firmly believe that Jack's cause is just, and that it is important that the world knows the ugly truth about Dan Brown's notorious and controversial book. Secondly, as a lawyer I am better qualified to speak on issues of law and evidence, as I do during the course of this book. Thirdly, because Jack's credibility has repeatedly and wrongly been attacked by attorneys acting for Dan Brown and Penguin Random House, I wanted to stand by him and say that I do not doubt him. Finally, as a signal to Dan Brown and Penguin Random House that if they want to go after Jack and his publisher, Silvertail Books, they are going to have to get through me first.

To be fair to Dan Brown, I must record that he vigorously denies having copied my client's book. He also denies having misled the court in *The Holy Blood and the Holy Grail* trial, and, by implication, also in Jack's US copyright claim. His lawyer has described the allegations made in this book as 'baseless' and 'already … rejected in a court of law'. His wife Blythe, who played a key role in writing *The Da Vinci Code* 'vigorously disagrees' with its content. However, neither has offered any alternative explanation for the myriad of similarities between *The Vatican Boys* and *The Da Vinci Code* to the one we set out in this book, which is that they are the product of plagiarism.

Penguin Random House, Dan Brown's publishers, also rejects the allegations, describing them as 'seriously defamatory' of him. It has said to me in correspondence that the 'allegations are extremely serious, false, defamatory and indefensible and should be withdrawn'. You will find a fuller response from Penguin Random House and Dan Brown in the final chapter of this book.

Penguin Random House has, via its lawyer, also written a series of threatening letters to me aimed at preventing the information which you are about to read from entering the public domain. So much for its claim to 'champion freedom of expression'. The last time I received such a series of letters was when I was legalling out a Sky TV documentary about the Church of Scientology. Penguin Random House has at the same time flatly refused to explain how it is that a book written by one of its authors can have a plethora of

commonalities with one that had been published shortly before it –
other than those commonalities being the product of plagiarism.

Penguin Random House is an immense and powerful publishing
empire which generates annual revenues of more than $4 billion,
but I have advised Jack to ignore all these threats against him – as
I have Silvertail Books, for which I also act – and proceed with the
publication of this book undeterred because of the obvious public
interest which is served by your being free to read its content. I leave
it to you to decide what the truth is; whether in fact the 100 million
plus people who read *The Da Vinci Code* or watched the film are
victims of *The Da Vinci Fraud*.

Jonathan Coad

London

September 2021

Preface

'It all began with a piece of cloth.'

Those are the words I sat down to write in the summer of 1996 that would open my third novel, *The Vatican Boys*, published by a small New England publisher, Modern Memoirs, in 1997. *The Vatican Boys* was a labour of love, and the second novel in which I had used my story formula, where painstakingly-researched historical facts were interwoven with historical fictions of my own creation; all wrapped up in a narrative driven by secrets from the past, codes and ciphers that needed to be de-encrypted, and desperate races against time. All these elements were intended to thrill and also to be faithful to the underlying historical truth in a vivid and authentic way. I had first used that formula in my debut novel back in 1982, and *The Vatican Boys* represented the best work I had done with it.

My book had narrowly missed out on publication by a major New York publishing house, as well as representation by a star literary agent, and so it was independently published, which meant I was not scything my way up the *New York Times* bestsellers list. But that did not bother me too much. I was ploughing my own contented furrow, writing stories on subjects about which I cared deeply, and into which I put my heart and soul. I was immensely proud of *The Vatican Boys*, and spent months visiting every bookstore in New England, hand-selling copies and making great connections with the booksellers there. I would find out later that a certain struggling local author called Dan Brown bought most of the books that he used as research for his novels at these very same stores.

The book did pretty well, and while I was by no means a household name, as a local author I was becoming pretty well-known, and I had *The Vatican Boys* to thank for it. The story the book tells had been percolating in my mind for some time. It was woven around a blood relic held by the Catholic Church to be as old as Christianity itself. It opens with the murder of a middle-aged Freemason who is killed to prevent him revealing a devastating secret that is being suppressed by the highest echelons of the Catholic Church because this secret has the power to contravene its teachings. It involves the shadowy Opus Dei organisation, and a murderous mercenary dispatched by its leader to hunt down the blood relic linked to the death of Jesus Christ. Two Westerners – a smart fortysomething American, a committed bachelor and expert puzzle-solver, and a beautiful thirty-something upper-class Parisian woman who works as a numbers' analyst – combine to compete with the Opus Dei's operatives for the prize, going on a chase through Paris and London which climaxes in London's historic Fleet Street, solving clues and cracking codes to prove who committed the murder and to expose a secret central to the true history of Jesus Christ.

Sounds familiar, doesn't it?

Well, of course it does. Because, as well as being the plot of my novel, it is also the plot of Dan Brown's 2003 mega-bestseller, *The Da Vinci Code*; a book which went on to sell around 80 million copies worldwide, to ignite the career of a struggling novelist and turn him into a world-famous name, and spawn a series of highly profitable Hollywood movies featuring Oscar winner Tom Hanks who unwittingly played the role of a character that I had created for *The Vatican Boys.*

Apart from the issue of originality there are only two differences of substance between Dan Brown's book and mine. The first is that while I believe that mine ultimately upholds truth about the single most significant event in history, the death and resurrection of Jesus Christ, his advocates the opposite by claiming that neither took place and that Christ was not divine.

The second is that the relic which is the centre-piece of Dan Brown's book is the Holy Grail, which is most usually identified as the cup Jesus drank from at the Last Supper and which Joseph of Arimathea used to collect Jesus's blood when He was crucified, while mine is the Turin Shroud, a length of cloth which some claim bears the image of Jesus and was His burial shroud. They are both 'blood' relics – though Dan Brown's lawyers argued before a judge that the Holy Grail was not a relic at all, despite it being described as a relic both in *The Da Vinci Code* and on his website. But guess what? In Dan Brown's original synopsis for his book, which he wrote in January 2001, his 'blood relic' was not the Holy Grail, but – you've guessed it – the Turin Shroud!

Although Mr Brown denies plagiarizing me and has powerful allies fighting his corner, I have spent the last fifteen years trying to have the world recognise that in writing *The Da Vinci Code* Dan Brown lifted wholesale characters, incidents, locations and plot from my novel into his. But the law of copyright has not come to my aid, just as it did not help Richard Leigh and Michael Baigent. The process for proving plagiarism to the point of a successful claim for copyright infringement, even plagiarism as blatant as I believe Dan Brown's to be, is expensive and exacting, and the bar – at least for the likes of me – is set prohibitively high, as Leigh and Baigent learned to their great cost. I believe that the law of copyright, which is supposed to protect the rights of authors, has failed all three of us.

And that is why at 72 years of age – still a writer in love with his work – I have set out my story to the public at large for the first time. Here, in this book, I am telling you and the world what happened to me and my work, and that Dan Brown's fame and fortune has been built on the work of others who have not enjoyed the credit which is due to them, nor the proper fruits of their labour. But the publication of the book you are about to read will be vindication enough for me. Our efforts to tell the true story of how *The Da Vinci Code* was written faced strong opposition from powerful forces, but we overcame them.

As I approach my twilight years I still value the truth as much as I did when I was a young man growing up in the shadow of the Great Depression and World War II, an era when our parents and grand-parents, having suffered through the trials and tribulations of those years, were committed to building better lives for their families and society as a whole. My family raised me to believe that honour, dependability, and honesty were the real measure of a person. The last few years have tested that faith in me. But I want to stand witness to it by means of this book which I believe to be a God-given opportunity for which I must in part thank that rarest of things, a God-fearing and truth-loving lawyer described in one legal directory as being 'an indestructible warrior for his clients', who took it upon himself both to pray for me and fight my cause.

I was brought up as a Catholic with Christian values which I still hold today. My family tried to follow the Ten Commandments. As the children of survivors of the most dreadful conflict the world has ever known, one of good against evil and truth against falsity, we all knew that if you followed them, you would be rewarded. Break them, and trouble would find you. Or as the writer of the Book of Proverbs observed (Proverbs 10.9), 'People with integrity walk safely, but those who follow crooked paths will be exposed.'

I believe that when he wrote his book Dan Brown broke the eighth commandment, 'thou shall not steal', which he did by stumbling upon a little-known author's work and cannibalising it for his own. In doing so he kick-started one of the most successful publishing careers of all time but he based it on the lie that *The Da Vinci Code* is an original literary work. This book is both the 'trouble' that has found him, and the 'exposure' that the Book of Proverbs talks about because in perhaps my final and most important act as a writer, I am revealing the dark secret behind one of the world's best-selling books. That is that it is not an original work at all, or the fruit of Dan Brown's imagination or creativity, or even one which he claims is based on real facts.

What you are about to read is the true account of my search for clues to expose a huge literary scandal which Dan Brown and his publishers have sought to suppress by trying to deter me and my publisher from publishing this book, telling us in a series of threatening letters to my lawyer that it is 'seriously defamatory' of Penguin Random House's golden goose. Fortunately Jonathan, my 'warrior' attorney, has told us both to ignore the threats and written letters back to Dan Brown's lawyers and Penguin Random House which more or less say, 'Go ahead, make my day.'

I will be curious to see if Dan Brown actually sues me for libel over the claims in this book. If he does, all well and good. Jonathan and I are ready for him and I will get another opportunity to prove the truth of my allegations in court, though without having to fulfil the exacting requirements of a copyright claim. If he does not sue, you can draw your own conclusion.

This, then, is the true story of my journey from thriller writer to literary detective. How I became a reluctant litigant, a bête noire to one of the biggest authors and publishers in the world, and was caught up in an international drama of my own which I believe to be worthy of its own non-fiction book.

You will discover in these pages an immense and dark secret which powerful forces deploy brutal mercenaries to keep hidden, along with assorted heroes and villains who lock horns over issues of truth and justice. Like any good thriller it is also an international 'David and Goliath' battle between right and wrong. It even has its own 'Holy Grail'. My story is also in part a legal thriller with elements of *Erin Brockovich* and *Dark Waters*, though in this case justice and vindication come not via a court but by the publication of this book, an event made all the more significant by the attempts made by Dan Brown and his publishers to suppress it.

I ask only that you read our book with an open mind as you consider the possibility that all that you have read about how *The Da Vinci Code* was written is a lie. The applicable US copyright test is whether an 'ordinary observer' would recognise that one copyright work has been copied by another. I hope that as you read this book you will be the 'ordinary observer' and judge for yourself whether we are right or wrong about the origins of Dan Brown's signature book and whether or not we have uncovered *The Da Vinci Fraud*.

Jack Dunn
Chicopee, Massachusetts
September 2021

1

My Writer's Story

It is difficult to pin-point the moment I first dreamed of becoming a writer – but I am certain that like most who go on to pick up a pen it began in those formative years when I was a child and discovering the wonder of books for the first time.

I was born in Holyoke, Massachusetts in 1948. Three years after the end of World War II it was a very different place to the one I know today. My grandfather and grandmother had come to America from Ireland fleeing the devastation of a failed family farm, and when their ship reached New York they were among the thousands who saw signs promoting Holyoke as a bright, new destination where they would build a new life by finding work and having a family.

James Dunn, my father, was their eldest son and grew up to fight in World War II. Like many of his generation, on his return to the United States he was determined to build a good life for his family. He bought a pharmacy that had been serving Holyoke since the 1890s, and my earliest family memories revolve around that store in the heart of the bustling downtown district. My father worked from 6am until 11pm every day to build his business so we did not get to see him much. No matter, because my mother Eileen was an Irish matriarch who looked after her four sons devotedly, making our home in the Elmwood district of the city a sanctuary.

That was until one awful day in 1956 when my youngest brother Billie – only three years old – wandered out into the street and was tragically hit by a speeding car. Billie's death made the front page of all the local newspapers, and has been the front page in the story of my life ever since. I was eight years old, the second eldest of the four boys, and the trauma of that day has never left me. None of us would be the same again.

The loss of a sibling in such terrible circumstances is no easy burden to bear. In a number of ways it came to define my existence. I do not like to draw lines between that event and the writing career I would go on to have, but there is little doubt in my mind that its shadow loomed over me long into my life. Immortality and escapism came to fascinate me and growing up I would picture a world where the turmoil around me was absent and where there was joy for all on God's earth.

Books became portals through which I could experience other times, peoples and worlds. Like most youths growing up in the 1950s and 60s, I devoured classics like *Moby Dick*, fascinated by the chase for the great white whale, man's battle against a noble creature. But it is *Peter Pan* that lingers most vividly in my memory. I was captivated by the possibilities of Neverland and the idea of boys who lived in an eternal childhood, and from those early books the potential of fiction would fascinate me. I still recall how in a graduate philosophy class I was confronted with this exam question: 'Did Pegasus Exist?' I was the only one who said that truly to answer the question we must root ourselves in the mythological world of the Ancient Greeks where winged divine horses could be real. From an early age I knew the power of imagination and this was to play a vital part in my writing career.

The idea which would underpin all my novels was that historical facts and credible fictions could be intermingled to create something rich and original. I came to professional writing relatively late, publishing my first novel in my mid-30s. Before that I had been building a career in the medical supplies business, and as a golfer, which was abandoned when my wife gave birth to our daughter Kim, the shining light and love of my life. This time was also marred by sudden and severe panic attacks. I foolishly took to medicating these with alcohol, a habit that took me lower than I thought possible and which would take many years to break.

I have heard other authors say that writing is the only thing that kept them sane during tumultuous periods in their lives, and perhaps I am fortunate that, in the middle of my own such period – with a young daughter, an increasingly perilous marriage, and reliant on alcohol to battle my demons – I stumbled across the story that would bring me back into the world of books and set me on course to become, in my modest way, a professional author.

I was asked by a man to whom I was delivering a hospital bed, and who turned out to be a fellow Political Science major from college, 'Have you ever heard of the Angel of Hadley?' When I said I hadn't, he began describing a ghostly appearance reported in the 1600s in Hadley, Massachusetts, involving settlers and Native Americans.

'You think I'm a Looney Tune, don't you?' he said, smiling at my reaction.

As politely as I could I told him I didn't believe in ghosts. But the man was sincere and interesting, and when he asked me to stay for coffee, I accepted. Soon he was describing what happened. In 1649 Charles I of England was beheaded by his subjects for his refusal to defer to Parliament. Three of the people who helped bring about his execution – now wanted for the crime of regicide – escaped to what were then the English colonies. My customer suspected that some or all of them ended up in Hadley. According to legend, when in 1675 the town was attacked by Native Americans one of these wanted men, General William Goffe appeared as a ghostly vision to rally the town's defences and lead the counter-attack which saved it, only to disappear into the ether.

As I was leaving my customer said, 'Go down to Forbes Library. On the second-floor landing there's a large painting of a man holding a sword warning the settlers of an impending attack. He's one of them, this Angel of Hadley.'

For some reason – perhaps because of the man's sincerity and enthusiasm – I became hooked on this story, and although I did not know it at the time, this fortuitous meeting would kick-start my writing career.

The idea of writing a novel had been in my mind for some time but this was the first time I would attempt it. Books had been such a large part of my youth, but in the years since life had been filled with so many other things – work, meeting my first wife and building our family – that any ambition I had to set pen to paper had been put on the back burner.

Nevertheless I still devoured novels. My favourite writers ranged from HG Wells to Herman Hesse, from the classics of American literature like Mark Twain, to the classics of Europe, like Leo Tolstoy. I loved writers who dared great flights of imagination like Jules Verne and Edgar Rice Burroughs who wrote before I was born, and others like Arthur C Clarke and Robert Heinlein who led the new wave of science fiction during the 1950s and 60s when I was growing up. These writers expanded my thinking and allowed me to visit new worlds and explore new frontiers.

It would take me two years to research and write my debut novel, *The Diary of General William Goffe* in which I would weave the story of the Angel of Hadley along with everything that had led up to it. But it would not be enough for me just to imagine this story. Part of the joy was merging facts I had researched with credible elements from my imagination to create something new, and, as far as possible, authentic.

It was one of the richest and most creative periods of my life. Most of the information about the killing of the English king and the travels of the three men in the colonies was buried in libraries and archives in Hadley and Springfield, Massachusetts, along with Hartford and New Haven, Connecticut. I dug it all out. This was my first experience of mining such archives and I loved it. While my baby daughter slept I spent countless nights over the next few months sitting at the Smith Corona typewriter on our kitchen table, building my story using the notebooks and news articles I had gleaned. I was learning a new craft and it made me feel vital and alive.

Writing the novel was a thrilling journey of discovery which in some sense is its own reward. The process of publishing it, however, was a journey of an altogether different kind. When I finished the book I sent it to a multitude of publishers in Boston and New York. I got tantalisingly close with some, of whom Little, Brown came closest to giving me a contract. In the end, I narrowly missed out on one of their coveted slots; I was the 'eleventh' choice in a list of ten titles for that year. I had a meeting, too, with one of New York's most feted literary agents, Scott Meredith, and although he ultimately declined to represent me, the opportunity to travel to New York and meet him made me feel I had a chance to break into the big time. Alas, it was not to be, and I decided that I would have to find another way of publishing my book.

In those long-ago days, before Amazon revolutionised what would come to be known as 'self-publishing', there was a plethora of indie publishers who would partner with writers to get their books out into the world. I agreed with a publisher based in Brattleboro, Vermont, the Book Press, that they would edit and produce my manuscript. Soon there were 5,000 copies of *The Diary of William Goffe* waiting to find readers.

I had been a salesman for many years so I took the skills I had acquired into this new arena, walking into every New England bookstore over the next six months, hand-selling the novel to the many booksellers I met – many of whom would go on to become friends. It was a rich and fascinating time in my life. The reviews were good, the books sold, I did book signings at stores and local historical societies, and soon began to receive praise and correspondence from the readers.

The writing bug had bitten. Seeing my book in the hands of readers had energised me in a way like no other, and although I was still battling demons in my private life, with my alcohol abuse unabated and my marriage falling apart, I felt I had taken my first stride toward realising my life's dream. In the following years, as the book continued to sell well locally, I focused on solving my personal problems, committing myself to my daughter, sobriety, and effectively becoming a so-called 'Mister Mom'. It was an enriching, restorative phase of my life.

The ambition to write never left me, however, and in the early

1990s a stroke of good fortune was to push *The Diary of William Goffe* back into the local public consciousness and rekindle the feeling that writing was my calling.

In 1989, Kitty Axelson, an editor from one of our local newspapers, the *Valley Advocate*, contacted me to say she would like to syndicate *The Diary of William Goffe*. The thought had never occurred to me and by then the book was several years old. But Kitty had discovered the novel in her local bookstore and loved it. It was just the kind of boost I needed, and we agreed that she would serialise the novel in weekly installments.

The effect on my fortunes as a writer was remarkable. The paper had a circulation of hundreds of thousands, all the way from Amherst, Massachusetts to New Haven, Connecticut, and suddenly my book was being exposed to more people than ever before. Kitty renamed it 'The Angel of Hadley', which we felt both appealed to the local audience and fed into the apocryphal story. The results were great. Everywhere I went people would stop me and say, 'Great story, Jack', which meant the world to me.

The syndication of my first novel turned my thoughts back to writing. So much had happened in my personal life in the intervening years that the urge to create something new had not yet emerged. But now it did, and I set my sights upon something bolder and more ambitious. That novel, inspired by trips to the Middle East – visiting the holy sites in Bethlehem and Jerusalem – would be *The Vatican Boys*.

It would take me a full six years to write that novel, which was the product of countless hours of research, both in the field and in the library archives, as well as a lifetime of imagination and, of course, my Christian faith. This is from the dedication in *The Vatican Boys*:

'This book is dedicated to everyone in the world who believes and lives according to the teachings of Jesus Christ … who do not condone the activities and religious institutions portrayed in this book.'

I decided it would adhere to the same formula I had devised for *The Diary of William Goffe*; interweaving documentary facts and invented elements to create a tapestry of clues, ciphers, and secrets.

And it would, I believe, come to be stolen wholesale by a fellow struggling writer by the name of Dan Brown, who used my material and that of others to win international fame and fortune, in an apparent attempt to strike at the very foundations of Christianity.

Allow me to show you how it was done.

2

The Vatican Boys

By the time publication day for *The Vatican Boys* arrived it had been fifteen years since my first circuits of the New England bookstores, hand-selling copies of *The Diary of William Goffe*, and seven years since the syndication in the Valley Advocate had revived its fortunes. I decided that *The Vatican Boys* should be published the same way; and, given how great our working relationship had been on *The Diary of William Goffe*, I asked Kitty Axelson to edit it.

In the intervening years Kitty had founded her own publishing firm, Modern Memoirs, which printed a first run of several thousand copies. Soon these were heading out to the same New England bookstores that had championed *The Diary of William Goffe*, including several large Barnes & Noble locations. In 1997 the bookselling landscape was about to be radically changed by what was back then a little-known website called Amazon, and *The Vatican Boys* became one of the first historical novels for sale on its website.

I was still in the business of medical supplies, and spent my time juggling the demands of that job with the joys and challenges of being a single dad to my beautiful daughter Kim. By this time she was old enough to be my sidekick on the many odysseys that would inform *The Vatican Boys*.

I had always loved to travel. It began when I was in high school –

my first ventures were across the United States and Canada and then, after college, in the Caribbean. It was not until I was twenty that I visited Europe, riding trains for six months from one country to another and soaking up the atmosphere and history of the marvellous old world that would one day suffuse my novel. Germany and Austria, Switzerland and the Netherlands, France, Italy and Spain – I wanted to absorb all the diverse cultures, and I became a sponge for local stories.

After devouring Penny Lemoux's book *People of God* I became fascinated by the controversial, but at that time still relatively unknown, Catholic organisation called the Opus Dei, Latin words meaning 'Work of God'. On a trip to London my daughter and I visited the Opus Dei House in the city's Bayswater district. Back then my daughter did not fully understand me when I said, 'I have to document some things here.' But I have never been shy asking for materials and the staff at the Opus Dei House were friendly and willing to provide me with whatever information I asked for, especially about Jose Maria Escrivá, the organisation's founder. I remember knowing even then that the Opus Dei Residence Hall would be a great location in the book I was intending to write. I didn't know it at the time, but it would eventually become the backdrop of the climactic scenes of both *The Vatican Boys* and *The Da Vinci Code*.

But the voyages I went on that most informed the writing of that book came a year later on a solo visit to the Middle East.

I was asked to speak at a medical conference and landed in the Israeli city of Tel Aviv. I had begun piecing together the first movements of *The Vatican Boys* and my extensive research on both the Opus Dei and their links with another secretive organisation, the Freemasons, had been rewarding. This however was my chance to see, feel and breathe the Holy Land, the kind of research I had always thought essential for any writer. And so it was in an old hire car that I went to explore the old city of Jerusalem and its mountainous environs.

The plot of *The Vatican Boys* had been forming in my mind for some time. I knew it would involve the Opus Dei, the Freemasons, and the most holy institutions of the Catholic Church. But I needed to be on location to help me formulate the story so my business trip to the Holy Land could not have come at a better time. I began at the Shrine of the Book in Jerusalem, inspecting the Dead Sea Scrolls. I was fascinated by the way the papyrus scrolls were stored inside glass cylinders to preserve them. When I walked through Jaffa Gate, I was greeted by armed guards who directed me to the entrance of the famous Old City.

Here a young boy led me along the Via Dolorosa (Latin for the 'way of suffering') to the Church of the Holy Sepulchre where the Rock of Golgotha is kept, the site where Jesus was crucified. As I walked that ancient road I remember thinking I could replicate my experience in the novel, and a picture formed of my lead character on this same route searching for a sacred ancient stone. It was a moment that would find its way into *The Vatican Boys*, with a boy giving my lead character a tour of the ancient church. A near identical scene would find its way into *The Da Vinci Code*.

I entered the church and kissed the Rock of Golgotha three times, as is the tradition – just as the Opus Dei assassin Jeremy would do in my novel. Standing there I felt dizzy and drained. Those feelings were normal, a Franciscan brother told me.

After seeing the Tomb of Jesus Christ I saw where a part of the cross on which Jesus died was found, which stirred something deep in me. So did my journey the next morning when I went to Bethlehem to see the place where Christ was born. Later that day I drove to the ancient city of Jericho whose walls were brought down by the Israelite musicians in the Old Testament, and from there I went to the Dead Sea.

That was my last night in the Middle East. But its hypnotic power would remain with me for years to come, and would find its way into the novel which I hoped would define my career. I did not know it would do so in the strangest of ways, and that it would also define another writer's career, catapulting him to stardom and riches.

All of that, however, was for the future. The following morning I climbed into my battered hire car and made the spectacular drive back down the mountain to catch my flight home. With me were notebooks filled with my observations of that history-rich locale, the pictures I had taken, and my memories of having been to the very place where Jesus had lived and died, though according to Dan Brown Jesus died somewhere different. It was one of the most magnificent drives of my life. I had felt something in Jerusalem – and especially in the Old City – that I had not experienced anywhere else. And since I had been there and imbibed its history, I felt I could write about it with the authenticity it deserved.

I was so proud of *The Vatican Boys*. 'Jack Dunn' might not have been a celebrity name, but I was becoming increasingly well-known as a local author. No doubt the advent of online bookselling helped. My local bookstores had been kind to me, as were readers and reviewers, and I sensed a bright future for my writing. I was regularly contacted by readers; and one day in 1999, I took a call that I believe was a turning point in the story I am telling you now.

Back then I spent much of my time flying back and forth to Belfast, Northern Ireland selling medical devices. Ireland was in my ancestry and I hold it dear. But I was always grateful for the opportunity to discuss my novel and when I received this call I was between trips and happy to spend some time chatting about *The Vatican Boys* and the research I had invested in it. As a local author – without the *New York Times* clamouring to interview me – I valued personal connections with readers.

The call came from a man who said his friend was writing a book and that the information about the Freemasons in my novel had intrigued him. He wondered if he might come from Amherst, and visit me the next day.

Early next morning a bearded young man arrived, and over a pot of coffee we discussed *The Vatican Boys* in great detail. I was pleased to meet somebody who knew my novel so well and who was so inquisitive about it. We discussed how I came to write it, all its various structural components, my historical research, including my trips to Jerusalem, Paris and London – as well my extensive research into the Opus Dei, the Freemasons, ancient Knights, and just about everything else that had gone into the rich historical broth from which *The Vatican Boys* emerged. As we talked the young man diligently made notes, filling page after page with all the information he gleaned from our discussion. I gave him an autographed copy of my novel and we said our goodbyes.

Hold onto this moment, because though I never saw nor heard from this man again I believe his visit is a key piece of the puzzle that connects *The Vatican Boys* to *The Da Vinci Code*, which was started just a few months later, was written by an author who attended Amherst College, has the Opus Dei, the Freemasons, and ancient Knights as key components, and which seemed to stem to an extraordinary degree from the same investigative and creative process as my book.

That meeting was in 1999, two years after *The Vatican Boys* was published. *The Da Vinci Code* would not be published until 2003, though according to Dan Brown he had his 'big idea' which led to his writing it only a year after this mysterious man's visit. That means that it would fit into the creative chronology for *The Da Vinci Code*, especially because according to Dan Brown himself, he wrote the synopsis for the book in 2001 and in it the 'relic' of his story was not the Holy Grail but the Turin Shroud – just like in *The Vatican Boys*.

Somehow I missed the fanfare for *The Da Vinci Code*, and it was not until December, 2005 that it exploded onto my radar, a tortuous moment that would upend my life.

It had not been an easy couple of years. I had been through the mill both personally and financially, and had decided to write my way out of these depths, which is what us writers do. My third novel, *Holyoke, the Belle Skinner Legacy*, followed the pattern of my two earlier books, mingling historical facts with flights of fancy. It was about the Skinners, a family of silk merchants who came from my hometown of Holyoke. It recreated a forgotten era in local history, focusing on Belle Skinner, the daughter of the family, who travelled to Europe as a young woman, spent time in France during World War I, and was later said to have unearthed a treasure trove of ancient gold coins.

I researched the novel in the same way as *The Diary of William Goffe* and *The Vatican Boys*, spending time in France and visiting the locations where Belle Skinner's story would be set and soaking up the environs. As Christmas 2005 approached I was ready to publish, again independently, and a December launch date was fixed.

And what a launch it was going to be. The Barnes & Noble bookstore in the Holyoke Mall had long been one of my favourite places, and the team there had championed my writing. On that December evening, as I looked up at the twenty-foot banner which hung from the bookstore's second floor landing displaying the book's front cover, I felt the wind beneath my wings again. This was a novel of which I was inordinately proud, and here was my favourite bookstore shouting about it to all their customers. It was the best of feelings.

But it was also to be one of the strangest and most seismic nights of my life, and one which would ultimately lead me to write this book.

My new novel had been published two weeks previously. To my joy and surprise it had already set sales records at that Barnes & Noble store, selling over 3,000 copies in six days. Tonight I hoped we would sell many more, and by 6pm I had taken my place at a signing table just inside the front door. It was the beginning of the Christmas rush, and book fans were busily buying gifts. A line of hundreds of people snaked away from the desk where I was sitting, going out of the door and into the wintry Holyoke night. It seemed that everyone in Western Massachusetts wanted to get a signed copy of my book.

And then it hit me like a lightning bolt.

'Jack,' said Henry, the store manager, as I worked through the line, 'I'm going to need another 2,500 copies delivered first thing tomorrow morning. I just can't keep it on the shelves!'

Henry had spearheaded my book's success in the store for which

I was very grateful, and I counted him as a friend. I felt I was on the cusp of something wonderful, akin to a rebirth. Little did I know that the next thing Henry would say to me would cleave me apart.

'This guy's from Amherst,' said Henry. I wasn't fully concentrating on what Henry was saying but could see that he was brandishing a book that was not mine. When I focused I saw that it was titled *The Da Vinci Code* and written by an author I had not heard of called Dan Brown.

'You ought to take a look at this, Jack,' Henry said. 'This guy's copied *The Vatican Boys* cover to cover.'

By now, the giddy joy of meeting so many folks in the line eager to read my new novel had cast a spell on me. I hardly heard, let alone understood, what Henry had said.

But Henry pressed his copy of *The Da Vinci Code* into my hands and went on, 'It's your story, Jack, told in your way; your structure, your characters, your concept. Take a look if you can bear it. It's a farce.'

Henry walked away, but I was so fixated on the cover of *The Da Vinci Code* that I did not register at first when the next customer in line said, 'He did copy your book. I'm a fan of your writing, Mr Dunn. I've read this *Da Vinci Code* too. It's bold as day.'

I looked up to see a middle-aged woman holding her copy of *Holyoke, the Belle Skinner Legacy* for me to sign. As I did the customer behind her chipped in, 'They're called "convergences" – any suspicious similarities between your book and his. If he did copy your work, there are potent laws against it.' Alas, as I was to learn to my cost, he was to be proved wrong.

The next few customers, who must have overheard the exchange, were silent about *The Da Vinci Code*, but this was not the last person that night to comment on the 'convergences' between my novel and Dan Brown's. Even now I am haunted by that night; face after face, peering into mine, commenting on the similarities between my work and the bestseller on the desk in front of me; the same words coming out from readers with my autographed novel in hand; 'It's *your* story, Jack.'

After experiencing many of these stinging observations I excused myself and went to find Henry to ask him what he knew.

'It's all between the covers, Jack. Read it and you'll see. You get coincidences in fiction. People stumble upon the same concepts and ideas. But not like this,' he sighed shaking his head. 'He's having a breakout bestseller with it, Jack. Like I said, he's a local New England writer. He used to come here trying to push the science-fiction thrillers he started out writing. They didn't click with readers. But this new book sure has ... and it's all down to your *Vatican Boys*. He's going to set records with it, and they're making it into a movie.' He paused. 'It's my job to read new books in case there are questions in the store. It was like reading *The Vatican Boys* for a second time. The story begins exactly the same: a renowned Mason is murdered because he knows a secret about a holy relic related to the life and death of Jesus Christ that might bring down the Catholic Church. The head of Opus Dei comes in, teams up with this lone mercenary to hunt that holy relic down. There's a smart forty-something American guy, good at solving clues – he teams up with a beautiful French lady who knows why the man was killed. And off they go – on a chase across Paris and London, solving clues and cracking codes to prove who killed the Mason and unearth the secret. Sound familiar?'

Of course it sounded familiar. I had published that story eight years ago.

'It doesn't stop there,' Henry went on. 'There's a scholar who knows all about Christian history, especially the relic, who teams up with the lead characters too. There's even a Knight who owns a private bank where the secret is hidden – just like in your story. The American man and his French sidekick have to figure out a two-digit combination number sequence code and a five-letter password to get into the bank's deposit box. This guy didn't just steal an idea from you. He stole the characters, incidents and the entire structure of your story. Everything is from your book and his story takes place in the exact same sequence.'

If I had been bewildered earlier in the evening, now I was stunned. Henry's description of *The Da Vinci Code* could just well have applied to *The Vatican Boys*. If he was right there was no doubt my novel had been copied.

I had begun the night on a glorious, otherworldly high. Now I was plunged into a mind-numbing low. I hardly remember the rest of the evening as I reeled back to the desk and continued to meet and greet all the readers and well-wishers who had come to get copies of *Holyoke, the Belle Skinner Legacy* signed. I smiled and made small-talk knowing that this ought to have been one of the crowning moments of my writing career. It would have been but for the sickening realisation that my years of research and honing my skills had been lifted without so much as an acknowledgement.

When I left the bookstore I was completely drained. I sat alone in the parking lot until the December night was frozen, thinking how quickly a person's world could change.

I tried to drive home but my hands were shaking on the steering wheel. I hardly knew what to think, and less than that what to do. I felt like I had been hit by a truck.

The book Henry had given me was on the passenger seat. I could not yet bring myself to pick it up, but knew that I would eventually have to do so to confront this nightmare.

3

The Da Vinci Fraud

It was a long, cold, lonely December.

I started reading *The Da Vinci Code* in the Barnes & Noble parking lot but I did not get far. The truth is I did not want to. The apparent theft of my precious work seemed too raw in that moment – as it did every time I picked the book up in the days that followed.

That December was also one of my busiest times as a writer. By Christmas I had done another two weeks of signings for *Holyoke, the Belle Skinner Legacy*, autographing up to four hundred copies at each event, and the effect was that the month was one of dizzying highs and paralysing lows. The thought of so many people devouring my new novel was the stuff of dreams. But between times the realisation that many more – eventually millions – were enjoying the fruits of my labours via a book credited to Dan Brown was too much to bear. It brought me as low as I have ever been.

Nevertheless, I fought my way through *The Da Vinci Code*.

I had to do it piecemeal – at least for that first read. It was too traumatic to read in one sitting because here were characters I had created, situations and mysteries I had developed, codes and ciphers I had crafted for my characters to unpick, and locations that I had visited and studied. This was my whole story rewritten and rephrased. The plots of the two novels were virtually identical, with his slightly modified to reach a conclusion which sought fundamentally to undermine the Christian faith, which mine did not. The clues and codes required to unlock the riddle of *The Da Vinci Code* seemed to have been lifted directly from my book.

Over the next months I set myself to chronicle the litany of ways in which *The Da Vinci Code* mirrored *The Vatican Boys*. The list went on and on.

I want to be clear here about what I am saying. They say ideas are 'ten a penny'. What they mean is that there is no copyright in them. Most stories have been told before. Some theorists, like the great Joseph Campbell, tell us that only a small number of stories exist and that for centuries writers have simply recast and reinterpreted them for different ages. Others, like Christopher Booker, argue there are only seven basic plots; and that every novel, film or television series is an iteration of one already told many times over.

It is also true that certain eras throw up certain types of story, and that artists are drawn to the same subject matter inspired by something in the air which the Germans call 'zeitgeist'. Hollywood will sometimes pump out two such movies in a year, such as in 2017 about Winston Churchill with Brian Cox in 'Churchill' and Gary Oldman in 'Darkest Hour', or two about asteroids in 1998, 'Deep Impact' and 'Armageddon'.

But what I was seeing in the pages of *The Da Vinci Code* was much more than this. I do not believe there could possibly have been anything in the ether that prompted both me and Dan Brown to write stories so closely aligned in concept, characters, locations and – crucially, as I was about to discover – the ordering of near-identical pivotal moments and events which were both original to my book and of considerable obscurity. Two stories, even one written shortly after the publication of the other by authors who in national terms were near neighbours, about the uncovering closely-guarded secrets around the life and death of Jesus Christ which have to do with His blood might have been 'zeitgeist'. But not two books which mirrored each other as precisely as these two did.

So let me tell you something of the conspicuous 'convergences' I discovered in the winter of 2005-6 as I trawled my way innumerable times through *The Da Vinci Code*, trying to stomach the literary fraud I was becoming convinced that I was unearthing.

It starts on the very first page.

The Vatican Boys opens with the ritualistic murder of a prominent Masonic figure, Roberto Calvi; *The Da Vinci Code* opens with the ritualistic murder of a prominent Masonic figure, Jacques Saunière.

In *The Vatican Boys,* a mercenary is dispatched by the head of Opus Dei to retrieve a relic intimately connected via his blood to the death of Jesus Christ; in *The Da Vinci Code*, a mercenary is dispatched by the head of Opus Dei to retrieve a relic intimately connected via his blood to the death of Jesus Christ. As I now know, in its first incarnation, *The Da Vinci Code* even centred its plot on exactly the same relic.

In *The Vatican Boys* a fortysomething American academic named Stephen Hathaway joins forces with Catherine Turrell, a beautiful upper-class Frenchwoman, aged 35, who is good with numbers. Catherine knows the Knight Banker who is holding the novel's core 'secret' in his private bank, having met him at a party at her family's French country estate 10 years ago, while on a break from graduate studies in London. In *The Da Vinci Code*, a fortysomething American academic named Robert Langdon joins forces with Sophie Neveu, a beautiful upper-class Frenchwoman, aged 32, who is good with numbers. Sophie knows the Knight Banker who is holding the novel's core 'secret' in his private bank, having met him at a party at her family's French country estate 10 years ago, while home on a break from graduate studies in England.

In *The Vatican Boys* the account number of the Knight's private bank where the relic is hidden is identified by the first two and last two digits being identical, and the password is a five-letter word, which is connected to a story from Catherine's past. In *The Da Vinci Code*, the account number of the Knight's private bank where the relic is hidden is identified by the first two digits being the product of the last two digits, and the password is a five-letter word, which is connected to a story from Sophie's past.

In *The Vatican Boys* the potential significance of a relic – revealed to be the Turin Shroud – is to prove that the cloth which was said to have been wrapped around Christ when He was taken down from the cross and which is stained with His blood, must be a fake, which is also potentially explosive evidence that a fundamental element of the teachings of the Catholic Church is incorrect. In *The Da Vinci Code*, the significance of a relic – revealed to be the Holy Grail (originally the Turin Shroud), which the book claims is Christ's earthly bloodline – is to prove that Christ was not dead when He was taken down from the Cross, explosive evidence that a fundamental element of the teachings of the Catholic Church is incorrect.

Think this all sounds suspicious? I haven't scratched the surface yet.

I had been prepared to discover two novels which were broadly the same in terms of themes and plots. Even then I do not think I could have dismissed it as mere coincidence; the 'convergences' were just so numerous and striking, and my novel was in the public domain six years before *The Da Vinci Code* was published – though the exercise of writing it must have begun much nearer to the publication of my book. But the breadth and specificity of the similarities I was observing were staggering.

It was not simply that those two novels featured principal characters with near identical personalities and backgrounds. Or that in both novels they go on cipher-breaking treasure hunts across Paris, London and Rome. It was not just that their quests – for a revered blood relic – and the catalyst for their journeys – the ritual murder of a Freemason – were also identical. *The Da Vinci Code* was replete with elements of detail that directly mirrored my novel. Both the means and chronology whereby the characters and locations were introduced closely emulated scenes I had written a decade before. In the opening pages of the novels every character from *The Vatican Boys* had a direct parallel in *The Da Vinci Code*, and they are introduced in starkly similar ways, and in *exactly* the same order.

It was not just the plot structures of the books that are the same. My very thoughts and phrases echoed out of *The Da Vinci Code* wherever I looked. The descriptions of the character and activities of the Opus Dei and its London headquarters Opus Dei House were nearly identical (as I later came to realise, even where I had made up elements of my portrayal of them).

A full compendium of the parallels between the two novels would overwhelm this book, but you will find comprehensive – though non-exhaustive – details of the plagiarism that we (by which I mean Jonathan and I) believe we have uncovered in an appendix at the back of this book. There you will also find the legal claim letter that was sent to Penguin Random house in the UK by Jonathan and its two schedules comparing the two books which highlight the sweeping similarities as well as the ones of detail. And we both believe it makes clear, beyond reasonable doubt, that the conspicuous commonalities between *The Vatican Boys* and *The Da Vinci Code* vastly exceed any credible coincidence hypothesis.

Where, I wondered, did that leave me? Compared to Dan Brown, who after various false starts with his earlier novels, was hurtling up the world's bestseller lists and about to take another quantum leap into mega-stardom with the cinematic release of *The Da Vinci Code*, I was small fry. He had immense riches and the might of a global publishing empire behind him. I had little idea where to go or what I could do with what I had just uncovered. All I knew was that I must do something to rectify the wrong I was certain had been perpetrated against me.

Nor was it greed that compelled me. Mine has never been a materialistic soul. I have always gotten by, and derived great pleasure from both being a father and friend and in a modest way by sharing my writing with the world. But honesty is integral to how my parents raised me. My family were devout in their faith. The Ten Commandments were the templates by which we ordered our lives. I had lived my life trying to honour the principle, 'Thou shall not steal.' I could not pass over the fact that somebody else had robbed me of the fruits of my labour.

I knew from the outset that I wanted to make public the evidence that I had unearthed revealing exactly how Dan Brown secured his fame and fortune so people could decide for themselves who was the real creative force behind *The Da Vinci Code*.

And I was not the only one.

In early 2006, soon after I finished compiling my first list of the parallels between *The Vatican Boys* and *The Da Vinci Code*, I was browsing the news on the internet and saw a headline which stopped me in my tracks:

AUTHORS SUE DAN BROWN IN LONDON

A story like this was bound to grab my attention. By following the link I was able to study a legal case which revealed the creative process behind *The Da Vinci Code* and made the proposition that Dan Brown had plagiarized *The Vatican Boys* even more credible.

Richard Leigh and Michael Baigent were British authors whose book *The Holy Blood and the Holy Grail*, written with a third author, Henry Lincoln, was published by Jonathan Cape in 1982 (the publisher would become part of what was then Random House in 1987). A US edition was published the same year under the title *Holy Blood, Holy Grail*. The authors had carved out a niche writing popular non-fiction which challenged orthodox historical tenets and the life of Jesus Christ. In *The Holy Blood and the Holy Grail* they advanced the hypothesis that Jesus Christ was not divine as He had claimed, and had not died via the crucifixion as per the gospel accounts. They claimed that Jesus married Mary Magdalene and had children whose descendants ultimately settled in southern France, intermarried with the local nobility and founded the Merovingian dynasty whose claim to the French throne was championed by an ancient society named the Priory of Sion. Leigh, Baigent and Lincoln concluded that the Holy Grail of legend actually refers not to the classical goblet that caught the blood of Christ while He was dying by crucifixion, but to a biological bloodline that still exists today in the form of His descendants. This became known as the 'bloodline theory'.

The book was a bestseller. Feted writers like Anthony Burgess showered it with plaudits and the authors went on to write a sequel, *The Messianic Legacy*, which was published in 1986. The 'bloodline theory' became a fiercely debated topic which spawned other non-fiction titles which expanded on the hypothesis. Serious scholars worked to debunk it. But others were apparently captivated by the authors' flight of imagination.

But Leigh, Baigent and Lincoln knew the idea of Christ's 'Holy Grail' being a bloodline stemming from his physical children was theirs, and when it appeared as one of the central historical pillars of Dan Brown's *The Da Vinci Code* in 2003, Leigh and Baigent believed they had a legal claim against him. Consequently, in 2005 the authors brought a copyright claim in the High Court in London which came to court in February 2006, only a few weeks after I discovered how much Dan Brown's book drew on mine.

You can imagine how their story piqued my interest. Clearly the truth behind the creation of *The Da Vinci Code* was far from as simple as Dan Brown made out.

Over the following weeks I followed the case as closely as I could. Leigh and Baigent believed, as I did, that Dan Brown had used their book as the basis for his own, liberally borrowing elements from it to construct his story. From a layman's perspective there did not seem any doubt about it, though as far as I could see he had not plundered their book to anything like the extent that he had plundered mine.

One recent commentator is still so angry about it he said this: 'Dan Brown is one complete fraudster. He copied, yes literally copied the major plotline of *The Holy Blood and the Holy Grail*. *The Holy Blood and the Holy Grail* is a massively researched book, written by 3 people, Michael Baigent, Henry Lincoln and Richard Leigh ... Do a favour and read the original ..."

Well, while you're at it, why not read my *The Da Vinci Code* 'original', *The Vatican Boys*, and see if you think the same thing about that?

Just as in Leigh and Baigent's book, *The Da Vinci Code* had a plot element based on a claim that there had been a romantic relationship between Jesus Christ and Mary Magdalene which had led to the conceiving of children and their bloodline persisting to the modern day, and a secret society, the Priory of Sion, which defended the secret and championed the holy descendants' apparently 'divine' right to rule.

The Holy Blood and the Holy Grail authors also made various related claims to support their thesis. They noted areas of close textual similarity between the two books – claims which the judge would later uphold – and also noted that *The Da Vinci Code* features a character named 'Leigh Teabing', Leigh being the name of one of the plaintiffs in the case, and 'Teabing', an anagram of the other's surname, 'Baigent'. But of all their claims, the ones that seemed most damning to me were those focused on the Priory of Sion.

The Priory of Sion was one of the few elements of *The Da Vinci Code* that did not have a direct parallel in my book *The Vatican Boys*. So I decided to do some research of my own. There seemed no doubt that these books were in some way interconnected, and it was in the Priory of Sion that I believed the key was to be found.

I discovered that far from being an ancient institution the Priory of Sion was founded in 1956 by Frenchman Pierre Plantard who sought to persuade France that he was a direct descendent of the Merovingians, a dynasty which had ruled Frankish Gaul in the Dark Ages. Plantard not only claimed that he was the direct descendent of this line, but that he was the 'Great King' prophesied by Nostradamus who would unite the world. The Priory of Sion was the fraud by which Plantard sought to prove it. According to him it was a secret monastic order founded in 1099 by the crusader knight Godfrey of Bouillon. The Priory's goal was to restore the Merovingians, of whom Plantard was the heir, to the throne of France.

It was the stuff great stories are made of. But it was also pure hokum. Nowadays it is recognised as no more than an elaborate hoax, and Plantard as one of the 20th century's most eccentric conmen. But not even Plantard could have anticipated that his tales of the Priory of Sion would be fused with the apocryphal idea of Jesus having propagated an earthly bloodline. And yet this was what Leigh and Baigent did in their book. According to them the Priory of Sion was not a hoax at all. It was a genuine institution whose aim was the protection and elevation of Jesus' natural descendants.

Neither Leigh nor Baigent – nor their co-author Lincoln who declined to join the court case – had been deliberately perpetuating a fraud. Plantard had been meticulous in crafting his hoax, composing forged histories of the Priory which would even be accepted into Paris's *Bibliothèque Nationale de France*, and Leigh and Baigent had used these sources in composing their book.

Had Dan Brown gone to those original sources? I suspect he went no further than Leigh and Baigent's book to document this part of the history he used. This is one of the 'Facts' which he sets out at the beginning of his book: 'The Priory of Sion – a European secret society founded in 1099 – is a real organization. In 1975 Paris's

Bibliothèque Nationale discovered parchments known as Les Dossiers Secrets, identifying numerous members of the Priory of Sion, including Sir Isaac Newton, Botticelli, Victor Hugo, and Leonardo da Vinci.' Unfortunately for Mr Brown this is all nonsense, a fabrication. He adopted a fiction and presented it as a fact, just as he did – I later realised – with my fictions.

By his own admission in the preface to *The Da Vinci Code*, Dan Brown had drawn on *The Holy Blood and the Holy Grail* as a source in writing his novel. This does not of itself constitute plagiarism. Authors of fiction legitimately draw on non-fiction all the time in the course of their research – just as I had done in writing *The Diary of William Goffe*, *The Vatican Boys* and *Holyoke, the Belle Skinner Legacy*. But Dan Brown seemed to have appropriated wholesale the way in which Leigh, Baigent and Lincoln had merged Plantard's story with the idea of a Jesus bloodline. This had become the key aspect of the trial unfolding in London in the early part of 2006.

As fascinated by this trial as I was, I knew that it had only limited bearing on the plagiarism of *The Vatican Boys* which I was sure I had uncovered. The points of 'convergence' this trial focused on were different from the ones I had found in my work and there seemed to be far fewer of them. But the trial reinforced my belief that *The Da Vinci Code* had not been the product of Dan Brown's imagination and creativity, but rather a covert re-working of the ideas of others. And by poring through his pre-trial December 2005 witness statement I felt better able to gauge the character of the man with whom I was confronted by reason of his mis-appropriation of my work. It is now to Dan Brown's story as a writer that I turn.

4

Dan Brown's Writer's Story

Daniel Gerhard Brown was born in 1964, sixteen years after I came into the world. Like me he grew up in a faith environment. Unlike me he rejected the Christian faith as a boy, though his journey appears to have followed something of a circular route. He said this in a 2009 interview with the headline, 'Life after *The Da Vinci Code*': 'I was raised Episcopalian, and I was very religious as a kid. Then, in eighth or ninth grade, I studied astronomy, cosmology, and the origins of the universe. I remember saying to a minister, "I don't get it. I read a book that said there was an explosion known as the Big Bang, but here it says God created Heaven and Earth and the animals in seven days. Which is right?" Unfortunately, the response I got was, "Nice boys don't ask that question." A light went off, and I said, "The Bible doesn't make sense. Science makes much more sense to me." And I just gravitated away from religion ... The irony is that I've really come full circle. The more science I studied, the more I saw that physics becomes metaphysics and numbers become imaginary numbers. The further you go into science, the mushier the ground gets. You start to say, "Oh, there is an order and a spiritual aspect to science."'

How tragic that the young Dan Brown was scolded for asking an entirely reasonable question about the Christian faith – the sort that any genuine seeker after truth might ask – rather than his being given a proper answer, which would include the fact that there is an army of great scientists who have been devout Christians.

I am going to let Dan Brown himself continue this chapter about his life and career by quoting parts of the main witness statement that he served in *The Holy Blood and the Holy Grail* case where he talks about his journey to becoming an author:

'My father is a teacher emeritus at Phillips Exeter Academy and also has published more than a dozen well-known academic texts used around the world. He received the Presidential Award for excellence in mathematics teaching. Both of my parents are musicians, and both have served as church choir masters. My mother has a master's degree in sacred music and was a professional church organist. My father sings and was an actor in musical theatre. To this day, both continue to sing and are members of a Symphony Chorus ... This love of music, like many things my parents loved, was inherited by me. When I was at Amherst I was very interested in music composition and creative writing. I also loved languages.

'I grew up on the campus of Phillips Exeter Academy, where my father was a teacher. By chance, the school has a very strong tradition of writing and has a number of famous writers as alumni, including John Irving, Gore Vidal, Daniel Webster, and Peter Benchley. It is also known for the strictness of its regulations and code of conduct, especially with respect to plagiarism. I notice from the school's website that plagiarism is still considered a "major offence", exactly as it was in my day.

'While at Phillips Exeter and Amherst College, I pursued advanced writing courses and was published in school literary magazines. At Exeter, I chose "creative writing" as my senior project. At Amherst, I applied for and was accepted to a special writing course with visiting novelist Alan Lelchuk.

'I took piano lessons since the age of six and wrote music throughout high school and college. Once I had finished college in May of 1986, I focused my creative energies on song writing. I left home and moved to Los Angeles, the heart of the song writing industry, where I had limited success in music and paid my rent by working as an English teacher at Beverly Hills Prep School. Over the course of the ten years after college, I wrote and produced four albums of original music. I met my wife, Blythe, through the National Academy of Songwriters, where she was the Director of Artist Development. Blythe, like me, loved art. She also was a very talented painter. Despite the Academy's best efforts to promote me, my music career never really took off.'

As their relationship developed Blythe used her influence in several unsuccessful attempts to further Dan Brown's musical career, which failed. His backers supposedly spoke of him as 'the next Barry Manilow', while others likened his music to the disgraced pop-rocker Gary Glitter. Regardless, in 1993 Brown returned to New Hampshire having secured a teaching job in English at Phillips Exeter Academy, where he grew up, and Blythe accompanied him. They were married in 1997.

In his witness statement Dan Brown traces the inception of his writing career to reading a copy of Sidney Sheldon's book *The Doomsday Conspiracy* which he found on a beach while on holiday in Tahiti in 1994. 'The Sheldon book was unlike anything I'd read as an adult. It held my attention, kept me turning pages, and reminded me how much fun it could be to read. The simplicity of the prose and efficiency of the storyline was less cumbersome than the dense novels of my schooldays, and I began to suspect that maybe I could write a "thriller" of this type one day.'

He then tells how first writing success came in 1995 using a female pseudonym. 'As an Easterner, I felt like a fish out of water in Los Angeles. I lived in a low-rent "artists" apartment complex, whose hallways overflowed with unusual individuals – aspiring rock stars, male models, drama queens, and stand-up comics. Amazed by this new world, I thought it might be fun to compile a list of some of the more bizarre sightings. Over the course of a few days, I wrote a list and called it *187 Men to Avoid*. Blythe thought the list was hilarious. She quickly wrote several literary agents and included a portion of the list. To my astonishment, I immediately got calls from a number of agents, including George Wieser, who told me he had already spoken to Putnam Books and could get me $12,500 for the manuscript. Having faced disappointment in the music industry, this quick success in publishing surprised and encouraged me. I agreed to sell the manuscript and chose to use a female pseudonym (albeit a pretty obvious one, Danielle Brown).'

Dan Brown then explains how the success of this book led his new agent to encourage him to write a mainstream novel, saying, 'He knew a novelist when he saw one.' But apparently Dan Brown was not ready to make the switch from music. 'Although I still had aspirations of writing a mainstream novel that was as fun to read as the one I'd read in Tahiti, I was still focused on song writing and felt I should give my music career a fair chance to catch on. In addition, I had no idea what I would write about.'

Dan Brown published his first science fiction 'thriller', *Digital Fortress*, in 1998, going on to write and publish *Angels & Demons* in 2000 and *Deception Point* in 2001. In the early pages of *Deception Point* there is an acknowledgement to 'Blythe Brown for her tireless research and creative input'. Likewise, *The Da Vinci Code* published in 2003 also benefitted from her 'research and input'.

In some ways Dan Brown's story mirrors my own. He was clearly a young man who yearned to write for a living, and despite the years and hundreds of thousands of words that he had invested in his craft he still was not getting his big break. Nevertheless, like me, he kept plugging away. The difference was that he eventually got the break that I did not get, being picked up by a New York literary agent and subsequently by a major publisher. But it did not immediately propel him to superstardom.

The period directly after the publication of his debut novel was difficult both financially and emotionally for Brown. *Digital Fortress* sold very few copies. Dan Brown was dejected by the publisher's lack of effort to publicise the title, and although he spent much of his own money promoting the book and doing interviews on hundreds of local radio stations it never translated into the hard numbers which are essential to any writer's career.

Nevertheless, to his credit he kept his nose to the grindstone and recommitted himself to his writing. Deciding he needed to change publishers, Brown was lucky enough to contract his second novel with Pocket Books, a division of Simon & Schuster, off a simple outline – what they call a 'synopsis'. Pocket Books seemed to be excited by this new project that was to be called *Angels & Demons* and which would be the first novel to feature the hero who would eventually become Brown's most famous character, the cryptologist Robert Langdon. He would later re-appear in *The Da Vinci Code*, and then be played by Tom Hanks on the big screen. Robert Langdon now seems destined to enjoy his own TV series. To this day, I maintain that Robert Langdon is a character drawn from my book.

In Brown's witness statement he relates how Simon & Schuster had promised him a substantial print run of 60,000, advertising in major newspapers and internet platforms, a twelve-city tour, an e-book release (when e-books were still in their infancy), and several other exciting prospects. As so often happens in corporate publishing though, few of those promises were kept. When *Angels & Demons* was published in 2000 the print run was a mere 12,000 copies, and the publicity provided by Simon & Schuster was virtually non-existent. The novel hardly sold.

Brown was naturally dispirited. He felt as if he had poured his heart and soul into *Angels & Demons*, and his motivation was running low. Nevertheless – and in part because he owed Simon & Schuster a second novel as part of his contract – he turned in a new novel, *Deception Point*, which when published in 2001 had similarly little fanfare and lack of success. By that time Dan Brown had written three novels, all of which had failed despite his having had the backing both of a top agent and major publishers. Of course this raises the question –– what new factor could have enabled his next literary endeavour to bring about such a dramatic change of fortune?

Failed ventures abound in the harsh world of publishing. Writers are built up by their agents and publishers only to have their hopes dashed when their publishers move onto whatever books look like their best bets for the next year. Publishing is a 'spread better's game' where a publisher banks on a roster of writers each year, knowing that most of them will fall by the wayside. But also knowing that should just one of those writers reach a critical mass of readers they will have a hot property on their hands for years to come, covering their losses on the failed books and propelling the company into profit.

It is not for nothing that many writers jack it in and go back to their day jobs after a string of failures like the ones Dan Brown suffered. Soldiering on in those circumstances is a lonely, emotionally debilitating business. It is entirely possible that Dan Brown's author story might have ended with the publication and failure of *Deception Point*. Even halfway through writing it, according to his own testimony, he was weary of the whole endeavour. He felt he had made a mistake in choosing its political subject matter, and was not enjoying writing about the lead character, apparently because she was female. He had no money, few prospects, and was plagued by the idea of giving it all up.

It was then – as Dan Brown claims – that he had his 'big idea', the one that would radically change his life, ignite his career and propel him into the top echelons of the literati, the idea that would become *The Da Vinci Code* – and the very same idea that I had a decade before when I started writing *The Vatican Boys*, all about 'a holy relic linked to the blood of Jesus Christ' (the Turin Shroud), though Dan Brown would replace it with the Holy Grail.

This is where the parallels between our writing careers end because according to his evidence in the Leigh and Baigent case, directly after the completion of *Deception Point* in 2001, Dan Brown set about writing a synopsis for a fourth novel, which he would produce by drawing – as I now believe – from the extensive notes taken by my mysterious 1999 visitor from Amherst who asked in such detail about my research for *The Vatican Boys* and the core thesis of *The Holy Blood and the Holy Grail*. The synopsis would win him a new deal with Doubleday, a division of the publishing giant Random House – now Penguin Random House, and open up a new chapter in his writing career.

While I went on toiling in relative obscurity, Dan Brown's rise was being driven by the powerful Random House publishing empire. *The Da Vinci Code* sold 6,000 copies on the day it was released, going to the top of the *New York Times* Best Seller list in its first week of publication.

I would not be human if I did not wonder whether given the same marketing power behind it *The Vatican Boys* would have enjoyed the same measure of success. However, as will emerge later in this book, Dan Brown insists that he had not even heard of my novel before he wrote *The Da Vinci Code*. For all the reasons which we relate in this book, Jonathan and I do not believe that to be true. You should of course hear Dan Brown's side of the story, though he and his publishers are determined that you should not hear mine. So these are the initial paragraphs of the lengthy account given by Dan Brown from his witness statement of how he came to write *The Da Vinci Code*. There is also some interesting personal detail in there about Dan Brown's lifestyle and personal habits:

Halfway through writing Deception Point *I began to think that maybe I had made a mistake with this palate cleanser. I was feeling bored by the topic. I was no longer keen on politics – which was part of the story in* Deception Point *– and I did not enjoy writing with a female lead. I had been far more interested in the Vatican, Langdon, codes, symbology, and art. I wasn't enjoying writing, I had no money, and I found myself wondering once again if I should give up. Fortunately, my wife has always been a tremendous support system and she encouraged me to keep at it. … My lone advocate at Simon & Schuster seemed to be my editor, Jason Kaufman, with whom I had developed a friendship and level of trust. He too had become deeply frustrated with the lack of publisher support I was receiving at Simon & Schuster.*

The day after I submitted the Deception Point *manuscript Blythe and I travelled on a much needed vacation to Mexico. It was thereon the Yucatan Peninsula, exploring the ancient Mayan pyramids and archaeological ruins of Chichen-Itza and Tulum, that I was (at last) able to leave behind the high tech world of* Deception Point. *We were immersed in ancient ruins and lost cultures, and this intriguing history was tickling my imagination again. I began to muster the sense that I might be able to write another novel. At that point, I had no doubt who my hero would be – I would return to the world of Robert Langdon. This sequel would ultimately become* The Da Vinci Code.

The Da Vinci Code *tells the story of professor Robert Langdon's race to decipher clues left for him by murdered Louvre curator Jacques Saunière. Many of Saunière's clues involve wordplay and relate to Leonardo da Vinci. The novel is, at its core, a treasure hunt through Paris, London, and*

Edinburgh. The story is a blend of historical fact, legend, myth, and fiction.

The novel's themes include: the sacred feminine; goddess worship; the Holy Grail; symbology; paganism; the history of the Bible and its accuracy, including the lost Gnostic Gospels; Templar history; the suppression of information by the church; the genealogy of Jesus; religious zealotry; and nature's grand design as evidence for the existence of God...

Many of the aforementioned themes from The Da Vinci Code fall in a category I often call "secret history" – those parts of mankind's past that allegedly have been lost or have become muddied by time, historical revision, or subversion. Of course, it is impossible when looking at secret history to know how much is truth, and how much is myth or fanciful invention... The Da Vinci Code has taken a lot of this information and put it forward in a different genre – that of a work of fiction, a thriller.

Researching and writing The Da Vinci Code

As with all of my books, so much time has passed since I researched each of the novels that it is hard for me to be exact about what sources I used at which precise point in the research and writing of each of the novels. In the case of The Da Vinci Code, Blythe and I spent a year or so travelling and conducting research during the writing of The Da Vinci Code. On the way, we met with historians and other academics and extended our travels from the Vatican and France to England and Scotland in order to investigate the historical underpinnings of the novel.

In preparing this statement, what I have done is gone back to my research books and notes and thought long and hard about how these big ideas came to the surface. In doing so, I see that more notes have survived from The Da Vinci Code *than from any of my previous novels. This is not surprising. I am not a pack rat; in fact, I'm the exact opposite. In the same way that I try to trim the fat from my writing, I am constantly trimming excess clutter from my life. I have discarded most of my life's memorabilia, including personal letters, grade school essays, early diaries, and even academic commendations. I trashed my first manuscript for* Digital Fortress *(which I now regret) and even disposed of most lyric notes and demo tapes from my years as a songwriter. This may sound surprising, but both* Digital Fortress *and my music career felt like creative failures (as did* Angels & Demons *and* Deception Point*), and big boxes of old notes felt like painful reminders of years spent for naught. Also, we have moved house four times since I began writing, and heavy boxes of old notes rank very high on my "to discard" list.*

I believe another reason that I found more notes from The Da Vinci Code *is that it has been the most research intensive of my novels to date. It was my fourth novel, and I was getting better at writing; in the same way a musician chooses to perform harder and harder pieces as he masters his instrument, I was eager to tackle more complicated plotlines. My research books for* The Da Vinci Code *are heavily marked with margin notes, sticky notes, underlining, highlighting, inserted pieces of paper, etc. A good portion of these notes (as with* Angels & Demons*) are in my wife's handwriting...*

With The Da Vinci Code, *however, she was reading entire books, highlighting exciting ideas, and urging me to read the material myself and find ways to work the ideas in to the plot... Looking back at the books, I can see that we were highlighting all the big concepts that eventually appeared in the final draft of the book...*

In beginning to write The Da Vinci Code, *I tried to place my head back in to the world of Robert Langdon – the world of art, religion, secrets, and symbols. In exploring his world anew, I began mulling over much of the information that had been leftover from my* Angels & Demons *research. This included my research on the brotherhood of the Masons and on The Knights Templar. As I have pointed out, the links between the Illuminati and the Masons are well documented, and one can hardly read about the Masons and not also read about the Knights Templar...*

At the outset of the project, one of my desires was to explore the origin of the Bible. The Bible is, in many respects, like any other compilation – it is a heavily edited collection of many authors' works. Even so, many people accept what is said in the Bible to be absolute fact. Another reason for selecting the topic of the Bible was my fascination with religion in general. To put it at its simplest, although religion often did good things and helped a lot of people, I could see that there were also many situations where any religion could be used for evil purposes. I found this clash to be potentially fertile ground in which to plant the seeds of my novel. I thought that perhaps this would be the theme, or "big idea" of the novel.

The theme of the Bible and religion took me to the Gnostic Gospels (essentially those parts of the Bible that were drafted, but ultimately did not appear in the final version and, therefore had not been widely read). Since visiting Rome while researching Angels & Demons *I remained fascinated by what could be buried in the Vatican secret archives – those miles and miles of books must contain something pretty interesting – what could it be? At this early stage I thought that the answer to this question would be, in essence, material contained in alternative drafts of the Bible and the Gnostic Gospels – the story we read in the Bible is a partial story and it is an edited story. Many historians believe that the Gnostic Gospels are one of the missing pieces.*

These paragraphs are followed by numerous others claiming that he meticulously accumulated the historical and geographical material that went into the writing of *The Da Vinci Code*, the main purpose of which is to persuade the judge that he did not plagiarize the ideas and supporting historical research of *The Holy Blood and the Holy Grail,* but rather personally undertook all key research which lead to his adopting that book's 'bloodline theory' independently of it. These paragraphs are replete with evidence of an impressive, erudite and painstaking historical research exercise which had been undertaken both by Dan Brown and his wife Blythe as part of the process of writing *The Da Vinci Code*. All this must however be set against the fact that a number of the events which he portrays in his book as being historical events, and on which his plot hangs, are actually 'facts' that I made up while writing *The Vatican Boys*, which, therefore, can only be their source. More about that later.

Dan Brown finishes his witness statement on this note: 'In closing, I would like to restate that I remain astounded by the Claimants' choice to file this plagiarism suit. For them to suggest, as I understand they do, that I have "hijacked and exploited" their work is simply untrue.'

Dan Brown's denial of having 'hijacked and exploited' my work is no less vehement. The purpose of this book is to enable you to make your mind up about whether his denial is true or false.

5

Leigh and Baigent Lose Their Case

As winter turned into spring in 2006 I followed the news about *The Holy Blood and the Holy Grail* case in as much detail as I could. It was not difficult because this was a high-profile piece of litigation which had turned into a publicity circus. Full trials of such claims about best-selling books are rare. The British media painted it as a David and Goliath story, with the less well-known authors, Baigent and Leigh, taking on the Goliath of Dan Brown and his publishing empire backers. The trial had an extra frisson because the two battling books were published by different imprints of the same company, Random House (Random House merged with Penguin in 2013), which sided with its much better-selling author. The whole thing was a promoter's dream, with the winner's booty being pitched at a hundred million dollars, and both books enjoyed a huge hike in sales during the trial.

By April 2006, after lengthy arguments and counter-arguments, with all three authors being subjected to damaging and revealing cross-examinations, the High Court in London was ready to announce its verdict.

It was not a good day for Michael Baigent and Richard Leigh.

The Judge, Mr Justice Peter Smith, ruled that their copyright infringement claim was not made to the satisfaction of the court; and that it had 'always [been] based on a weak foundation'. The judge said that a comparison of the language in *The Holy Blood and the Holy Grail* and *The Da Vinci Code* did show some copying of the text. 'However this is not alleged to be a copyright infringement [because it did not constitute the requisite "substantial part"] ... so does not assist the claimants. Such copying cannot amount to substantial copying of the text of *The Holy Blood and the Holy Grail* and the claimants have never said it does,' said Mr Justice Smith.

Since there was little copying of the actual text of *The Holy Blood and the Holy Grail*, Baigent and Leigh's claim was premised on what is called 'non-literal' copying of a substantial part of their literary work, by which they meant that Dan Brown had copied the way in which they had structured the facts which they claimed supported the bloodline theory.

The court held that, while the evidence was clear that Dan Brown and his primary researcher (Blythe Brown) had drawn on *The Holy Blood and the Holy Grail* to a greater extent than he had admitted, this did not amount to copyright infringement. Rather they had used *The Holy Blood and the Holy Grail*, and other books, merely to provide source material for *The Da Vinci Code*, an exercise which is a legitimate element of the creative process.

The judge decided to engage his creative skills in writing his judgment by including a coded message of his own. Using a simple cipher, including a keyword based on the Fibonacci Sequence employed in *The Da Vinci Code*, the judge's message refers to a World War I British admiral. He subsequently explained that the admiral was a hero of his, and that the trial coincided with the centenary of the launch of one of the admiral's ships.

It was clear to me by his ruling that because *The Holy Blood and the Holy Grail* was published as a work of history – neglecting the fact that much of its central thesis had a fictitious premise because of the Priory of Sion hoax – it could be freely exploited in subsequent fictional work without infringement of copyright. Therefore, Dan Brown had been free to base significant parts of his novel on the ideas, albeit original, laid out in *The Holy Blood and the Holy Grail* in the same way that an historical author might base a novel about the life of Henry VIII on the work of a Tudor historian, or how I had based my novel, *Holyoke, the Belle Skinner Legacy* on the local histories I had researched.

Leigh and Baigent appealed the judgment unsuccessfully and by March 2007 they faced legal costs of around £3,000,000 – nearly $5,000,000. This was despite the fact that the judge discounted them, presumably because he concluded that Dan Brown had been less than candid in his evidence, and that he had taken more from The *Holy Blood and the Holy Grail* in writing *The Da Vinci Code* than he had been prepared to admit. Leigh died of a heart attack that year, his death no doubt hastened by the stress of litigation against a ruthless opponent with limitless resources. Baigent lived the six next years harried by Random House's lawyers for their costs until his own untimely death in 2013.

A little later in the spring of 2006 as I observed the fallout from the trial, I tried my best not to become disheartened. There was little doubt in my mind that the findings of the High Court in London did not impact directly on the case I intended to bring against Dan Brown. While there was logic in the idea that Brown could not infringe copyright in a work published as a 'factual' account of the bloodline theory by just lifting the key elements out of it, *The Vatican Boys* was very much a novel filled not only with my own historical research but also with creative and invented expressions.

As I understood it, historical facts can be 'copied', but original characters, situations, ciphers, codes and other plot points are all the products of a writer's imagination and therefore do enjoy legal protection. I was certain Dan Brown had lifted all of these from my novel.

Mr Justice Smith accepted that, 'The facts and the themes and the ideas cannot be protected but how those facts, themes and ideas are put together ... can be.' He added, 'It must be shown that the architecture or structure is substantially copied.' Surely, I thought, I must therefore have a winnable copyright claim in the UK, though I had not the slightest idea how I could pursue one.

Moreover, although the court's ruling was in Dan Brown's favour, some elements of the judgment did seriously call his credibility into doubt, suggesting that at least some of his evidence was fiction. That too was an encouragement to me as I assumed that this would be taken into account in any future copyright action against him.

The judge also criticised Dan Brown's defence team for not calling his wife to the stand, who he was told did the research for his books. 'All of this could have been clarified had Blythe Brown given evidence,' he wrote in his judgment. The judge made it clear that he suspected that Blythe Brown had used *The Holy Blood and the Holy Grail* extensively, and much earlier than Dan Brown had admitted. 'Accordingly I conclude that her absence is explicable only on the basis that she would not support Mr Brown's assertion as to the use made of HBHG and when that use occurred in that evidence.'

Justice Smith's comments now seem to be prescient given what Bythe Brown has said recently both about her husband's honesty and his account of how he came to write his books.

The judge also found Brown's insistence that the Langdon/Teabing lectures delivered in the novel had been created from sources that were explicitly *not* the work of Baigent and Leigh to be 'completely unsustainable', i.e., in layman's terms, *untrue*. 'It flies in the face of logic,' declared the judge. 'The conclusion is irresistible: Blythe Brown provided the material for the lectures with HBHG in her hands.'

These are the relevant paragraphs of the Justice Smith judgment:

'315 ... I reject Mr Brown's evidence that [*The Holy Blood and the Holy Grail*] was acquired later and was not used in any significant way. Blythe Brown's underlinings (absent any other explanation from her) tell their own story. In my view as I have said this is overwhelmingly supportive of the view that when Mr Brown came to write the second part of [*The Da Vinci Code*] the historical context that was then inserted was the Langdon and Teabing lectures. At that time Sophie was linked to Saunière (he was then given a name). Teabing was similarly created from the anagram of the Claimants and the textual insertions show that they were drawn from [*The Holy Blood and the Holy Grail*].

'316. I regard the suggestion that Mr Brown and Blythe Brown created the Langdon/Teabing lectures from the other sources as completely unsustainable. It flies in the face of logic and the documents as carefully demonstrated by the Claimants in the annex of language similarities set out in their closing submissions. The conclusion is irresistible. Blythe Brown provided the material for the lectures with [*The Holy Blood and the Holy Grail*] in her hands.'

On the witness stand, Dan Brown repeated the denial in his witness statement that he had a copy of *The Holy Blood and the Holy Grail* when preparing the synopsis for *The Da Vinci Code*. Mr Justice Smith did not believe him. 'What is extraordinary about Mr Brown's evidence is that he appears to have acquired all of the books that cover this area apart from the one that is described as essential reading.'

On another point he observed that Brown during the course of his cross-examination 'looked like he was making the answer up', i.e. he was inventing evidence to suit his case. In other words, he was lying on oath.

At paragraph 294 of his judgment Mr Justice Smith makes this additional emphatic judgment against the veracity both of Dan Brown's witness statement and sworn testimony from the witness box: 'I have rejected Mr Brown's evidence that he acquired [*The Holy Blood and the Holy Grail*] late in the process of writing [*The Da Vinci Code*].' In other words, the judge concluded that Dan Brown's evidence on this issue was untrue.

The judge appears however to exonerate Dan Brown from having 'consciously lied' when preparing his witness statement – the one of which you have read parts – as opposed to his oral evidence. However he also said this: 'It ought to have been obvious to Mr Brown that if he had carefully prepared his witness statement that his case on [*The Holy Blood and the Holy Grail*] as he put it would simply fall apart on an examination of [*The Holy Blood and the Holy Grail*], the copying similarities and the other documents to which I have referred."

To be clear then: although Mr Justice Smith found the copyright claim against Dan Brown not to be made out, he did find a) that some copying had taken place of Leigh and Baigent's book; b) that

Dan Brown gave oral evidence under oath to the contrary that the judge felt obliged to 'reject' – i.e. he did not believe it; c) that he found another part of his oral evidence to be 'completely unsustainable' (i.e. untrue), and (d) that he thought that for at least some of his oral evidence, Dan Brown was 'making the answer up' (i.e. it was mendacious).

To put this into perspective, Perjury is a crime in the U.K., defined in the Perjury Act 1911 in these terms: '*If any person lawfully sworn as a witness ... in a judicial proceeding wilfully makes a statement material in that proceeding, which he knows to be false or does not believe to be true, he shall be guilty of perjury.*'

The punishment for this crime can be up to two years in prison. But that does not matter to Dan Brown. He has never even been charged with perjury, let alone found guilty of it, and he denies it. He still enjoys his international fame and the millions of dollars that he has made from his books, as he enjoys the prestige of being perceived to have earned all this through his skills as an author. To this day, he also retains the full support of his publishers.

In evaluating all of this, the key aspect of the ruling became clear to me: Dan Brown was free to use the ideas, research and infrastructure of *The Holy Blood and the Holy Grail* in his novel, both because it had not been copied 'literally', and because it had been presented as historical fact. I did not, however, believe he was free to use the plot lines, characters, and narrative structure from *The Vatican Boys* because they were the fruit of my own creativity. Those belonged to me by what I understood was my constitutional right.

The Holy Blood and the Holy Grail trial had been a wake-up call to me and probably for others, highlighting that the burden of proof in cases of copyright infringement is set high. But I was determined not to give up because it seemed clear to me that the story behind the writing of *The Da Vinci Code* was of a willingness to piggyback on the hard work and imagination of other people.

The High Court might have ruled that Dan Brown's exploitation of Leigh and Baigent's ideas was not unlawful in the sense of breaching their copyright. But it had demonstrated clearly to me at least that Dan and Blythe Brown had appropriated other people's literary work to construct theirs. As far as I could see, to catch them I had to show simply that my fictional *The Vatican Boys* – with both its actual and created (or 'fictional') facts – was the primary source they plundered to write *The Da Vinci Code*. To me, this seemed viable based on the detailed analysis that I had already undertaken.

I was pumped. I was sure that I had caught Dan Brown with his hand in the proverbial cookie jar. All I had to do to prove it was show the world they were my cookies that he had taken, how he had done it, and where he had put them. I knew I could do it. This felt like a huge moment, and I couldn't wait to get started on what I felt certain was an incontrovertible claim for breach of copyright.

Little did I know how long and arduous was the journey on which I was about to embark.

6

The Empire Strikes Back

Between the end of *The Holy Blood and the Holy Grail* trial and the late summer of 2006 I decided to mount my own case for copyright infringement against Dan Brown and his publishers through the US Federal District Court in Springfield, Massachusetts, confident that I would succeed where Leigh and Baigent had failed. I enlisted Gary Ensor, who though he was not a copyright specialist, was a well-known lawyer in the area having filed many cases in federal courts, even having argued one in the Supreme Court in Washington. We had met years before and spent many days playing golf together at the same country club. He sadly passed away in February 2021.

Our first line of attack was to write to Random House and Dan Brown outlining our case and demanding that the literary fraud perpetrated against me be acknowledged and restitution made. We added Sony Pictures for good measure since they had made *The Da Vinci Code* film. When we received their lawyers' curt dismissal by return, we were not surprised. Gary advised me these were just the opening salvos in the longer battle and we were just getting started.

It is far from unusual for successful novelists and their publishers to receive letters claiming plagiarism, and most of them come from writers whose claims of 'convergence' are speculative at best – or where the 'convergence' is so general that copyright theft is ruled out.

My claim, however, did not fall into this category. After months of studying *The Da Vinci Code* and comparing it to *The Vatican Boys* I had created a voluminous list of similarities: identical structures, characters clearly lifted from my novel, specific plot lines, as well as the concept and ethos of the story. My claim was well-founded, and we had compiled the evidence that proved it.

I like to think that somewhere in the offices of Random House a lawyer pored over my letter and their heart sank at the realisation that this was a claim with merit from somebody who had genuinely been wronged, and who had produced compelling evidence of that wrongdoing. But they will have perceived it as their responsibility – in Jonathan's view wrongly – to respond nonetheless to the effect that my claim had no legal merit. Whether that was ethical conduct on their part I leave you to judge. Should an ethical lawyer write a letter denying the validity of an obviously well-founded claim? Jonathan would say not because in his view a lawyer crosses the line when they are covering up wrongdoing.

The lesson I had taken from *The Holy Blood and the Holy Grail* trial was that in Great Britain at least, establishing that a book has been plagiarized is not enough. One must satisfy a court that the claim is a good one according to the exacting legal definition of 'copyright infringement'. To prove copyright infringement in the US the plaintiff must (inter alia) show both that the defendant had access to the plaintiff's work, and that the defendant's work is substantially similar to protected elements of the plaintiff's work. My case was to be tried on the First Circuit of the US Federal Courts where to win my case I had to prove four things:

1. That I owned the copyright in the original work;

2. That the subsequent author had had access to that work;

3. A reasonably apparent degree of sufficient similarity to the original work existing in the subsequent work and that copying is determinable to actually exist or can be inferred; and

4. The manner of expressing the constituent elements of underlying themes and ideas is substantially similar between the books.

… which looked like a walk in the park.

In the District Court of Massachusetts the test they apply is that whether an 'ordinary reader' of *The Da Vinci Code* would regard it as "substantially similar" to *The Vatican Boys*; in other words that it 'rendered the works so similar that the later work represented a wrongful appropriation of expression.'

I already knew the answer to that question, because so many 'ordinary readers' of the two books had independently come to the conclusion that Dan Brown's book was a flagrant copy of mine. Surely, I thought, that means that we must win our case. Gary and I felt we were well prepared and that, once our evidence was presented, no reasonable judicial official could find against us. Jonathan, who was not involved in this case, has looked at our evidence and agrees 100 per cent.

Since at the time of filing we knew that Dan Brown was denying that he had read my book before he wrote *The Da Vinci Code* we decided we also needed to show 'opportunity' on his part; i.e. that Dan Brown had in all likelihood both accessed and read my book. I felt that the 'opportunity' part of that equation was clear cut. I would never be able to *prove* that the young man from Amhurst who visited me to talk about the Opus Dei, Freemasons, Knights and the Catholic Church was connected to Dan Brown, but it was a matter of record that Dan Brown had graduated from Amherst College and lived in Amherst. He had been there at around the same time as my early writing was being syndicated to hundreds of thousands of readers in the local newspapers. It seemed pretty clear to me that – as a fellow local author who had a devoted and well-sized following – I must have come onto his radar during this period.

There was also the fact that my book was on sale in the very bookshop from which, according to him, Dan Brown used to buy his research material. In the acknowledgements page of *The Da Vinci Code* he says this: 'My gratitude also to Water Street Bookstore for tracking down so many of my research books.'

Dan Brown also says this at paragraph 68 of his witness statement in the copyright case brought against him in England: 'The store where we buy most of our books, The Water Street Bookstore in Exeter New Hampshire, was hand selling my books ..."

If Water Street Bookstore was searching for Dan Brown books on subjects like the Opus Dei, the Freemasons, and the Catholic Church then it would have been bound to send him my book. Dan Brown was looking in New England bookstores in 1998-1999 when *The Vatican Boys* was selling in the Water Street Bookstore and it is still listed for sale on their website now. Who knows, I might have even signed a copy for him.

We filed the lawsuit in August 2006. I can still picture Gary and me walking down Springfield's Main Street on the day. Gary was not just carrying paperwork. Holstered to his belt was a gun. When I asked him why, he explained, with a deadpan expression, 'This is a five-hundred-million-dollar lawsuit, Jack. People do strange things when this much money is involved.' Those unsettling words echo in me even today. I was later to learn that my opponents would indeed deploy a different kind of force against me, thankfully not involving guns.

After filing our carefully-prepared legal documents we began the long wait imposed by the US legal system. But I put my trust in the judicial processes of our democracy and waited expectantly for news. After some months during which the court evaluated our filings and Dan Brown's New York City lawyers' rebuttals, the Federal District Court judge who had been appointed to the case scheduled a hearing to be held in May, 2007.

In December 2006 the three mighty Defendants whose commercial interests I had the temerity to threaten had filed a motion for what is called 'Summary Judgment'. This is a judgment entered by a court for one party and against another party summarily, i.e. without a jury trial. Summary Judgments may be issued on the merits of an entire case, or on discrete issues within that case. The presiding judge generally must find there is 'no genuine dispute as to any material fact and the movant [i.e. the party applying for Summary Judgment] is entitled to judgment as a matter of law.'

This is from the guidance given on Summary Judgment applications in copyright cases, in a book entitled *First Circuit-Second Circuit Copyright Infringement Standards*: 'Summary Judgment ... Courts in the First Circuit apply the ordinary observer test to determine substantial similarity in both the summary judgment and preliminary injunction contexts. Courts grant summary judgment for the defendant "only where the only finding that could be reached by a fact finder, correctly applying the applicable legal standard, is that there is no substantial similarity between the two works." The dissimilarity of the works at issue must be "readily apparent" for the court to grant summary judgment for the defendant ... when there is no possibility that a reasonable person could find any similarity.'

Surely, I thought, based on those stringent tests which on the evidence the Defendants could not possibly meet, we could see off any such application at a canter and get our jury trial which we should win at a gallop. On the 'ordinary observer' test, we already knew the answer from the small army of readers of both books to whom the copying had been obvious. I was confident that our written submissions were compelling to the extent that there was 'no possibility that a reasonable person could [fail to find] find any similarity'.

We must have stirred something in Dan Brown and Random House because they decided to send an expensive crack team of four attorneys against us, which I take as testament to the strength of our case. Three of them were from a smart New York firm, Davis Wright Tremaine, which is one of the top 100 firms in the US with eight offices around the country, and which, ironically given the quality of its submissions in my case, prides itself on 'excellence'. The lead counsel was Elizabeth A. McNamara, who, among many professional accolades, was selected as one of the 'New York Super Lawyers' by Thomson Reuters from 2006 to 2020, and is a member of the Copyright Society of the USA.

Like the Leigh and Baigent case, this was another David and Goliath battle with the heavyweight attorney hit-squad hired by the Defendants serving a '*REPLY MEMORANDUM OF LAW IN SUPPORT OF THE DEFENDANTS BROWN AND RANDOM*

HOUSE ... MOTION TO DISMISS OR, IN THE ALTERNATIVE, FOR SUMMARY JUDGMENT'.

When Jonathan read the submissions in the case fifteen years later, and looked at the disproportionate and intimidating attorney power on show he said it was clear to him that the Defendants had invested tens of thousands of dollars to knock me out before I could get in front of a jury, sums that were way beyond my means.

This intimidating and frequently misleading document ran to 33 pages, and you can read it in full at *The Da Vinci Fraud* website in the 'materials' section. It had obviously been an expensive piece of legal drafting which was either incompetent or – as Jonathan thinks – more likely replete with sophistry and guile. Its main points were that no Discovery (i.e. exchange of documents between the parties) was warranted, expert testimony should be excluded, and that the two novels were not substantially similar.

Jonathan describes this document as 'a really nasty piece of work', and one that he, as an ethical lawyer, would be thoroughly ashamed of. Using his legal analytical skills, he has contributed greatly to the following critique of it, as he has that of the defective judgment which resulted from it – just so you know that both have been scrutinised by a lawyer and not just by me!

In their *PRELIMINARY STATEMENT* the Defendants' attorneys say this: 'The only similarities are highly abstract ideas or *scènes à faire* that cannot form the basis of copyright infringement ...'. *Scène à faire* is a French term which means 'scene to be made' or 'scene that must be done'. It is a concept in Copyright Law which holds that certain elements of a creative work are held to be not protectable because they are mandated by or are customary to a particular genre, i.e. generic.

That claim was right in principle, but wrong in fact, and is therefore a claim that should not have been made. It is by no means true that the similarities between the books are merely 'highly abstract ideas or *scènes à faire*'. Furthermore, in this case these two novels also have a large number of near identical specific ideas and *scènes à faire*, which are used in virtually the same chronological order, which can be the basis of a copyright infringement claim.

In their *PRELIMINARY STATEMENT* the Defendants' attorneys urge the judge just to read the two books, and ignore my evidence while urging the judge to take account of theirs. They conclude: 'In the end, when one reads the actual works ... only one conclusion can reasonably be reached: *Vatican Boys* and *Da Vinci Code* are not similar.' That proposition is an absurdity to anyone who has read the two books. It is also plainly untrue.

The first part of the Defendants' key document setting out their case is a detailed legal argument citing rules of precedence for the First Circuit. Several authorities are cited in support of the Defendants' claim that all that the judge does is read the two novels in coming to his decision. It asserts that the First Circuit 'employs a ... straightforward test assessing substantial similarity of protecting material from the perspective of an "ordinary reasonable person" or "ordinary observer"'.

It was presumably obvious to the Defendants' attorneys that if the two books were to be shown to 12 'ordinary reasonable people' that the myriad of similarities would have been obvious to them. It was therefore essential for the Defendants' attorneys that a jury be kept out of the legal process at all costs.

On the issue of 'opportunity', the Defendants aimed to have their cake and eat it. In their motion for Summary Judgment their attorneys stated that while Dan Brown denied ever having even heard of my book before writing *The Da Vinci Code*, for the purposes of their motion, what they called 'access' to my book was 'admitted'. This was a tactical admission to comply with the requirement that in a Summary Judgment application there must be no material fact in dispute; in this case the issue of whether or not Dan Brown had read *The Vatican Boys* before writing *The Da Vinci Code*.

One of the 'big points' made in this shoddy document to emphasise the difference between the two books is this: 'Dunn tries to create the misleading impression that the illegal banking activities, the Opus Dei, the Knights and the Catholic Church is mentioned in multiple places in [*The Da Vinci Code*].'

This is nonsense. A search of *The Da Vinci Code* shows that the word 'Catholic' is used 28 times, and there are 27 references to the Knights Templar. The Opus Dei is mentioned no fewer than 86 times, also taking up around half of the 'Fact' page of the book, where it states: 'The Vatican prelature known as Opus Dei is a deeply devout Catholic sect that has been the topic of recent controversy due to reports of brainwashing, coercion, and a dangerous practice known as "corporal mortification." Opus Dei has just completed construction of a $47 million World Headquarters at 243 Lexington Avenue in New York City.'

Here by way of example is an extract from pages 40-41 of *The Da Vinci Code*: '"The head of Opus Dei?" *Of course I know of him. Who in the Church doesn't?* Aringarosa's conservative prelature had grown powerful in recent years. Their ascension to grace was jump-started in 1982 when Pope John Paul II unexpectedly elevated them to a "personal prelature of the Pope," officially sanctioning all of their practices. Suspiciously, Opus Dei's elevation occurred the same year the wealthy sect allegedly had transferred almost one billion dollars into the Vatican's Institute for Religious Works – commonly known as the Vatican Bank – bailing it out of an embarrassing bankruptcy. In a second manoeuvre that raised eyebrows, the Pope placed the founder of Opus Dei on the "fast track" for sainthood, accelerating an often century-long waiting period for canonization to a mere twenty years. Sister Sandrine could not help but feel that Opus Dei's good standing in Rome was suspect, but one did not argue with the Holy See.'

Any two books which (among other things) both make frequent references to the Knights Templar, Freemasonry, the Opus Dei, that centre around a secret about a famous blood relic and its relationship with the teachings of Catholic Church, and the covert payment of vast sums of money in dubious circumstances to secure the sainthood of Opus Dei's founder cannot possibly be said to share nothing substantial in common or not be 'similar'. And this is without considering the other litany of conspicuous similarities.

The attorneys for Dan Brown and his publishers really run aground in one of their footnotes where they say this: 'Dunn strains to reach this conclusion from two brief mentions on page 40 and 416 of *The Da Vinci Code*. There, Brown merely references the actual historical fact that the Opus Dei lent the Vatican Bank money in 1982 when the Vatican Bank was in bankruptcy (in exchange for Pope John Paul II granting Opus Dei the status of a personal prelature).'

The problem for Dan Brown's elite attorneys is this. The lending of a vast sum of money by Opus Dei to the 'bankrupt' Vatican Bank in 1982 is not an 'actual historical fact' at all. It is a 'fact' which was made up by me for *The Vatican Boys*, and which therefore does not appear anywhere else, and which therefore has no other plausible source for its appearance in *The Da Vinci Code* than my book.

It also gives the lie to the claims made by the Defendants' attorneys about Dan Brown's 'thorough research in works of popular history and other non-fiction works – the very type of research that any good author of historical fiction would undertake.'

Unfortunately for Mr Brown the evidence suggests his research into the Opus Dei, the Freemasons and the Catholic Church largely comprised reading my book, sending an emissary to pick my brains (as I believe he did), and then piggy-backing on my six years of research. He came unstuck when, doubtless because of that lack of research, he unwittingly uploaded into his book several of my 'fictional facts' – just as he did fictions from *The Holy Blood and the Holy Grail*.

There are more false claims in this unworthy document: 'At the outset of his opposition [to the Summary Judgment Application], Dunn argues that Brown "abruptly changed his writing style in the course of writing *The Da Vinci Code*," implying that he must have come upon *Vatican Boys* while doing his research... This is a gross distortion of Brown's annexed Witness Statement from an unrelated English action, which traces the uniform elements and writing style that Brown has employed in his prior books, <u>all historical-fiction thrillers featuring codes, and reviews the advances he made as he progressed from book to book</u>.' (Emphasis added.)

However, Dan Brown's book *Digital Fortress* is not a 'historical-fiction thriller featuring codes' at all. It is not even a work of historical fiction, but a techno-thriller novel set in the present and published in 1998. It explores the theme of government surveillance of electronically stored information on the private lives of citizens, and the possible civil liberties and ethical implications of using such technology. Nor is his book *Deception Point* historical fiction. Brown himself in his witness statement says it occupies a 'high-tech world'. It traces White House intelligence analyst Rachel Sexton's involvement in corroborating NASA's discovery of a meteorite that supposedly contains proof of extraterrestrial life.

In page 14 of the REPLY, Elizabeth McNamara tells the court that unlike the relic (the Turin Shroud) that I associate with the 'Blood of Jesus Christ', the Holy Grail that Dan Brown associates with the Blood of Jesus Christ 'is not a relic'. The problem for Ms McNamara is that apart from that proposition being obviously wrong, she omits to tell the court that *The Da Vinci Code* itself refers to the Holy Grail as a 'relic', and that consequently in this assertion she is directly contradicted by her client in his own book. She is also contradicted by her client on his own website where he describes the Holy Grail as 'a vastly important religious relic'. It is also referred to as a 'relic' thirteen times on its Wikipedia page. Either by accident or design, Ms McNamara has misled the court on yet another key issue in the dispute in attempt to persuade it of the obviously untrue proposition that there are no significant similarities between the two books.

Ms McNamara also claims that *The Da Vinci Code* is not a 'religious' novel, but is a 'secular work'. Her client appears to disagree. This is from his witness statement in *The Holy Blood and the Holy Grail* case: 'The novel's themes include: the sacred feminine; goddess worship; the Holy Grail; symbology; paganism; the history of the Bible and its accuracy, including the lost Gnostic Gospels; Templar history; the suppression of information by the church; the genealogy of Jesus; religious zealotry; and nature's grand design as evidence for the existence of God.'

Ms McNamara also claims this: 'The two books share nothing in common regarding the use of codes', apparently forgetting at that moment the title of her own clients' work which includes the word 'code', and that the word 'code' appears nearly 90 times in *The Da Vinci Code*. This is from Chapter XXIV of *The Vatican Boys*: 'The password, too, was ludicrously simple. The account number combinations went together too easily; the first two and last two digits of each set were exactly the same.'

And: 'Christ, he's (Michael Macheras) just about piecing the fucking numbers together for us and giving us the code word.' In *The Vatican Boys* Chapter XXIV, 'the five-letter password is IBIZA.'

Ms McNamara also makes this claim: '*The Vatican Boys* does not discuss any of this material about Mary Magdalene, the Gnostic Gospels.' Once again Ms McNamara tries to mislead the court because the text of the two books reads differently. This is from Chapter VII of *The Vatican Boys*: '... the discovery of the seven Dead Sea Scrolls in 1947 in a cave in Qumran, near Jericho and the Dead Sea and about 50 kilometers from Jerusalem. The scrolls had been found inside jars that protected them from the humidity, a practice which was described in the Bible and the Apocrypha.' (The Gnostic Gospels are found in the Dead Sea Scrolls.)

And this is from Chapter 55 of *The Da Vinci Code*: '"Fortunately for historians," Teabing said, "some of the gospels that Constantine attempted to eradicate managed to survive. The Dead Sea Scrolls were found in the 1950s hidden in a cave near Qumran in the Judean desert. And, of course, the Coptic Scrolls in 1945 at Nag Hammadi."'

She is also economical with the truth in the sentence: 'Dunn also tries to create the impression that Brown has been judged to have improperly incorporated into his book when, in fact, the two copyright claims against Brown's successful novel have been forcefully dismissed.'

The Defendants' lawyers must have known that Dan Brown had been found by Mr Justice Smith to have copied parts of The *Holy Blood and the Holy Grail*, and to have tried to mislead the court about having done so on oath.

The same attorneys served a Reply on behalf of Sony Pictures, which was no better than the one served for Dan Brown and Penguin Random House. After telling the court that it should 'just read the books' to determine substantial similarity, Elizabeth McNamara then tries to persuade the judge by means of another set of dubious submissions that the books share nothing in common.

In asserting 'There is No Genuine Issue to be Tried' at page 2 of the SONY REPLY Ms McNamara tells the court that *The Da Vinci Code* has 'an ending that does not remotely echo anything in *Vatican Boys*.' However, Ms McNamara does not tell the court what actually happens at the ending of *The Da Vinci Code* where there is a family reunion, which closely mirrors what happens at the ending of *The Vatican Boys*. She also omits to tell the court the following:

1. At the end of *The Da Vinci Code* Sophie is reunited with her grandmother. At the end of *The Vatican Boys* the family reunites with an old Gypsy woman.
2. In both books the old woman is the other high-ranking member of the brotherhood protecting the secrets of the relic, and at the end of both books it is she who reveals its secrets.

3. In both books it is revealed at the end that there are two relics, not just one, and that they are identical.

4. Both books end with the two relics coming together.

5. In both books this joining of the two relics at the ending is necessary to prove a central theme of the book, in *The Vatican Boys* that Jesus was divine, and in *The Da Vinci Code* that Jesus was not divine.

6. In both books the family member reunion at the ending is with a male character who is 'the keeper of the relic'. In *The Vatican Boys* he is the old woman's brother, and in *The Da Vinci Code* he is the old woman's husband.

7. In both books this character is the one who had the relic and knew its secret in the beginning of the story.

8. At the conclusion of both books the story returns to the same place as its commencement.

In pages 3-5 of the SONY REPLY Ms McNamara says this: 'One is ... transported to Paris (and London ...) in *The Da Vinci Code* Motion Picture in a way that is simply absent in *Vatican Boys*.' Here are two of *The Vatican Boys*' Chapter Headings: 'Paris' and 'London'. Ms McNamara appears to be trying to distract the court from the striking commonality of London's Fleet Street being the transition of the story in both books.

Ms McNamara later says: '*The Da Vinci Code* Motion Picture and *The Vatican Boys* quite simply tell two entirely different stories. At its very core the [*Da Vinci Code* novel] revolves around solving complex clues to figure out a secret.' This, however, also describes the story of *The Vatican Boys*.

Ms McNamara's next departure is this: 'The secondary plot [of

The Vatican Boys] of the sacred shroud does not involve a religious secret to be discovered. Rather, the shroud is safely in the hands of Father Rovarik from the onset of the novel.' Yet again, she is wrong. This is from Chapter XXIII of *The Vatican Boys*: 'To publish evidence strongly questioning the validity of church teachings was not considered to be in the best interests of the church and the reports had been suppressed by the Vatican.' The 'sacred shroud' which holds the 'religious secret' being sought in *The Vatican Boys* does not stay safely in the hands of Father Rovarik. That is the very reason why he along with Catherine Turrell and Stephen Hathaway are looking for it, and why the Opus Dei's Jeremy and Peter Zagranski oppose them – just like Sophie Neveu, Robert Langdon and Leigh Teabing fight the Opus Dei's Silas and Bishop Aringarosa in *The Da Vinci Code*.

It is of course not difficult to create even a *bona fide* document which itemises differences between one substantial novel running to around 470 pages, as *The Da Vinci Code* is, and another which is about half its length, *The Vatican Boys*. When the text has grown to be twice as long it is bound to include new elements. Nobody with sufficient intellect to write a novel which was copied from another would be foolish enough not to make at least some attempt to inject differences between the two books in an effort to cover their tracks. In the case of *The Da Vinci Code*, the main differences come from many of the elements of his book that Dan Brown plagiarized from *The Holy Blood and the Holy Grail*.

Nor is it sufficient to point out – as is a key theme in these documents – that some at least of the convergent elements are common in a particular genre, though none that I am aware of in this genre have any way near this degree of similarity, and, tellingly, no such example is offered by the Defendants' attorneys – something which Jonathan always does when he is defending copyright claims. The point is if all the common features in a genre are ordered according to the same chronology, then that is at least proof of 'similarity'.

In fact, even if you restrict your assessment simply to the convergences between the two books which are effectively conceded by Ms McNamara and her colleagues in the two Replies, the books still have a great deal in common, and the statistical likelihood of that being the product of mere chance is infinitesimal.

By May 2007 Dan Brown's publishers had been victorious in the appeal lodged against the ruling in *The Holy Blood and the Holy Grail* trial in London. But we did not let that deter us. We were sure that we had right on our side and I had a God-fearing man's faith that eventually the truth about how Dan Brown attained his literary success would come out. That was why, when the day of the hearing came around, I was confident that our cause would succeed. There was no way, or at least so I thought, that any judge who studied the evidence could find that there was 'no possibility that a reasonable person could find any similarity', which is what was being asked of Judge Michael Ponsor by the Defendants.

It is difficult within the constraints of a book to do justice to the thoroughness and cogency of the 65 pages of written evidence that we prepared in response to the Defendant's Summary Judgment motion. You can read it in full at the "materials" link on the website. Here are just some of the convergences that we highlight in that document:

1.   '... both begin with a ritualistic murder of a Mason-Knight,

... who knows a secret involving the Catholic Church, the Knights, the Opus the Dei, a lot of money and a relic linked to the blood of Christ ... [which] is passed on in both stories'.

2. '... the secret is kept in a Knight's private bank. The banker is a friend of the central female character's father/grandfather and they were all at a party at the family's French country estate. Even though the banker knows they are fugitives, he helps the male and female characters get into the account at his bank ... They access the secret in the bank account using a number sequence code that utilises the number two'.

3. 'After [the two mercenaries] are introduced ... the first thing they ... do is examine the floor in a famous church searching for the relic linked to Jesus Christ. There is a nun associated with each of these characters at the same time ... in both stories [the lead male and female character] band together to follow the clues left by ... the murdered Mason-Knight ...'.

4. 'The password [required to access the secret] is kept in the Knight's bank'.

5. Both books then feature an eccentric Catholic Priest and historian who gives a tutorial on church history and the blood relic of Jesus Christ, and explains 'how the Catholic Church hides truth from the world that threatens its power'.

And so it goes on. The document also cites a number of other small but significant clues that Dan Brown's book plagiarizes mine:

1. 'Descriptions of the world's condition as "going mad" are in both books almost on the same page, and the descriptions occur in exactly the same sequence with regard to the progression of the story. Furthermore, both characters speaking in [the two books] are arriving at airports in the same famous city and then riding in a taxi or hired car.'

2. 'In both [books] the characters go through a mansion, a "safe place". In [*The Vatican Boys*] ... it is described ... as "a haven and ... a safe place" ... In [*The Da Vinci Code*] ... it is "an ideal harbor".'

3. 'In both books the mansion is a safe place and the characters discuss matters relating to the Catholic Church and the Opus Dei that are suspicious. These matters have been supressed by the Church because they threaten the Church's doctrines and teachings. This ... supports the central theme, ... identical in both books.'

4. 'At this point in both stories all of the historical information regarding the Dead Sea Scrolls, the Gnostic Gospels, the Turin Shroud and the Holy Grail all relics linked to the blood of Christ have been introduced. Everyone, including the Opus Dei, is going to London to find them.'

5. The lead characters in both books then go to Fleet Street in London.

6. The mercenaries are both healed by means of a miracle.

7. Later both mercenaries are depicted running through the streets of London in a state of crazed frenzy.

8. In both books, '[the] Opus Dei is defeated in London'.

9. In both books the Opus Dei disgorge ill-gotten gains to compensate victims of Opus Dei crimes.

10. In both books, 'The Characters go to a Famous Holy Church'.

11. The Defendants ... claim that the Knights ... do not feature in Dunn's plot line ... [but] References to Knights in TVB include:

  (i)   A Knight-Mason is murdered in a ritualistic killing ...

  (ii) The Knight murdered left clues behind ...

  (iii) The Knights have a relationship with the Opus Dei ...

  (iv) The clues lead to a Knight's private bank ...

  (v)   Turrell's family is historically linked to the Knights ...

  (vi) The Private Bank is run by a Knight Banker who is a friend of Turrell's father...

  (vii) Turrell met (or was seen by) the Knight Banker at a Party at her family's French Country Estate ...

  (viii) The code needed to access the secrets in the account at the Knight's Bank is a number sequence code and a five-letter password ...

  (ix) The Knight helps Hathaway and Turrell get in and escape from this bank with the secret.

Given this veritable tsunami of evidence in my favour, the events described in the next chapter may come as something of a shock. They certainly did to me and my attorneys.

7

The Ponsor Scheme

On the fateful morning of the hearing I met Gary and my other attorney, Howard Safford, outside the federal court building in Springfield. Howard was a college fraternity brother and one of the most remarkable people I have ever met. He had been hurt badly in an accident in high school and lost the use of his legs. Since then he had been in a wheelchair, but that had not stopped him from going to college, graduating law school, and then becoming a highly respected and brilliant assistant district attorney in Springfield. The three of us had a short meeting before we went into court to make sure we were fully prepared. As the courtroom filled with my friends and local reporters Judge Ponsor entered and instructed Gary to begin.

I was sure the wind was in our sails. But we were about to hit a reef and sink.

'Your Honour,' said Gary, 'we recognise that ideas cannot be copyrighted, but we also know that the expression of ideas can be.'

'There are deep pockets in this courtroom,' Judge Ponsor declared, rather stating the obvious given the billions of dollars ranged against us, though that was something to which justice should have been blind. This is the judicial oath which Judge Ponsor swore on his appointment: 'I do solemnly swear (or affirm) that I will administer justice without respect to persons, and do equal right to the poor and to the rich, and that I will faithfully and impartially discharge and perform all the duties incumbent upon me ... under the Constitution and laws of the United States. So help me God.'

As well as being a departure from Judge Ponsor's sworn duty, that comment was an ominous opening salvo. Gary was then cut off by Ponsor mid-way through his opening. 'I'm going to award heavy legal fees against the loser. Continue, Attorney Ensor.'

Gary was a consummate professional and quickly regained his composure in the face of this wholly inappropriate judicial interruption. There was no doubt that the interjection had startled many of the onlookers in the courtroom – including me. Gary resumed his argument, outlining initially in broad terms the comprehensive plagiarism we were certain had taken place.

'And what do you have to say, Attorney Safford?' Ponsor interjected once again.

By that time my puzzlement had receded. Now I was livid. There seemed to be an insinuation that this was just a meritless plagiarism claim made against a 'reputable author' (as his publisher would later describe him to my UK attorney) and their prominent international publisher, a sense of *how dare he make these outrageous allegations against such distinguished defendants.*

Watching from the back of the room behind the bar which separated the judge and lawyers from everybody else, I felt my heart sink. If there was a predilection on the part of the judge favouring power and status, what hope was there of a fair hearing for an underdog?

Against court protocol I got up from my seat to confer with Gary and Howard. I needed to know if this was a fair way to conduct a hearing, and if there was any objection we could raise over this bias against us on the part of the judge. There were clear signs of greater power than mine being wielded in the court room, and a judge who lacked the moral courage to stand up to it. What I did not realise at the time was that Judge Ponsor had been a frustrated novelist since his college days some forty years before, and that perhaps he also wanted to curry favour with a prospective future publisher of his work.

I will never know if this was Judge Ponsor's motivation in being so confrontational at the hearing that day, or whether he was just in thrall to the awesome power and resources on the other side of the court from us. But to me there seemed little doubt that he had decided both the tone and outcome of the hearing before he even walked into the court – despite the much greater potency of our written submissions. Scolded for daring to breach protocol and speak to my representatives, I was sent back to my seat at the back of the courtroom.

'Perhaps you should have a conference with your client, Attorney Ensor, and convince him to give up this action?' Judge Ponsor went on.

But my attorneys rightly ignored this unjudicial invitation. 'Might I proceed?' asked Howard.

'If you must,' the judge answered dismissively to my attorney who was just doing his best for his client, who in turn was exercising his constitutional right to a fair trial of his claim.

Not intimidated, Howard manoeuvred his wheelchair closer to the judge and proceeded with his account of the plagiarism that we had uncovered.

'The novels both begin with the murders of Masonic figures, a respected cryptologist teaming with a glamorous French woman to solve a mystery, and with Opus Dei assassins being hired to hunt down a holy relic before the lead characters do. The transition chapters in both *The Vatican Boys* and *The Da Vinci Code* are set on Fleet Street in the City of London with all the characters coming in from Paris, France. They're there because they've solved clues and codes that point them to London as the location of a holy relic linked to the blood of Jesus Christ and which could destroy the Catholic Church. In both novels the lead characters team up with a scholar who is an expert on Christian history. Meanwhile, the head of Opus Dei and his hired killer are racing them for the relic. By the end of both novels, the code gets solved by the middle-aged academic and his glamorous French sidekick – and they, not the sinister Opus Dei characters, reveal the true history of Jesus Christ.'

There was much more to say once the general sweep of the similarities was set out and we were ready to take the judge through all the plethora of specific similarities between the two books which was the key evidence supporting my copyright infringement case. But at this point Judge Ponsor stopped Howard in his tracks long before he could complete his submissions. 'That's enough,' he said.

'I'm not finished,' Howard told him.

'Yes, you are.' Ponsor turned to Elizabeth McNamara, the lead attorney for Dan Brown, Random House and Sony Pictures.

'We're going to rely on your judgment, your honour,' McNamara replied, who could see which way the judge was leaning. 'We ask that you deny the Plaintiff his request of a jury trial and grant our motion for Summary Judgment.'

Judge Ponsor declared he would not rule on these points that day, and there would be investigation by him with a decision in the coming months. My team and I knew his decision was crucial. If we were granted our request for a jury trial I felt certain that the legal process would work in our favour.

I had already seen that night in the Barnes & Noble bookstore how convinced the 'ordinary reader' had been by the numerous 'convergences' between the two books. Having seen the way the legal system in the UK, where decisions are made by a judge alone, determined the claims of copyright infringement in *The Holy Blood and the Holy Grail* trial, I felt certain that a US-style jury trial better served our cause, especially because in the US a copyright claim is made out if it is evident to an 'ordinary reader' that one work is derived from another. So, evidently, did Dan Brown's legal team. The fact that they were pushing to exclude a jury only confirmed that they would rather rely on a judge's interpretation of the 'ordinary reader' test, perhaps because a single judge is easier to sway than a jury of 12.

'All rise!' barked a court officer as Judge Ponsor got up from the bench and exited the courtroom. The hearing had lasted only a few minutes.

At last I was free to converse with my legal team without fear of being scolded by a judge who seemed to think my attorneys and I were trespassers in his court.

'What the hell was that?' I asked Gary and Howard as the courtroom emptied around us.

Howard just stared at me with a concerned expression.

'I've never seen anything like it,' Gary replied.

It was a bad omen.

That was a long summer darkened by uncertainty. The hardest part was that Judge Ponsor's aggressive attitude towards my case had prompted unanticipated doubts in my mind about the fairness of the US justice system. Though I never doubted the merits of our claim, I had reluctantly become wary of the judicial process in which I had previously had such confidence.

Even so I remained sure that given the opportunity to try the case in front of a jury we would win. The books were identical in so many aspects that any reasonable jury would dismiss any 'mere coincidence' argument – as the Defendants had no choice but to claim as their defence.

You can imagine how my heart was stirred when in September 2007 on the long drive to Montreal for a business conference my cell-phone flashed with Gary Ensor's number. I was in considerable pain that day. I had almost cancelled the trip because I had just had a dental procedure and my jaw was throbbing, so I was not ready for any news Gary was about to convey. Nevertheless, I pulled over. The leaves were turning to russet and red all over Vermont. It should have been a beautiful day.

Gary's news was stark.

'What do you mean we don't get a jury trial?' I exclaimed.

Attorneys are adept at breaking bad news to their clients gently, but this crashed over me like a storm breaker. I knew how much more difficult it would make our case – especially with the kind of hostile reception we had received from Judge Ponsor. But worse was to come.

'Judge Ponsor took it upon himself to evaluate all of the evidence himself and he's granted their Motion for Summary Judgment. It means not only there won't be a jury, Jack, but no trial at all. I'm so sorry.'

'But what was his justification for the decision?' I asked, trying to make sense of it.

Gary was brief. '*There are NO substantial similarities between the two stories,*' he said, quoting Ponsor's words verbatim. I leave you to judge when you have finished this book if that is a conclusion that any fair judge could have come to.

'None?' I replied, angrily. I do not like being angry – it does not suit me and it is not ordinarily in my nature. But I felt real rage bubbling in me now. 'Jesus Christ, Gary, there are too many to count.'

'He also says that he could find no precedent regarding copyright protection for structural copying.'

I looked at the mountains that surrounded me. In other circumstances it could have been beautiful and peaceful environs. But this news made the world seem noxious.

'Come into my office when you get back and we'll discuss everything,' Gary told me. I could hear the disappointment and frustration in his voice. Then he hung up.

That night I stayed at the Hilton in downtown Montreal. I could not eat dinner, no matter how hard I tried. I almost got sick in the restaurant. I spent the night restless and sleepless, afraid about what might happen next. I kept hearing Judge Ponsor's words, 'I'm going to award heavy legal fees against the loser', by which he clearly meant me.

For the first time I wondered if I should have just rolled over and accepted from the outset that power and status were always going to defeat me, and if fighting this thing had been worth it. But I had thought that the prospects of our success were absolute, not just because we had right on our side, but we could also prove it. What I was just beginning to realise was that right could be a malleable thing in the American legal system – and that, where money and power are concerned, judicial decisions can be bought by financial muscle being used to hire expensive, smart and mercenary attorneys – just as in *Erin Brockovich* and *Dark Waters*.

I did not have the money to lose this case. I was fighting it because I was in the right and I thought the world should know the true story about how that best-selling thriller came to be written. But to lose would crush me – not just emotionally, but financially as well. I could hear the judge's warning about 'heavy costs against the loser' ringing in my ears.

It did not take long for Dan Brown's attorneys to show me exactly how to use money as a crude weapon against justice.

Only days after Michael Ponsor issued his decision Elizabeth McNamara called Gary to tell him that unless I signed away my right to appeal her clients would voraciously pursue me for the 'heavy costs' with which the judge had threatened me at the hearing, just as they had Michael Baigent.

Faced with this exercise of brute force by my much more powerful opponents raising the possibility of my financial ruin, I did what I never thought I would have to do. I beat a retreat, which meant that I had first been robbed of my constitutional right to a jury trial, and then hustled out of my right to appeal against a judgment that was fundamentally flawed both in its analysis of the facts and the law.

You can read the Ponsor judgment in full in the materials section of the website. Here are just some of the reasons why it is wrong, and why I believe the attorneys representing Dan Brown and his publishers were so keen to bully me into signing away my right to appeal.

Judge Ponsor based his extraordinary finding that, 'no substantial similarity exists between *The Vatican Boys* and *The Da Vinci Code*' on seven findings of fact as set out these numbered paragraphs. Each and every one of them is wrong, as we explain in bullet points after each one:

1. 'Brown's hero, Stephen [*Jack: In fact his name is Robert – Stephen is the Christian name of my hero; not a good start*] Langdon, is a Harvard professor, baffled and overwhelmed at times, but likeable and trustworthy. In the end, the central female character begins to fall in love with him, and the two agree to meet after the action in the novel concludes. Dunn's central male character, Stephen Hathaway, is a greedy, macho rat. At the end of *The Vatican Boys* the central female character wisely cuts off contact with him.'

   - In both books the central male characters are 45-ish American, handsome and smart.
   - Their main role is to assist the central female character in figuring out her family's secrets.
   - Both the male characters find themselves 'baffled and overwhelmed' at one time or another; not just Robert Langdon.
   - In *The Vatican Boys* there is a relationship bond between the two lead characters Stephen Hathaway and Catherine Turrell, just like there is in *The Da Vinci Code* between Robert Langdon and Sophie Neveu.
   - In both books the couples come together solely to solve the riddle of why the man was ritually

murdered in the opening of the story, and to uncover a secret he left behind, which they do it by solving clues and codes, and they become involved in a search for a blood relic linked to the life of Jesus Christ, which originally was the Turin Shroud for both books.

2. 'The central female character of Dunn's novel, Catherine Turrell, is a con artist and recovering drug addict, saved during the course of the novel by religion. The central female character in *The Da Vinci Code*, Sophie Neveu, is a distant offspring of Jesus Christ, a trained cryptographer, a resourceful and reliable sidekick for Langdon, and the granddaughter of the curator of the Louvre. Plaintiff's suggestion that these two characters are in any way similar is absurd.'

Actually, it is the judge's conclusion which is absurd because:
- The central female characters play near identical roles in the two books.
- They are both glamorous.
- They are both savvy.
- They are both 35ish.
- They are both French.
- They are both upper-class.
- They both have ties to a Christian brotherhood.
- Even though both are estranged from their father (my book) grandfather (Brown's book), they are both connected to a friend of his, a debonair banker

who is also a member of the Christian brotherhood and owns a private bank.

- In both books they are the character who knows why the man was murdered at the beginning of the story, and how to extract the secret from the private bank where it has been hidden.
- They both team up with the central male character to find the secret by solving a series of clues/codes, which also bear striking similarities.
- Along with their equivalent male characters they join up with a Christian Scholar (Father Karl Rovarik in my book and Leigh Teabing in Brown's).
- Together the three characters search for a blood relic that the Opus Dei is also trying to track down, which then becomes a desperate race between them.

3. 'The villain in *The Da Vinci Code*, Leigh Teabing, a cultivated and calculating killer, has no parallel in *The Vatican Boys*. Plaintiff's attempt to suggest that his character, Father Karl Rovarik, a Benedictine priest who embodies goodness and holiness in *The Vatican Boys*, was somehow copied by Brown to create Teabing is patently ridiculous.'

- Ponsor is wrong here because he makes a glaring error about the roles of the characters by equating Leigh Teabing with Father Karl Rovarik, ascribing to them the parallel roles as villains in the stories.

Perhaps he would not have made this error had he let my attorneys finish their oral submissions, though their respective roles are clearly explained in our written submissions.

- In *The Vatican Boys* the main villain is the Opus Dei leader Archbishop Peter Zagranski, 'the head of the Opus Dei', who hired the mercenary killer Jeremy Willoughby to find the missing relic. He is totally unscrupulous in his quest to get it, and condones the use of murder and treachery, and uses the Vatican Bank's money to obtain it.

- In *The Da Vinci Code* Teabing is a villain who is chasing after the relic. But the Opus Dei Bishop Manuel Aringarosa is obviously the parallel character to Peter Zagranski in *The Vatican Boys*, as 'the head of the Opus Dei'. They are both introduced at the beginning of the story.

- Just like Zagranski in *The Vatican Boys*, in *The Da Vinci Code* Aringarosa is immediately hooked up with the Opus Dei mercenary killer to seek the relic. He performs the same functions as Zagranski, and Aringarosa's appearances occur both in similar physical locations and at the same chronological points in both stories.

- In *The Da Vinci Code* Aringarosa is following the Opus Dei killer's actions and knows he is committing crimes to get the relic. Just like Zagranski in *The Vatican Boys*, Aringarosa in *The Da Vinci Code* is the one who has access to the Vatican Bank's money as the means whereby they can and get their hands on the relic.

4. 'Plaintiff's attempt to draw parallels between his character, Jeremy Willoughby, a "steely-eyed Yankee" mercenary totally uninterested in religion, and Brown's fanatically religious, homicidal albino monk Silas is utterly lacking in support from the texts.'

Judge Ponsor picks out two differentiating elements between the two characters, but ignores all the numerous common features:

- Both are engaged by the Opus Dei.
- Both are members of the Opus Dei.
- Both therefore have at least some faith allegiance.
- Both have been elevated from a regular member of the group.
- Both are mercenaries.
- Both have become fanatical killers.
- Both perform the same roles and appear in the same places.
- Both commit ritual murders in the opening of the books.
- The purpose of both murders is to keep a dark religious secret from being discovered.
- They are both hired by the Opus Dei to find a missing blood relic linked to the life of Jesus Christ.
- The first place they both go to find the relic is a famous holy church.

- They both look in its floor for a sacred rock.
- In *The Vatican Boys* Jeremy goes to the Church of the Holy Sepulchre on the Via Dolorosa and finds the Rock of Golgotha.
- In *The Da Vinci Code* Silas goes to the Church of Saint Sulpice, on the Roseline and finds the Keystone.
- In both books they chase after the female lead, the male lead and Scholar who are trying to secure the relic.
- This eventually leads both characters to London, but they do not secure the relic for the 'head of the Opus Dei'.
- A 'miracle' happens in London to both of them.
- At that point both exit their respective books in London and are last seen near a hospital.

5. 'The timing and setting of the two novels are entirely distinct. *The Da Vinci Code* takes place over a few days in Paris, London, and Scotland. *The Vatican Boys* extends from 1964 to 1997, with the bulk of the action taking place over several months in 1996, sometimes in Paris and London, but also in Vermont, Ontario, Jerusalem, Madrid, Toronto, Martha's Vineyard, Monte Carlo, and Tibet.'

This is a highly selective and misleading analysis because:
- The period of the events in both books is in the second half of the 1990s.

- In both books there is a papal Catholic conclave in the 1990s in Rome, an event made up by me.
- Both books portray significant events in Paris and London, and have a climactic scene at the Opus Dei House in London.
- Fleet Street is a key location in both stories.
- The code is cracked in London in both stories.
- The characters are seen in the tiny principality of Monaco in *The Da Vinci Code*, and Monaco's capital Monte Carlo in *The Vatican Boys*.

6. '*The Da Vinci Code* relies on a series of clues and puzzles to draw the reader along and allow the plot to unfold. *The Vatican Boys* uses no such device and follows a traditional thriller format.'

Again, Judge Ponsor is simply wrong:
- *The Vatican Boys* in fact has numerous 'clues and puzzles', and their parallels in *The Da Vinci Code* are legion.
- The first clue in *The Vatican Boys* is in 'Buddy's glass eye' – tiny bits of microfilm containing account numbers.
- The second clue in *The Vatican Boys* is hidden in 'the slit in the backing of a painting.'
- *The Vatican Boys* has a 'puzzle' in the form of a number sequence code to get the secret out of the Knight's private bank involves the number 2, with the first two and last two numbers being related.

The password has five letters and it is related to the central female's life.

- In *The Vatican Boys* the puzzles, number code and password are described as being 'simple' to figure out.
- In *The Da Vinci Code* the first clue is also hidden in 'the slit in the backing of a painting'.
- In *The Da Vinci Code* the number sequence code to get the secret out of the Knight's private bank involves the number 2, with the first two and last two numbers being related. The password has five letters and it is related to the central female's life.
- In *The Da Vinci Code* the number code and password are described as being 'simple' to figure out.

7. 'As noted, *The Vatican Boys* expresses an allegiance, both implicit and explicit, to traditional Catholic doctrine, whereas the central tenet of *The Da Vinci Code* is precisely the opposite. Much more could be said along these lines, but no more is necessary. Far from being similar, the characters, plot devices, settings, pacing, tone, and theme of the two books are entirely different. Even if a theory of copyright infringement could be based on a similarity of general thematic or structural elements, which is doubtful, no such similarity exists here. One could as easily claim (if the authors had lived contemporaneously) that Hemingway's *Old Man and the Sea* violated the copyright of Melville's *Moby Dick* (aging seaman encounters large

fish), Hardy's *Tess of the d'Urbervilles* violated the copyright of Tolstoy's *Anna Karenina* (woman succumbs to passion, suffers consequences), or Joyce's *Portrait of the Artist as a Young Man* violated the copyright of Dickens' *David Copperfield* (troubled childhood leads to writing career).

- As I acknowledge in the Preface, there is one fundamental theological divide between my book and Dan Brown's which is the one legitimate point of divergence that Ponsor identifies in his judgment.
- If by 'traditional Catholic Doctrine' the judge means the Apostle's Creed, then he is right. The divergent and controversial elements of Brown's book which deny Christ's divinity and his death by crucifixion and resurrection which ride a coach and horses through the Apostle's Creed are, however, not original to Dan Brown, but are also taken from the work of others – the writers of *The Holy Blood and the Holy Grail.*
- But *The Vatican Boys* also describes serious errors in the teaching of the Catholic Church and portrays profound conflicts within it. It also recounts its unethical and immoral practices and shameful elements of its past – just as does *The Da Vinci Code.*
- These failings within one of the most powerful institutions on the planet is central to the story of

The Vatican Boys, which – like *The Da Vinci Code* – tells how the Catholic church has been involved in murders, Vatican Bank scandals, with members of its hierarchy and brotherhoods engaged in illegal activities all around the world.

- To illustrate conflicts in the Catholic Church doctrines my book uses plot devices such as a seminal blood relic (the Turin Shroud), and especially the Dead Sea Scrolls (Gnostic Writings) to show that the Catholic Church 'suppresses' information that potentially conflicts with its teachings and doctrines.

- Likewise, Brown's book uses plot devices such as a seminal blood relic (the Holy Grail – though originally the Turin Shroud), and especially the Dead Sea Scrolls to show that the Catholic Church 'suppresses' information that conflicts with its teachings and doctrines.

- Another significant convergence between the books which derives from the ructions in the Catholic Church comes from the murky nature of its history in 1982 which is hugely significant in the plots of both *The Vatican Boys* and *The Da Vinci Code*.

- Before launching into a series of false literary analogies, Ponsor says this: 'Even if a theory of copyright infringement could be based on a similarity of general thematic or structural elements … no such similarity exists here.' I am at a loss to understand how anyone who has actually read the two books can possibly claim that there are no thematic or structural similarities, when in a plethora of instances the two books are pretty well thematically and structurally identical.

- The literary analogies that he goes on to deploy are absurd and completely misrepresent my case against Dan Brown.

Even according to the skewed submissions made on behalf of the Defendants – either by positive admission or lack of challenge to our evidence – the two books have these unchallenged factors in common:

1. The theology, history and ethics of the Roman Catholic church;
2. The nature and role of the Opus Dei in the Church;
3. The role of the Freemasons both in both Opus Dei and the Church;
4. A ritualistic murder in opening scene;
5. Its purpose is to protect a secret;
6. The murderer is an Opus Dei member and operative;
7. He is a mercenary;
8. He is a ruthless killer;
9. He then pursues the two main characters;
10. He also seeks the religious artefact sought by the main characters;
11. The context of his pursuit is a race between those representing religious authority against a team comprising an American male and French female;

12. The respective roles played by the American male and French female are closely related;

13. The American male and French female in both books have much in common;

14. The subject of the race is ancient artefact with huge religious significance because its association with the blood of Jesus Christ;

15. The use of the 'cilice' (spelled 'celice' in *The Vatican Boys*) as a self-torture device;

16. The cilice being in form of a barbed *belt* which is progressively tightened to inflict pain;

17. Such use of this device deriving from the teachings of Opus Dei;

18. The historical context is a vast payment by Opus Dei to the Vatican Bank;

19. The payment is required because the Vatican Bank is in severe financial difficulty;

20. As an apparent consequence of that payment the founder of Opus Dei is fast-tracked to sainthood;

21. Opus Dei Headquarters as a setting;

22. Fleet Street (London) as a setting;

23. Paris as a setting;

24. Monaco/Monte Carlo as a setting;

25. At the end it is revealed that there are two parts of the relic being sought, and that they are identical.

In addition to his absurd findings of fact, Judge Ponsor also gets his law wrong and is selective in his quoting of precedent cases. He cites the famous 1930 Nichols decision and the seminal Judge Learned

Hand's advice from that case about experts, but does take account of what he says about how literary copyright cases should be decided. Ponsor says on page 5 of his judgment:

> 'No less an authority than Judge Learned Hand has observed that expert opinion in this arena "cumbers the case and tends to confusion, for the more the court is led into the intricacies of dramatic craftsmanship, the less likely it is to stand upon the firmer, if more naive, ground of its considered impressions upon its own perusal." Nichols v. Universal Pictures Corp.'

But in the same judgment 'No less an authority than Judge Learned Hand' makes these observations which Ponsor ignored:

> 'It is of course essential to any protection of literary property, whether at common-law or under the statute, that the right cannot be limited literally to the text, else a plagiarist would escape by immaterial variations. That has never been the law ... Then the question is whether the part so taken is "substantial," and therefore not a "fair use" of the copyrighted work; it is the same question as arises in the case of any other copyrighted work ... As respects plays, the controversy chiefly centers upon the characters and sequence of incident, these being the substance.'

Yes indeed. No plagiarist should be able to escape by 'immaterial variations' Judge Ponsor. If only it had been the great Judge Learned Hand presiding in his place I am sure the outcome would have been different. Had Judge Ponsor undertaken a proper character 'sequence of incident' analysis, he would have compared the characters in *The Vatican Boys* and *The Da Vinci Code* in (a) order of appearances, (b) places of appearances (c) how and why the characters are paired up, (d) identifying correctly the protagonists and antagonists, (e) evaluating their roles and motivations, (f) comparing their conflicts, (g) documenting the information they each give in the story, (h) identifying the locations where they act in the story, not just the cities but the actual physical streets and buildings, (i) showing what they are each after and where, and (j) comparing all of their outcomes. This would not have been hard, because all the work was done for him in our written submissions.

If Judge Ponsor had done what Judge Learned Hand had said he should do in a case which appears in his judgment, this would have absolutely ruled out the granting of Summary Judgment to the Defendants. If he was going to grant Summary Judgment to anyone it should have been to me. The question then arises: why he did not do so, and not even let my attorneys finish their submissions?

Judge Ponsor goes on to say this at pages 5-6 of his judgment:

'Second, it is noteworthy that the central argument offered by Plaintiff in support of his copyright claim – that the two works have substantial thematic and structural similarity – has little or no support in the law as a basis for a copyright claim. Plaintiff offers no allegation of verbatim, or near verbatim, copying; rather, Plaintiff asserts that the basic outlines of the two books are sufficiently similar that the latter book must, or at least may, be seen as violating Plaintiff's copyright. No prior case recognizing a theory of copyright infringement based on the sort of thematic or structural similarity posited by Plaintiff has been offered in his memorandum opposing summary judgment, nor has the court found one.'

In the highlighted section Judge Ponsor says that 'the court' (i.e. he, Judge Ponsor) has not found a case which is founded on 'a theory of copyright infringement based on the sort of thematic or structural similarity posited.' But not only was there such case in our memorandum, Judge Ponsor both cited and quoted it in his judgment – the decision of Judge Learned Hand in Nichols v. Universal Pictures.

Furthermore, though in a later case, in his 2008 Judgment Robert Patterson Jr., in a copyright case brought by JK Rowling, had no difficulty in finding that both Structure and Fictional Facts are protectable in copyright. In the UNITED STATES DISTRICT COURT SOUTHERN DISTRICT OF NEW YORK; WARNER BROS. ENTERTAINMENT INC. and J.K. ROWLING, – against – OPINION & ORDER RDR BOOKS, at Page 37 of his decision the judge says this:

'Although the entries proceed chronologically and do not use the same plot structure as do the Harry Potter novels (which structure the plot so as to create an interesting drama), the entries do provide a skeleton of the plot elements that hold the story together.

In Castle Rock Entertainment, Inc. v. Carol Publishing Group, Inc., the Second Circuit explained that such invented facts constitute creative expression protected by copyright because "characters and events spring from the imagination of [the original] authors."... ; see also Paramount Pictures

107

Corp. v. Carol Publ'g Group, (stating that "[t]he characters, plots and dramatic episodes" that comprise the story of the "fictitious history of Star Trek" are the story's "original elements," protected by copyright).'

By a strange (and I have sometimes thought suspicious) twist of fate Judge Ponsor later combined his legal profession with a career as a novelist himself. His first novel was published by Open Road Integrated Media in 2013, and was called *The Hanging Judge*. He certainly hung me.

8

The Aftermath

To sum up my experience of US justice as administered by Judge Ponsor: he appears to have ignored our written submissions, he did not give my attorneys time to plead my case in court, nor to point out all the flaws in the Reply lodged on behalf of the Defendants, and in his judgment he made seven findings of fact, all of which are wrong. He was also wrong in his interpretation of the law, and seemed to have contravened his judicial oath by siding with the powerful against the weak. Would I have won an appeal? Surely the answer is yes. But I will never know because I was forced to sign away my right to appeal because of the threat of financial ruin made by the attorneys acting for Dan Brown and his publishers.

In the year that followed I took solace in the only thing that would lift me out of the bitter disappointment of having been strong-armed out of my constitutional rights by the SWAT team of attorneys hired by Dan Brown and his publishers and a grossly incompetent (or worse) judge: I started writing again.

My fourth novel, *Babylon's Tablet of Destiny*, describes a race to find an object from ancient Assyria, one foretold by a series of stories committed in cuneiform script to stone tablets, and which has the power to change the world. It is a story written using the same formula I had been honing since *The Diary of William Goffe* – mingling historical fact, invented fiction, codes, ciphers and breakneck races across the globe. I published it in 2008, again using an independent press, and this time edited by the talented Fletcher Poret.

In March 2009 I had a call from my publisher – based in New York's Empire State Building – to tell me that the novel had been nominated for an Independent Book Publishers National Writing Award. Thousands of titles are put up for consideration and only three medals for each category are awarded. *Babylon's Tablet of Destiny* had won one of the medals for the 'Historical Fiction' category and I was invited to an awards ceremony in Manhattan in May. To say it was one of the proudest moments of my writing career would be an understatement.

I had been trying to put aside the immense disappointment of being comprehensively trounced by force of arms in the US judicial process, and this was exactly the tonic I needed to feel again that writing was worthwhile. Writing can be a lonely business and moments like these make you realise that there is a thriving literary community out there of which you are a part.

I still remember how excited I was walking into the restaurant where the IPPY Awards were held. Though we knew that we had been awarded a medal none of us knew who would be awarded the 'gold', 'silver' and 'bronze' award, so there was a frisson in the air. I had invited my editor, Fletcher Poret, to come along with me, and the first person I saw as I got through the door was my cover designer, Mike Williams. I felt strongly that whatever happened tonight the award belonged to all three of us. Writing is solitary but publishing is a communal endeavour and they deserved praise every bit as much as I did.

We were discussing the independent publishing scene – it had moved on so much in the years since *The Diary of William Goffe* driven by the monumental success of Amazon and the upsurge in e-book publishing – when a man approached us and asked if I was Jack Dunn.

'I read *The Vatican Boys*,' he told me. 'You look just like your pictures!'

I always find it humbling to meet people who have read and enjoyed my novels. I have never lost that feeling of surprise and honour that comes with it. And it was no different this time. The man introduced himself not as a writer but as a journalist and book reviewer. He had come to cover the IPPY Awards and we soon got talking about *The Vatican Boys, Belle Skinner,* and *Bayblon's Tablet of Destiny*. Meanwhile Fletcher and Mike drifted towards the bar. The names of the winners had started to be announced, but this journalist seemed so keen to speak to me that I did not let myself get distracted.

'I read about your trials and tribulations with Dan Brown,' he said. 'You know, he's got a new novel coming out soon called *The Lost Symbol*. Some friends of mine got pre-release copies.'

But this was supposed to be a celebratory night. 'I've had quite enough of Dan Brown, thank you', I censured him.

'I'll bet. Tell me, Jack, how does it feel to have Dan Brown make billions off your stories ... and all you get is this lousy little medal?'

It was not a 'lousy little medal', not to me. To me it was an honour and an acknowledgement that, though I was not troubling the New York Times bestseller lists my writing was living in the minds and imaginations of readers, and that I was worthy of being recognised as what I had always wanted to be – a writer.

'What do you mean my *stories*?' I snapped. 'It was in *The Da Vinci Code* where he lifted one of my books wholesale.'

'It's not the only time he stole from you, Jack.'

I could feel my anger bubbling up. I wanted to grab this guy by the throat and throttle him for bringing the spectre of Dan Brown into what was supposed to be a joyous occasion.

Luckily I didn't, because at that moment Fletcher and Mike had returned from the bar. Mike, sensing a change in the atmosphere, handed me a Coke.

'Are we getting close?' Fletcher asked me, noticing I was seething.

I had been given a list of the awards as they would be called out and when I held it up my hands were shaking.

'We're five prizes away,' Fletcher said, taking the list from my hands. 'Maybe another thirty minutes.'

Then I looked back at the journalist who had retreated a short distance. He was standing by a round table watching the award winners and taking notes. My Irish temper got the better of me. I weaved my way through the crowd towards him.

'You're just trying to provoke me, aren't you? Something for one of your stories?' I said forcefully, my fists clenched.

'I didn't mean to spook you, Jack,' he said. 'I figured you already knew. It's like this. He didn't just mine *The Vatican Boys* for *The Da Vinci Code*. He used the entire first part of it in *Angels & Demons* as well. That book came out in 2000, a full three years after *The Vatican Boys*. They've just made a movie out of it.' He stopped. 'You really didn't know?'

For the first time he looked taken aback.

'No,' I muttered, trying to stay calm. The fact was I was so sick of Dan Brown and his *Da Vinci Code* that I had not been able to bring myself to read any of his other novels.

'*Angels & Demons* is the first novel where he writes about Robert

Langdon. You know, the character he cribbed from your Stephen Hathaway. Take a look at it, Jack, and you'll see. Go to the first chapter in *Angels & Demons* which replicates the "Bridge of Dread" section at the start of *The Vatican Boys*. Anybody can see it. There are specific words used in Langdon's description along with scenes and locations all taken from your book.'

I was in the middle of a crowd but felt as if there was silence all around me. I felt a fool for not having discovered it myself. It was like being pummelled to the canvas for a second time.

I couldn't utter a word. I just stared blankly at him, still trying to process what he had told me.

'Jack, Jack!' Fletcher's words brought my mind back into the moment. 'You're up!'

The master of ceremonies announced, 'This year's IPPY Silver Award for Best Historical Fiction goes to Jack Dunn, with editor Fletcher Poret!'

I cannot say that the idea of bringing a second lawsuit against Dan Brown had never entered my head in the years since Judge Ponsor had crudely dismissed my initial claim and threatened to award heavy costs against me. Yet every time my thoughts drifted that way the same fear of financial ruin at the hands of a legal system that seems to favour power and money over justice and truth drove the idea out of me.

Now, however, I could feel the old fire in my belly. The passages I had been alerted to in Dan Brown's *Angels & Demons* corroborated my conviction that I was the victim of literary robbery. The similarities between the opening of *Angels & Demons* and the 'Bridge of Dread' scene in *The Vatican Boys* were so startling and specific that it seemed to me and my close friend, Tom Kenefick, a fraternity brother who had gone on to be a brilliant attorney and who agreed to counsel me going forward, that the commonalities could not be coincidental.

Both scenes open with a terrifying dream sequence from which the lead characters are rudely awoken by a telephone call from the director of a research facility. In my book the telephone call comes from a man named Maxwell; in *Angels & Demons*, from a man named Maximillian – not very subtle. After the telephone call both characters get up and, upon looking in the mirror, see their reflections as ghosts of their youthful selves. Both characters are described as forty years old, American, handsome and athletic who like to dress casually and love good clean fun – especially involving water. In my book the character is called Stephen Hathaway, and in Dan Brown's book Robert Langdon.

I am only scratching the surface here. The overall plot of *Angels & Demons* does not mirror *The Vatican Boys* as *The Da Vinci Code* does, but the first forty pages of the novel have numerous direct parallels in my book.

This revelation about *Angels & Demons* allowed me to build up a clearer picture of what must have happened for the books to 'converge' as they had. Because *Angels & Demons* precedes *The Da Vinci Code* by three years, having been published in 2000 – three years after *The Vatican Boys* – it seems likely that *The Vatican Boys* was bought soon after its publication, possibly at the Barnes & Noble where Dan Brown bought his research material, and then found itself on his desk and that of his wife. Perhaps it had inspired Brown to move from the science-based genre of his earlier novels to the kind of religious historical thriller that I had written.

Elements of *The Vatican Boys* suffuse the early parts of *Angels & Demons*, but the book then follows its own plotline. I contend that only later, after publishing another science fiction novel (*Deception Point*), when Brown decided to write a religious-themed thriller, did he decide to plunder *The Vatican Boys* again. We know from his own testimony that he had hit a creative block and needed something to help him to overcome it. We now also know that *The Vatican Boys* had been used to launch an earlier novel. It takes only a short leap of the imagination to piece together what happened next. *The Vatican Boys* was lodged in his mind and so was transported into the pages of one of the most successful novels of all time.

I brought the second copyright infringement action *pro se*, representing myself, against Dan Brown and Simon & Schuster, the publisher of *Angels & Demons*, in August 2010; another 'David and Goliath' fight. Remembering my earlier bitter experience, I pursued the claim through the Boston Federal District Court to ensure it was not heard in Springfield by Judge Michael Ponsor. Yet within weeks the Boston court had moved it back to the Springfield court where Ponsor presided.

This time, however, the situation was different. There had been developments in copyright infringement cases that I was confident would work to my advantage. In 2009 a federal judge had found in favour of JD Salinger who had sought to ban publication of a sequel to his classic novel, *The Catcher in the Rye*. Previously, in 2008, JK Rowling had, in a joint action with Warner Bros who made the Harry Potter movies, launched a lawsuit against a US publisher, RDR Books, which had published an encyclopaedia of JK Rowling's fictional world called *The Harry Potter Lexicon*. JK Rowling won and RDR Books was compelled to publish a cut-down version. The aspect of the case which was pertinent to me was that the Federal Judge, Robert R. Patterson Jr., wrote this in his judgment:

> 'Furthermore, the law in this Circuit is clear that "the concept of similarity embraces not only global similarities in structure and sequence, but localized similarity in language", and "Invented facts constitute creative expression protected by copyright".'

I wondered what Michael Leigh and Richard Baigent might have made of the ruling that 'invented facts' are protected by copyright given how many there were in their book. But by this time their case had concluded, and one had passed away with the other soon to follow. For me the critical thing was that successful copyright claims based on similarities of structure had a precedent in law. In his ruling Judge Ponsor had said that 'the court' could find no laws providing copyright protection for structural copying. Well, he was wrong then. But by 2010 I thought even he could no longer hold that to be the true state of the law.

Certain that Judge Ponsor's perceived impartiality at least had by this time been undermined – not just because of his open hostility in my last lawsuit, but also because in pursuing his own writing ambitions he had established relationships with other Random House and Simon & Schuster authors – I petitioned that Judge Ponsor recuse himself and allow another judge to preside in his stead. By September 2011 Ponsor had stepped aside and had called in a federal judge from Worcester, Massachusetts named J. Dennis Saylor, to preside.

It did not make a blind bit of difference. Judge Saylor, like Ponsor before him, declared that he had read both books 'line by line' along with all the submissions made by both parties within twenty-four hours, and that just like Ponsor he had found '*NO substantial similarities*' between them.

So it was that I failed for a second time to prove via a court case that Dan Brown had plagiarized *The Vatican Boys*. I was less surprised by my second defeat because it was only a claim about a part of a Brown book, and I was always on the back foot because I could not afford legal representation.

This time, unlike in the first defeat when I was strong-armed into submitting to Judge Ponsor's decision, I was able to appeal to the Boston Federal Appeals Court. But it made not one iota of difference, doubtless not helped by the fact that I was again forced to represent myself. People who can afford them hire lawyers because they are trained for this kind of work, which I am not. Even though they brought in three judges to officiate, they affirmed Ponsor and Saylor's decision in favour of an immense international publisher and mega-star author, and against an unknown unrepresented writer from out of town. It seemed I had run out of road.

You would be forgiven at this point for concluding that I was barking up the wrong tree, just a crank who had subsided into self-delusion and that what I believed about these books was simply untrue. There is an old adage which says that if the same ill-fortunes keep befalling you, at some point you have to acknowledge that the problem is not out there; the problem lies with you.

I had to take a deep breath and level with myself. Was I just plain wrong about all this? But I couldn't see how that was possible. I knew I was not going mad. There were too many people who had read the two books and had independently concluded that the writer of one had plagiarized the other, and there were my two brilliant US attorneys who had no doubt of the justice of my cause. Take a look at the litany of 'convergences' between *The Vatican Boys* and Dan Brown's signature book *The Da Vinci Code* in the appendix which is not only my work but also that of an expert lawyer, and tell me that it does not evidence literary theft.

It seemed that the US justice system was unable to find in favour of the little guy against the rich and powerful, which was a bitter disappointment to me. So it was that when in 2012 the US Supreme Court decline to review the Saylor judgment and my claim that my Civil Rights were violated, I was left where I had been seven years before when I first learned about *The Da Vinci Code* and its uncanny similarities to *The Vatican Boys*: unwavering in my belief that my novel had been stolen, but completely unable to have the crime publicly acknowledged via the US judicial system.

It seemed that I had reached the end of the road because the US judicial system did not seem to protect the constitutional rights of a little-known and financially challenged author like me when confronted by the combined might of Dan Brown, Penguin Random House and Sony Pictures.

That just left me, standing alone and wondering what I should do next. Where was my Erin Brockovich when I needed her to fight my corner?

9

The London Lawyer

It is difficult to let something go when you know you are in the right, and justice has been denied you. It was even harder when in 2013 the book review pages were lauding Michael Ponsor's debut novel *The Hanging Judge*, the cover of which was adorned with an ecstatic quote from a Random House author as it went on to become a *New York Times* bestseller. But I have always known bitterness to be self-destructive and that Jesus Christ is very clear about my obligation to forgive those that wrong me. The last few years had tested my resolve, but I was ready to accept the past and move on with my life.

Between 2009 and 2016 I launched myself into a frenzy of writing, independently publishing six new novels. The energy required was immense, but while researching these stories and committing them to paper I learned a lot about myself. Part of the reason I worked so hard was that I wanted to prove to myself that the crushing experiences I had been through, and my inability to turn on the TV, go to a movie theatre or browse a bookstore without seeing the name 'Dan Brown', had not robbed me of my ability to write. I felt like part of my soul had been abducted and monetized for another's gain. But I worked hard, writing by night and designing medical devices by day.

Nevertheless, the burden of the last decade often weighed heavily on me. While Dan and Blythe Brown seemed to be feasting on the fruits of my labours, my life savings had been depleted by my US courts battles and there were bills to pay. I sometimes wondered if I would end up like *The Holy Blood and the Holy Grail* author Michael Baigent; financially and emotionally wrecked because of his failed attempts to prove that his work had been copied into *The Da Vinci Code*.

But this story is not finished.

In November 2016 I travelled to Düsseldorf in Germany to attend the Medica Trade Fair which focuses on the kind of medical devices I created. My business partner Eric and I were greeting visitors when a man in a flashy dark suit asked me in broken English what our new product did.

'It takes away pain by stimulating nerves and muscles,' I explained, holding my hand out for the stranger to shake. 'My name's Jack Dunn.'

'Árpád Burányi,' he said taking my business card and our literature. I noticed by his badge that he was another exhibitor.

The convention hall was noisy and I could hardly hear him. All I could ascertain was that he had a deep voice, friendly face, and an accent I did not recognise.

'Where are you from?' I asked.

'Hungary,' he replied. 'Can you tell me how this technology works?'

After a thirty-minute discussion Árpád left to view other displays.

I stayed in our booth through the long day greeting other prospective buyers until the show ended at around 6pm. Eric and I then took a bus back to the hotel for dinner.

We returned to the arena the next morning and when we reached our booth I was surprised to see Árpád waiting with a big smile on his face.

'You're Jack Dunn,' he shouted out as we approached. 'The famous author! I learned about you on the internet last night.'

'I'm not famous,' I replied as I shook off my backpack.

As Eric began setting up for the day Árpád went on, 'Yes you are! I read about you suing Dan Brown. Hey, did he *really* copy your book?'

I had heard that '*really*' word far too many times before. I had also learned over the years to forgive it. It is natural that people who hear about a story like mine assume it must be me who is deluded or just plain wrong. But I have not yet met a soul who, when confronted with the full breadth of similarity between my work and Dan Brown's, has not had an epiphany like my mine. I exclude of course a small number of US judges, and the lawyers representing Dan Brown, Sony Pictures and his publishers.

'The whole damn thing,' I replied.

'Then why are you here, still working in this business? Surely you received compensation?'

I liked Árpád's tone. It reminded me of when I had faith in a justice system which would right such wrongs; and a kind of naivety which I too once enjoyed.

Eric was still setting up our booth and it would be some time before the trade fair was back in full swing. 'If you have time for a coffee,' I told Árpád, 'I can explain everything.'

It took me an hour, sitting in the refreshments area, to tell Árpád all that had transpired since the bomb-blast at Barnes & Noble bookstore when people were queuing up to tell me that Dan Brown had stolen my book. He was as appalled at the way the behemoth of corporate publishing had tooled up with expensive attorneys and quashed my case. So much so that sometime later Árpád reappeared, speaking animatedly on his cell-phone and gesticulating for me to listen.

'Yes,' he was saying, 'it's Jack Dunn standing right here in front of me, Jonathan. It's exactly like I said – there was no justice for him in the United States. Maybe you could speak to him?'

Though I did not know what he was up to I stood there until he took the cell-phone from his ear and said, 'This is a friend of mine in London, Jack. Jonathan Coad – he's a celebrity lawyer, and he represents a lot of very well-known people. I've been telling him about you and Dan Brown. Here,' he said, handing me the cell-phone, 'you should talk.'

I was apprehensive because I was reluctant to re-open old wounds. It had taken a monumental effort of will over the last few years to suppress ill-feeling about Dan Brown and my failed court cases, and I was not keen to go back to a place of pain and frustration. But Árpád's animation was infectious, and more than anything, I did not feel I could rebuff his obvious desire to help me, which I later learned was what also prompted the lawyer to whom I was about to speak to be generous with his time. So, with some hesitation, I took the cell-phone and said, 'Hello Jonathan, it's nice to meet you.'

I didn't know it then, but this was the opening scene in the next chapter of the story.

Over the next few months I had several transatlantic phone calls and email exchanges with Jonathan. It turned out that as well as being a leading UK-based reputation and privacy lawyer for both companies and individuals, his practise included copyright law and he had done intellectual property work for some of the world's biggest companies. He had also followed closely Leigh and Baigent's failed copyright claim against Dan Brown.

I immediately owned up to the fact that my claims had been tried and found unsubstantiated in the USA. But as Jonathan explained an opportunity still existed to pursue a claim for copyright infringement through the UK legal system because *The Da Vinci Code* was published there, as well as pretty well everywhere else on the planet. I had already learned how difficult that would be, and still smarting from my American defeats I was wary about stepping back into a ring where I had already suffered two knock-downs. But my faith in ultimately securing justice was not entirely dead and there had to be a reason that Árpád and I had crossed paths, so I decided I would give Jonathan Coad a chance. Perhaps he would be my Erin Brockovich and overcome the powerful forces ranged against me.

Jonathan, too, had to deliberate on whether he would give *me* a chance. He would later confide in me that during our initial conversations, although he had been sympathetic to my plight, he was also highly sceptical about my plagiarism claims against Dan Brown. I suppose as a lawyer his natural state of mind is to be sceptical; and, of course, he had also been told that his US counterparts had failed to persuade the US courts of the validity my claims. Hell, we hadn't even got close. But during the course of our initial dialogue he agreed both that my claims were credible and that there was something that did not add up about the United States proceedings.

Jonathan is not an expert on US law, though he has experience of the US law of copyright and our legal process having successfully defended some high-profile copyright litigation about who owned the format of a highly successful TV programme which had fought on both sides of the Atlantic. He was also an international expert on the application of copyright law to television formats. He asked me to send through all the documents I retained generated by my US legal claims. He also asked me to send him a copy of my book.

Over the following weeks Jonathan read up about the US proceedings and reviewed the two novels and the record of 'convergences' I had prepared. As he said at the time, 'The first person you have to convince is me'. It was my detailed study of the convergences between the two books, which he could cross-check in the books themselves, that started to win him over. This was the process of his performing his due diligence, as every good lawyer must, working out if this was both a case and a client that he should take on. I came to learn that Jonathan was picky both about his clients and the causes that he would fight.

Eventually he declared himself convinced by the evidence that I had sent him that my book had indeed been copied by Dan Brown, and invited me to meet with him in London to plan how to find a remedy, assuming that after our meeting he was confident enough in our cause to mount a copyright claim in the UK.

I made my first trip to meet with Jonathan in April 2017, my first visit in ten years. I know London well and it gives me a rush every time I return to that great history-rich city.

I booked into the Apex Temple Court hotel, close to Blackfriars Bridge, a stone's throw from Fleet Street which plays such a prominent role in both *The Vatican Boys* and *The Da Vinci Code*. I wanted to stay close to the area I had visited in 1996 when researching *The Vatican Boys* and it all came rushing back. Blackfriars Bridge, just off Fleet Street, had been the place where the murder victim was found in the opening of my novel. Those had been rich, energising days, before *The Da Vinci Code* had marred my life.

I checked in on a Sunday, which Jonathan explained was a church day for him. The following morning I was to meet him in the hotel lobby which was only a few hundred yards from his offices and try to persuade him to take my case on. The nerves were back. I had not felt this way since pleading my case in front of Judge Ponsor. I spent the day pottering through the streets of old London town, reinhabiting the sights and sounds of my novel, trying not to recall that they were also the sights and sounds of Dan Brown's. Fleet Street, Blackfriars Bridge, the Chelsea Embankment were both the settings of my imagination and the scenes of the crime. But somehow by being here I felt I was a step closer to uncovering it.

The following morning I woke early and after breakfast took myself to the hotel lobby to pore through some documents I had brought with me while I waited for Jonathan to arrive. My jitteriness was not just caused by the four cups of coffee I had drunk at breakfast, but also by my being nervous about meeting Jonathan.

I need not have been. When Jonathan presented himself at precisely 9am I knew straight away that here was a rare thing among lawyers: a grounded, decent man, committed to fairness and honesty, and with true generosity of spirit. Jonathan is younger than me and a family man living with his wife and two children in London. After studying law at Jesus College, Cambridge, and training as a solicitor he established a practice specialising not only in copyright, acting for both creatives and content commercial exploiters, but also in PR and media law.

In that capacity he has worked for corporate clients such as Amazon, Gucci, Procter & Gamble and the Universal Group, and represented individual clients including celebrities like Lady Gaga, the Beckhams, Geri Halliwell, formerly of the Spice Girls, the best-selling author Paul McKenna, the Duchess of York and two other royals. Outside work he is a keen musician, playing in a jazz quintet and with his church's gospel band. He is also a devout Christian and we were able to bond over this aspect of our lives because my family's Christian faith still ran strongly through me.

Jonathan and I spent a while getting to know each other. The relationship between a lawyer and their client is so important, and while that does not mean they must be best friends it is always helpful when they chime on some fundamental level. Soon I became certain that this was where Jonathan and I were headed, and most importantly that we were going to develop a relationship of trust.

At the appropriate moment, Jonathan said, 'Tell me all you know, Jack. We've already discussed much of this via our emails, but it's always instructive to hear it from the horse's mouth. Let's go back to the beginning – *The Vatican Boys*. I want to know all about how you came to write it, especially your historical research.'

Little did I know at the time, but Jonathan was doing what all good lawyers should do and subjecting his prospective client to a gentle cross-examination so that he could form his own opinion about my credibility and the justice of my cause. As he said to me later, it is no good to me if he takes everything that I tell him at face value, only to come unstuck either just before or (worse still) during a trial.

We talked for hours about the events of the last twenty years, going all the way back to *The Diary of William Goffe*. Jonathan listened carefully, taking notes, and when that was done, he outlined both the challenges and opportunities that were likely to present themselves on the way ahead, based in no small part on his experience of fighting many 'David and Goliath' battles for other clients.

One of the first things he explained was that while in the US civil disputes are still usually tried with a jury, in England jury trials in civil actions were restricted to only a couple of types of claim, the main one being defamation, though they had become rare in those claims too. So, if we wanted to win a copyright case on the east side of the Atlantic we were going to be dealing just with a judge. Jonathan, however, assured me that the quality of the judiciary in London was generally good, and that there were specialist judges for copyright cases. Thank goodness, I thought. I am not going to be confronted by another Judge Ponsor.

'The challenge facing us isn't to prove that Dan Brown has acted unethically, which on the basis of the evidence you have shown me, I believe he has by plagiarizing your book,' Jonathan explained. 'Michael Baigent and Richard Leigh felt they had moral right on their side in their copyright claim and reading the judgment you can understand why. The question we have to concern ourselves with isn't whether he has plagiarized your book, as I am convinced he has. We must establish that according to the exacting stipulations of the UK law of copyright, Dan Brown has infringed your rights in your book and crossed the threshold where a merely derivative work has become a copyright breach. That means we must prove that Dan Brown has lifted a "substantial part" of your book into his. Books are made up of tens of thousands of words, and no "copy" is going to be exactly the same as the original. In this case *The Da Vinci Code* is about twice the length of *The Vatican*

Boys which means that it is bound to contain new elements. That makes our job trickier still.'

Jonathan then illustrated how the law of copyright works as simply as he could to an American non-lawyer. He took Charles Dickens' great novel, *Oliver Twist* as an example (Jonathan being a big Dickens fan, he made sure to tell me that the ground on which the hotel where I was staying was built is a part of ancient London which featured in his books). He said, 'On a basic level there's a story about the mis-adventures of an orphan boy alone in 19th century London. That's Mr Dickens' one-line pitch. Next are the elements of Dickens' world – the richly imagined surrounds of 19th century London, the workhouses and slums, the homeless and destitute, the criminal underbelly of the city. Next, think about the plot: young orphan Oliver is sold from a workhouse to an undertaker and, after running away from there ends up with a gang of street thieves led by the cruel taskmaster Fagin before ultimately – after the murder of a cherished friend by the wicked Bill Sikes – he finds a new adoptive father in the kind Mr Brownlow. Finally, look at some iconic lines from the book: Oliver daring to say to the workhouse beadle, "Please sir, may I have some more ..."'

'The law,' Jonathan continued, 'cannot prevent somebody from reading Oliver Twist and then writing their own novel about the misadventures of an orphan boy in 19th century London. Ideas as broad as this rightly belong to nobody, existing in the ether for us to harvest as we wish. All creative endeavours borrow from its predecessors, and creatives often speak of "standing on the shoulders of giants". Breach of copyright might arise if somebody were to write a near exact copy of this novel quoting numerous specific lines like the one I've quoted which clearly belong to

Dickens and this wonderful novel. Think of two ends of a spectrum; at one end a broad idea that nobody can own, and at the other, a compendium of specific and original expressions coined by one writer and clearly belonging to a literary work, which the law of copyright is there to protect.'

These propositions are clear enough at least in theory, and the law can apply them. It is the in-betweens, Jonathan explained, where difficulties arise. The question for a judge is, when does plagiarism cross over into becoming a breach of copyright, an issue in which inevitably connotes some degree of subjectivity?

One of the first things I was going to have to understand was the difference between mere 'plagiarism' and 'copyright infringement'. 'Plagiarism', Jonathan explained, differs from 'copyright infringement' in crucial ways. 'Plagiarism' occurs when another author's ideas are passed off as your own. Morally indefensible though it might be, it is not unlawful, and of itself does not meet the legal standard of 'copyright infringement'. This only occurs when specific and original elements are reproduced without acknowledgement and permission, when the infringing author has not just borrowed the ideas of another, but has also appropriated a 'substantial part' of their expression of those ideas.

Jonathan explained that Baigent and Leigh had sued the publishers of *The Da Vinci Code* claiming that Dan Brown's novel had 'appropriated the architecture' of their historical work. They also claimed that Dan Brown had 'hijacked' and 'exploited' their book, which had taken them five years to create. The judge said that a comparison of the language in *The Holy Blood and the Holy Grail* and *The Da Vinci Code* did show some limited copying of the text of the Leigh and Baigent book.

'However, this is not alleged to be a copyright infringement ... so does not assist the claimants. Such copying cannot amount to substantial copying of the text of *The Holy Blood and the Holy Grail* and the claimants have never said it does,' said Jonathan, quoting Mr Justice Smith.

He went on to explain that the judge determined the Claimants' analysis of the structure of the book's central themes had been designed retrospectively to help their case, and that there was in fact no 'architecture' or 'structure' to be found in *The Holy Blood and the Holy Grail* as contended by Baigent and Leigh.

'Even if the central themes were copied, they are too general or of too low a level of abstraction to be capable of protection by copyright law,' the judge said. 'Accordingly there is no copyright infringement either by textual copying or non-textual copying of a substantial part of *The Holy Blood and the Holy Grail* by means of copying the central themes.'

As Jonathan observed, here was an example of a judge both finding that copying had taken place, but not in a way which constituted copyright infringement because it was merely of the 'central themes'.

As Mr Justice Smith also observed: 'When a book is put forward as being ... non-fiction ... and contains a large number of facts and ideas it is always going to be a difficult exercise in trying to protect against copying of those facts and ideas because as such they cannot be protected. It is the effort and time that has gone into the way in which those ideas and facts are presented that is capable of protection.'

But as Jonathan emphasised, mine was not a non-fiction book, and it was much more than the 'central themes' that had been copied.

We later identified passages in the judgment which seemed to chime with my claim. The judge quoted parts of an earlier judgment which appeared to support my case: 'Copyright protects the skill and labour employed by the plaintiff in production of his work. That skill and labour embraces not only language originated and used by the plaintiff, but also such skill and labour as he has employed in selection and compilation. The principles are clear from the cases … Another person may originate another work in the same general form, provided he does so from his own resources and makes the work he so originates a work of his own by his own labour and industry bestowed upon it. In determining whether an injunction should be ordered, the question, where the matter of the plaintiff's work is not original, is how far an unfair or undue use has been made of the work? If, instead of searching into the common sources and obtaining your subject matter from thence, you avail yourself of the labour of your predecessor, adopt his arrangements and questions, or adopt them with a colourable variation, it is an illegitimate use.'

The judge went on to say this: 'In other words the facts and the themes and the ideas cannot be protected but how those facts, themes and ideas are put together (this is the Claimants' "architecture" argument) can be. It follows from this that the Claimants must show that there is a putting together of facts, themes and ideas by them as a result of their efforts and it is that which Mr Brown has copied.'

Surely, I said to Jonathan, that is exactly what Dan Brown did in plundering characters and plotlines from my book to write *The Da Vinci Code*.

It had always seemed clear, to me at least, that *The Da Vinci Code* represented much more than a mere 'plagiarism' of *The Vatican Boys*, which even parts of Dan Brown's witness statement seemed to suggest. How about this, from paragraph 79: '*The Da Vinci Code* tells the story of professor Robert Langdon's race to decipher clues left for him by murdered Louvre curator Jacques Saunière. The novel is, at its core, a treasure hunt through Paris, London, and ... a blend of historical fact, legend, myth, and fiction.' If you just change the names to refer to the main characters of *The Vatican Boys*, you have an exact summary of my book.

Another writer is of course free to read *The Vatican Boys* and be inspired to write their own holy relic thriller. They are even free to write one based on the core thesis of somebody else's historical work, as Baigent and Leigh discovered to their cost. But what they were not free to do was to write one which comprehensively copies the plot, scenes, dialogues, and characters.

'It's a difficult area of law, Jack, which is one of the reasons why it is so fascinating to practice in,' said Jonathan. 'Where art and creativity are at issue, legal principles don't always dovetail as neatly as we'd like them to. Making a clear distinction between mere ideas which cannot be protected, and the expression of ideas which can be protected, is by no means easy. This is what the Court of Appeal said in *The Holy Blood and The Holy Grail* case: "Copyright does not subsist in ideas; it protects the expression of ideas, not the ideas themselves. No clear principle is or could be laid down in the cases in order to tell whether what is sought to be protected is on the ideas side of the dividing line, or on the expression side."'

Jonathan went on, 'I have done a lot of work in TV formats both in the UK and internationally where intellectual property issues are even harder than they are in books. There are cases where the copyright infringement is clear and incontrovertible, but they are few and far between. If Brown had taken *The Vatican Boys* in its entirety – its ideas, its prose, its *everything* – and republished it under his name, there could be no doubt about it. But where it's a case of somebody using another person's novel as a resource, even if it is the primary resource, assessing what a "substantial part" of the original work means in law is inevitably to some extent subjective; not least because it is a test of not of quantity, but of quality.'

I said, 'This all started when readers of my book told me that Dan Brown had copied the whole thing, Jonathan. I didn't go looking for this fight.' I told him about the first signing at the Barnes & Noble bookstore and the journalist at the IPPY Awards. All those readers who followed my work came to tell me, entirely of their own volition, that my work had been copied.

After a lunch interspersed with more family discussions, we got back down to business until at around 4 I suggested that we adjourn to my room so I could show Jonathan some more material which was on my laptop.

Jonathan watched the screen as I took him through my comparison of the Bridge of Dread sequence in *The Vatican Boys* and the parallel scene in Dan Brown's *Angels & Demons* – the same section I had shown my friend Tom Kenefick and which formed the basis of my second US lawsuit. In my side-by-side analysis my main character awakes from a nightmare to a call from a man named Maxwell, while Brown's character wakes from a nightmare to a character named Maximilian; both are called from a facility with the word research being used; both get up, look into the mirror and consider their lost youth. Both sections are even headed with the same line: 'It's April 1996, New England' in my book, and 'It's April 1999, New England' in Brown's book, which was written about three years later.

It was at that moment that Jonathan stepped back and said, 'You've got him.'

I had been waiting to hear those words for years. After being shut out of the justice system for so long, every person whose eyes I opened to the fraud felt like a major step forward – especially if they were a lawyer. I needed some encouraging voices on my side. Being told by the judicial authority that you are in the wrong about something so unarguably right can instil a kind of madness.

'We must start again from the beginning and build this case painstakingly from the ground up, deploying as much probative detail as we can.' said Jonathan. 'I've got some work to do. I'll need to go back to the judgments in The *Holy Blood and the Holy Grail* case and study them closely. I'll also need to revisit the key texts on literary copyright. There's no reason why you can't bring an action in the UK just because you haven't been successful in the USA. But we should develop a clear view of where things went wrong over there, and learn from any mistakes.'

Jonathan returned to the plethora of materials I had brought with me to win him over to my cause. 'This Bridge of Dread sequence is certainly incriminating, Jack, but it's in *The Da Vinci Code* that your real case lies. *Angels & Demons* is just its prelude. It's in *The Da Vinci Code* that everything happens sequentially – the same characters being introduced, the same incidents, the same mystery unfolding. That's clearly where the major lifting was done. We need to show that Brown has imported a substantial part of your book into his to the extent that a court will find that your copyright has been infringed which is no easy task and will require a great deal of work. I have learned that litigation is usually won by the side that prepares their case best. The burden of proof is firmly on us, so we must spare no effort to discharge it.'

'So what now?' I asked.

'We get to work,' said Jonathan.

10

High Stakes

Abraham Lincoln said this: 'I see in the ... future a crisis approaching that ... causes me to tremble for the safety of my country ... corporations have been enthroned and an era of corruption in high places will follow, and the money power of the country will ... prolong its reign by working upon the prejudices of the people until all wealth is aggregated in a few hands.'

As a young man growing up I believed that despite Abraham Lincoln's fears about the immense power that big business would ultimately wield in my beloved country, ultimately justice would always prevail. As a matter of fact, I still do, despite the fact that my experience of the US justice system suggests otherwise. But what my first attempts at having my case tried taught me was the difference between moral and legal justice. To attain the first, you just have to be in the right; to attain the second, you generally have to be rich.

That appeared to be one of the determining factors in my defeat in the US cases. Money endows its possessors with power, which it is the job of a justice system to attenuate. I had little of it, and – between them – Dan Brown, Penguin Random House as it now was, following the 2013 merger of Penguin and Random House, and Sony had billions. In my opinion, Judge Ponsor had not done his job in the face of this immense imbalance of power.

Despite knowing that my claim had failed in the US, Jonathan had decided to commit himself to my cause, even knowing that I could not pay him. He felt both that I had suffered a grave injustice, that *The Da Vinci Code*'s central thesis about Christ not being executed and establishing an earthly 'blood line' was an evil myth, and that my lawsuit might help further expose it as such. Jonathan has told me that he also believed that God's call was on him to do the job.

He told me that despite the good work that my US attorneys had done, to give us a real chance of winning a copyright claim in the United Kingdom I had a lot more 'homework' to do because our case was going to have to be advanced with yet more detail and rigour. Consequently, over the following months I devoted my every spare moment to going back through *The Da Vinci Code* adding to the already lengthy list of 'convergences' with my book that I could find. The catalogue I eventually compiled would form the basis of our proposed case in the United Kingdom.

Jonathan proved to be a hard task-master, just as he has been in co-writing this book. Like a school master he not only kept sending my homework back deemed unsatisfactory, but he also always wanted yet more work from me. He did not think that the analysis that we had used in the US claim had nearly enough detail. He kept both rejecting evidence that he deemed not to be sufficiently compelling, and demanding additional material and analysis. This went on until the schedule of convergences had begun to resemble the compendious 27-page document that you will find in the appendix at the end of this book. Explain those away if you can, Mr Brown and Penguin Random House.

After a further five months of hard work Jonathan and I felt that we were ready to progress the case. By the fall of 2017 it felt as if things were moving forward again. At the end of the process Jonathan sent Penguin Random House the claim letter he had drafted along with the two schedules that we had prepared, which you will find in the appendix. Jonathan raised two points which were absent from my US lawsuits.

The first was that, although Dan Brown had submitted a roster of titles he had consulted in his 'research' for *The Da Vinci Code* during *The Holy Blood and the Holy Grail* trial, he had not included *The Vatican Boys*, and that by not doing so he had opened himself up to new accusations of perjury.

The second point that Jonathan's letter took was the conspicuous absence of Dan Brown's wife Blythe in the trial over *The Holy Blood and the Holy Grail* which had been criticised by Mr Justice Smith. Our contention was that Blythe's absence was a legal device to obfuscate, and mislead the court over the true provenance of the disputed elements of *The Da Vinci Code*.

Penguin Random House's lawyers sent back a relatively short letter in response to Jonathan, and have made it clear that despite 'championing free speech' they do not want you to read it, saying it is 'Private and Confidential', so you will not find a copy in the appendix. You will, however, find quotations from it and Jonathan's summary of its not very convincing arguments in the last chapter of this book. The conclusion is as follows: 'Your client's allegation is rejected in its entirety and our client will vigorously defend any claim brought by your client.'

The inevitable question that arose was how we would finance such a claim given the brute exercise of financial muscle that had killed off my US case. No copyright claim is inexpensive, and one about a book against opponents as well-resourced as ours would be costlier still, even though Jonathan was venturing his time by agreeing to be paid only if I won. The months of work that he and I had already put into it would have to be supplemented by that of expensive specialist barristers.

Jonathan explained to me that unlike the US in the UK the legal profession is split into two halves. On the client-facing side there are solicitors, and on the court-facing side there are barristers, who are the equivalent of the US trial counsel. He also told me that we would need to hire a top Queen's Counsel (an elite barrister) and top 'junior' who were specialists in the law of copyright, and that none of the best practitioners would take a case on via a 'no win, no fee' basis because they would have more than enough work for which they were guaranteed payment. For that reason he needed to raise a lot of money to fund my case, and said he would go out into the then relatively new UK litigation funding market to try to secure the financial backing we needed.

It was with a sense of deep gratitude that in July 2017 I learned from Jonathan that a major litigation funding firm, Harbour, to whom he had pitched the claim, had expressed interest in my case, which was apparently much influenced by the fact that Jonathan was prepared to do the work at his own risk, and that consequently they only had to finance the work of the barristers. They reckoned that if Jonathan was prepared to put his skin in the game, so were they.

Jonathan had a good record for winning cases on a 'no win, no fee' basis, choosing to fight them because of his personal convictions about the rightness of the cause, and Harbour had faith in his judgment about *The Vatican Boys*. Within days they sent me a

Letter of Intent which outlined how they would finance my case should the evidence we provided satisfy them that the case was winnable. The moment I signed it we had a potential fund running to a million plus pounds with which to fight our legal battle. I was sure we would need it as I fully expected Dan Brown and his publishers to fight us hard.

The two barristers that Jonathan hired to determine our chances of success came from London's Hogarth Chambers, leading experts in copyright law and the same chambers which had fought Dan Brown and what was then Random House in *The Holy Blood and the Holy Grail* case, and who Jonathan hoped would relish a return match on the assumption that Dan Brown and his publishers hired the same legal team.

In late October I returned to London for a meeting Jonathan had scheduled with Andrew Norris of Hogarth Chambers, whom he had chosen because he was one of the barristers who had brought *The Holy Blood and the Holy Grail* claim.

It was good to see Jonathan again, who had become my friend as well as my lawyer. Using his extensive links with the media Jonathan had also made contact with a journalist at the *Daily Mail* who was eager to write a feature, anticipating the media circus that would surround our lawsuit. For the first time in years it felt as if I had a formidable team who believed and trusted me. That support counted for so much and gave me the faith to continue.

I met Jonathan at the hotel to run through the events of the day. From there we walked the short distance over Fleet Street to Hogarth Chambers, past the historic High Court of Justice on London's Strand, another of Dickens' settings.

Hogarth Chambers had about it the same kind of rich old-world air that I have come to love in London. It is in the famous Lincolns Inn, a beautiful building that is steeped in history. It was built in the 17th century and is a place where barristers had worked since well before the time of Dickens, who included legal themes in his wonderful novels which often featured lawyers as both heroes and villains. Before becoming a successful author, the young Charles Dickens was a solicitor's clerk whose tasks included looking after the petty cash and delivering documents, doubtless to Lincolns Inn.

Andrew Norris welcomed us warmly and escorted us to a conference room that had an excellent view of the well-tended gardens where they still employ beautiful hawks to chase away the ubiquitous London pigeons. We were joined by Andrew's senior colleague Nick Caddick, who was what the English call a 'Queen's Counsel', and a lawyer named Marcus who was there as the representative of Harbour. The prospect of my claim being discussed by top experts in the English law of copyright gave me fresh hope that I might at last achieve recognition as the real creative behind *The Da Vinci Code*.

As is the custom in England Jonathan opened the 'consultation' (as meetings with QC's are called) by introducing everyone and outlining the key elements of his Instructions to Counsel – the detailed document he had prepared for the two barristers which delineated the breadth of the copyright infringement we were convinced had taken place, along with the applicable elements of the law as Jonathan perceived them. That is what happens in the UK. A solicitor like Jonathan prepares a brief which analyses the facts and applies the law, which is accompanied by bundles of the key documents for the barrister to study and advise on the chances of a case being won at trial. It is the barrister who then takes to the case to trial with the solicitor sitting behind (literally and metaphorically) giving instructions and providing support.

Jonathan said he thought Dan Brown and his publishers would employ the same tactics in the UK as they did in the US, and apply to strike the claim out or seek Summary Judgment to avoid a full trial. That was not because there would be a jury trial, but Jonathan believed that Dan Brown's deficiencies in cross-examination at *The Holy Blood and the Holy Grail* trial would be exposed even more starkly in our trial if and when he was asked to explain the myriad of convergences between his book and mine. He would have to persuade the judge that they were not the result of plagiarism, something which he not had managed to do in *The Holy Blood and the Holy Grail* trial. Both he and his lawyers would know that any judge in our claim would assess his credibility in the context of an earlier judge having had serious doubts about it.

Jonathan was also sure that should there be a trial Dan Brown and his lawyers would have no option but to call Blythe Brown as a witness in an attempt to prove that he had written *The Da Vinci Code* without assistance from my book, given the strong judicial criticism of Brown and his lawyers about her absence at the earlier trial. Jonathan thought that there was plenty of scope for uncomfortable cross-examination of both Mr and Mrs Brown (as they then were) about why there were so many convergences in terms of characters, settings and themes, and the fact that they also appeared in near identical order.

Jonathan also made the point that there were grave risks for Dan Brown at any trial, ones that could even affect his liberty as well as his reputation as a writer, because if the court found against him that would be a second instance of his sworn evidence being found to have been errant, and he risked being charged with perjury. The most obvious risk arose from both his written and oral evidence about how he came to write *The Da Vinci Code*, because even if we lost our copyright claim but the court concluded that he had read and plagiarized parts of my book then parts of his evidence in *The Holy Blood and the Holy Grail* trial would then be proven to be lies. The same would go for his evidence in the US proceedings that I had brought against him.

There was also a contempt of court issue. Jonathan explained that in England there is a strict legal obligation to disclose all relevant documents. We in the US call it 'discovery', as it used to be called in the UK. He explained that UK's Civil Procedure Rules required Dan Brown to sign a declaration that he had disclosed all the relevant documents both to the other side and to the court. If you knowingly sign such a declaration which is false then you are in contempt of court, which is also a criminal offence for which you can be sent to jail.

So Dan Brown could be jailed for perjury and/or contempt at the earlier trial, or even perverting the course of justice, which had happened to the prominent author and politician Jeffrey Archer who in 2001 was found guilty of perjury and perverting the course of justice at a 1987 trial, and was sentenced to four years' imprisonment. It had also happened to an Member of Parliament called Jonathan Aitken who was convicted of perjury in 1999 and received an 18-month prison sentence.

Jonathan concluded that if we could survive an application for Summary Judgment Dan Brown would settle rather than face a trial. Andrew and Nick listened attentively to Jonathan's analysis, and seemed particularly interested in his idea that Brown might be proven to have perjured himself and been in contempt of court at the earlier trial.

When Jonathan finished I had my opportunity to weigh in. I had been trying to refine my description of what Dan Brown had done and had boiled it down to this: 'If you dissect the books into parts the same things happen in the same order and sometimes even in the same places. The same characters, incidents, motivations, and settings appear in both books. He used *The Vatican Boys* to construct the opening section of *The Da Vinci Code*. He used *The Holy Blood and the Holy Grail* to construct its middle section, the Teabing Lectures which featured at the trial. But then he returns to my novel. Everything from France to London, with the Fleet Street transition ...' I had walked down Fleet Street the previous afternoon; it was only a stone's throw from where we now sat. 'From that point on the chapters run virtually in parallel. The clues and codes that get the characters into the Knight's bank are almost identical; the confrontations at Opus Dei House, the journey to the holy church in another country – where both my characters and his meet with a holy woman who reveals there are two relics, not one ...'

I stopped when I realised that Andrew had begun to look uneasy, which was when I knew bad news was coming. 'Nick and I have read both books, Jack, along with everything that you and Jonathan have provided,' Andrew said. 'I'm afraid we don't think that your evidence meets the present UK legal criteria for proving copyright infringement.'

Have you ever been sucker punched? Well, I have. And that was exactly what it felt like. I had flown across the Atlantic anticipating a breakthrough only to be knocked down flat.

Nick explained that they had come to this conclusion based on the judgments in *The Holy Blood and the Holy Grail* case in which the lawyers acting for Baigent and Leigh attempted unsuccessfully to make the argument that in the UK there can be non-literal copying of a work of literature. But I was barely listening. 'But you both agree that he copied my book, right?'

There was no doubt on their faces. Even Marcus from the litigation funder agreed.

'We're in a tricky area of law. *The Holy Blood and the Holy Grail* made the law somewhat clearer but this is still a problematic area. All of the things you've shown us prove a clear correlation between the texts which pretty well rules out coincidence. But the thing we have to address is when plagiarism crosses over into infringement of copyright? According our law copyright is infringed when "a substantial part" of your work is taken without your permission.'

I felt quite certain that with everything Brown had taken from *The Vatican Boys* there was more than one 'substantial' part of my book embedded in his. But I also knew that words have different definitions in the legal world than they do in common parlance. 'What does it mean, from a legal perspective?' I asked.

That was the moment when things got even more bewildering.

'Well, Jack, that's the 64-million-dollar question. The answer is, nobody is exactly sure ...'

If, like me, this makes you feel lost in some legal labyrinth it is probably worth stepping out of the story to understand what my team were trying to communicate when talking about a 'substantial part'. It seemed to me that the elements of 'convergence' between my book and Dan Brown's were substantial enough to show beyond any reasonable doubt that copying had taken place, at least in terms that we lay folk would see it. You do not have to have a forensic legal mind or be overly cynical to decide something fishy is going on when two stories feature a hunt for an ancient religious secret solved by accessing a deposit box at a Knight's bank, where the two clues to opening that box are a number sequence and a five-letter word. Any reasonable human being (except, perhaps, Judge Ponsor) would agree that two novels based on a holy relic about the life of Jesus Christ, both opening with the murder of a significant Mason, and where both sets of near-identical main characters are being hunted by an assassin hired by Opus Dei, are similar enough to prove the point.

But, as they explained, the UK's legal definition of 'substantial part' is not always easy to apply in practice. It was that uncertainty that we were doing battle with here. How can the law define 'substantial', when every instance of copyright infringement is different to another?

It seems that things get hazier still. A 'substantial part' can be as little as a few sentences – *if* those sentences are copied literally. There have been cases in both the US and English legal systems where a court has found a copyright infringement for exactly this reason. The problem I had was the way Dan Brown had plagiarized *The Vatican Boys*. Even though there are countless instances where his images and scenes mirror mine, and manifold moments where the same actions are described in remarkably similar ways, there are no instances of direct sentence-by-sentence copying in the novels. Brown had not pillaged my prose but my imagination. His characters were mine, as was the trajectory and movements of his story. But his sentences, a few suspicious clauses aside, were his own. My writer's creativity pervaded his book, but my actual words did not. That made identifying the 'substantial part' trickier still.

There is a long and inglorious history of plagiarism in literature, though no instance comes close to the one that I describe in this book. Mrs Beeton wrote her famous *Book of Household Management* in the 19th century, which is mostly made up of recipes. It was later discovered that she had stolen nearly all of them from other authors including Florence Nightingale. 95 per cent of a biography of Alexander Graham Bell by an author called James MacKay was found to have been taken from an earlier biography of the great inventor of the telephone. It seems the first known example of plagiarism occurred in the 1st century AD where a poet called Martial discovered that other poets were using his work without his permission. Even Dr Martin Luther King was alleged to have plagiarized his famous 'I have a dream' speech from another political writer, there being some strikingly similar passages.

It may be worth comparing how copyright infringement in popular music is dealt with as my impression is that musicians enjoy a better level of protection for their work than we writers of literature.

It might surprise you to learn just how many cases are brought in any given year, and not just for obscure acts. When luminaries like George Harrison, Led Zeppelin and Madonna – along with current stars like Ed Sheeran, Sam Smith and Bruno Mars – have been found guilty of copyright infringement, it almost seems plagiarizing somebody else's work is a well-trodden route to musical superstardom.

The 'substantial part' rule also exists in the world of music, and it was instructive for me to look at this because songs, by their nature and limits, are much less complicated to police than books. Certain chord progressions and song structures are 'owned by all'. One songwriter cannot accuse another of plagiarism because they have written a song in which a verse is followed by a chorus, another verse, a bridge, and then a second chorus. Certain chord progressions pervade popular music. Believe it or not, the epic ballad 'Let it Go' from Disney's 'Frozen' has the same chord progression as U2's 'With Or Without You', which also has the same chord progression as Elton John's 'Can You Feel The Love Tonight', The Beatles' 'Let it Be', and Journey's famous 'Don't Stop Believing'. Yet none of these songs infringe the copyright of another.

Whether it is a novel or a piece of music the 'substantial part' must be both original and copied. It seems that in music it is easier to identify than in a novel. The same 'quality' vs 'quantity' test applies. A few bars of identical bassline can qualify as a 'substantial part', a single riff or guitar lick. So, when the guitar player Joe Satriani sued the British band Coldplay for imitating the guitar line from his track 'If I Could Fly', the band chose to settle out of court – even though Satriani's was a purely instrumental track, and therefore shared no lyrical content with Coldplay's 'Viva la Vida'. And when the 1960s songwriters Albert Hammond and Mike Hazlewood successfully sued the British band Radiohead for infringing the copyright of their song 'The Air That I Breathe' with their debut single 'Creep', it was the song's identical 'middle eight' (or 'bridge' as it's called in the US) that they relied on to win their claim.

But what if somebody borrows your story wholesale and yet it is of scant importance in their own work? Has copyright then been infringed? Conversely, if somebody borrows a small incident from your book but adapts it into a three-novel saga are they then in breach of the copyright? How substantial does the 'part' have to be in the original novel, and how correspondingly substantial does it have to be in the second novel for a court to find a copyright infringement? At their extremes it is easy to judge. But because of the breadth and scope of novels, there exists a grey area. This was apparently where my case was located – lost in the great legal unknown.

You can be forgiven if you are scratching your head right now. I certainly was. In fact, it felt like I was pounding my fists against a brick wall and getting nowhere. Ranged in front of us was this wealth of evidence that the plots of the novels progressed in parallel, and that their ideas, motifs, characters and plot points corresponded with such depth that it could be nothing other than wilful copying. But as I understood it, to prove to the satisfaction of a court that according to the strict copyright principles a 'substantial part' of my book had found its way into *The Da Vinci Code* I would have to identify what amounted to the literal copying of a 'substantial part' of my book, which looked to be beyond me.

But at least, I told myself, I had a lifeline. Before I left London Jonathan told me that he would not give up the fight. Marcus, from the litigation funders, also assured us that if I could identify the 'substantial part' that satisfied Hogarth Chambers they would still consider funding us.

And so like my characters Stephen Hathaway and Catherine Turrell and Brown's characters Robert Langdon and Sophie Neveu, I found myself embarking on a quest for a kind of mystical treasure of my own. But unlike the lead characters in *The Vatican Boys* and *The Da Vinci Code*, I would not be hurtling across Europe and the Middle East in search of my quarry. I would be returning to the fictional world I had created which had somehow incarnated itself in Dan Brown's world as well.

My quest was for the fabled 'substantial part' of my book in *The Da Vinci Code* so I could prove in court that Dan Brown had passed off my work as his own.

11

A Part of Substance

By now I had been living with *The Vatican Boys* for twenty-five years, from its inception to when I sat down with my much-annotated and dog-eared copy and began to read it for the hundredth time to try to find the evidence that I needed to win a copyright case in the English courts.

But how do you find something when you are not sure exactly what you are looking for? I had been cataloguing and re-cataloguing the convergences between the two novels for so long that I could barely see what was in front of me. By January 2018 I had whittled down the vast list of potential candidates to those that seemed strongest. But when I presented my findings to Jonathan, he would say they were 'interesting, but not substantial'. That word was really beginning to bug me.

Something about the challenge kept taking me back to JK Rowling who had been both defendant and plaintiff in lawsuits concerning her *Harry Potter* series. Many commentators noted similarities between JK Rowling's *Harry Potter* series and the English writer Jill Murphy's *Worst Witch* novels which, published years before the first Harry Potter novel, feature a young witch, Mildred Hubble, who goes to a witchcraft school where she gets involved in all kinds of adventures while her principal enemy is a fellow student named Ethel Hallow. Some commentators also observed that JK Rowling's secret platform at King's Cross Station, Platform Nine-and-Three-Quarters, bears a striking resemblance to Eva Ibbotson's 1994 novel *The Secret of Platform 13*, in which a secret platform at – you guessed it – King's Cross Station in London leads to a magical world of wizards and witches. Neither of these cases led to court cases; and in fact, both Jill Murphy and Eva Ibbotson have been gracious. But it got me to wondering about the difference between 'qualitative' and 'quantitative' copying, and why neither of these 'convergences' met the legal definition of copyright infringement.

It seemed clear to me that although the *Harry Potter* and *Worst Witch* series shared a strikingly similar backdrop (some commentators pointed to the fact that 'Ethel Hallow' is redolent of the 'Deathly Hallows' from JK Rowling's creation), this would still not constitute copyright infringement. The idea of a 'witchcraft' school obviously cannot be the exclusive property of one writer. For the same reason I could never successfully make an accusation of copying against Dan Brown arguing purely on the basis that we had both written holy relic thrillers involving a secret about the life of Christ, which was the absurd and disingenuous rationale of the Ponsor decision.

To me the moment where *The Da Vinci Code* most clearly imitates *The Vatican Boys* is when the lead female character – Catherine Turrell in my novel and Sophie Neveu in Dan Brown's – attends a party at her family's French country estate. In both novels she goes there on a break from her graduate studies in England ten years before the story is set. Both characters meet a debonair Knight Banker who has a private bank, and it is here where both novels' defining secret is hidden. The account at both versions of the bank is accessed by a number sequence – a secret code – in which the first two digits have a relationship with the last two digits, and a five-letter password directly related to the life of Catherine/Sophie. In both books, the code is described as 'simple'.

I kept asking myself if this was the 'substantial part' I was looking for?

Jonathan thought not because the copying of that part of my book was not sufficiently literal or slavish to meet the strict requirements of UK copyright law, and so my quest continued.

The next theory I developed was that the key role of Opus Dei was the substantial part I was looking for. In both books Opus Dei killers hired by its leader search for a relic linked to the blood of Jesus Christ. The first place the killers, Jeremy in my book and Silas in Brown's, look is the site of a famous ancient church. In my book Jeremy searches on the Via Dolorosa, looking for a sacred stone, the Rock of Golgotha; in Brown's book Silas searches on the Rose Line, looking for a sacred stone, the Keystone. They both find the ancient stone in a hollow cut-out in the church's floor.

'Interesting,' Jonathan mused when we talked it over, 'but it does not constitute a "substantial part" which has been copied in a way which is virtually literal. If you add these points to all the other similarities it's clear in layman's terms your book has been copied. But I still don't think a judge would find that the stipulations for copyright infringement have been met, so keep looking Jack.'

By the end of January 2018 I had whittled my dossier down to a handful of other suggestions that I hoped might qualify as this fabled 'substantial part', including the uncanny similarities in the way Dan Brown described the Scottish Rosslyn Chapel in *The Da Vinci Code* compared with how I described an ancient Jerusalem church in *The Vatican Boys*. I thought this example particularly telling because of the descriptions of the Rosslyn Chapel that Brown had employed. In *The Da Vinci Code*, he claims that the Rosslyn Chapel is a replica of Solomon's Temple in Jerusalem, then uses elements of my portrayal of the Jerusalem Church of the Holy Sepulchre to describe it. The problem is that the Rosslyn Chapel is not a replica of Solomon's Temple at all, and this claim has been thoroughly debunked by authors much more learned than me. In their book *Rosslyn and the Grail*, Mark Oxbrow and Ian Robertson scorn Brown's claim. 'Rosslyn Chapel,' they say, 'bears no more resemblance to Solomon's or Herod's Temple than a house brick does to a paperback book. If you superimpose the floor plans of Rosslyn Chapel and either Solomon's or Herod's Temple, you will actually find that they are not remotely similar.' The authors explain that the design of the Rosslyn Chapel is actually more akin to Glasgow Cathedral.

The fact is that it is not modelled on one of the ancient holy churches at all. Yet Dan Brown is adamant in his introduction to *The Da Vinci Code* that the architecture that he presents in its pages comprises 'Fact'. Well, his claims about the Rosslyn Chapel certainly aren't facts, and the only explanation I could come up is that Dan Brown had concocted the idea that the Rosslyn Chapel is modelled on an ancient Jerusalem Church, and then imported my descriptions of an actual Church from Jerusalem into his novel.

I took this idea and others to a meeting with Jonathan at the end of January accompanied by Árpád, who had now become a friend and one of the close team championing our cause. Jonathan, however, remained unconvinced that any of the permutations I had compiled satisfied the criteria to be the 'substantial part' on which our litigation funding depended.

Árpád, who was not looking at it through the same legal lenses, needed less convincing. 'You *don't* think Jack's established that a substantial part of his book has been copied yet Jonathan?'

'We all agree that Jack's identified a multitude of elements taken by Dan Brown which prove beyond any real doubt that he had plagiarized Jack's book. But as to the literal "substantial part" that the law in its wisdom requires; no, not yet.'

'It's legalistic gibberish,' Árpád countered. 'Either his book was copied or it wasn't.'

'I am sure that the "substantial part" is in there.' I replied. 'But which is the singular piece of evidence that passes the legal tests?'

'You need money,' Árpád concluded. 'I have an idea.'

Árpád was one of the most enterprising men I have ever met. He smiled as he said, 'Dan Brown's gained international stardom and made hundreds of millions of dollars on the back of *The Da Vinci Code* and its movie. What if you were to beat him at his own game?' You've got your book, but you don't have a movie. Time to change that.'

Initially I did not see his point. Eventually it became clear that he meant that rather than risk another courtroom defeat I should turn my attention to the court of public opinion, which in the end is the one that really matters.

Over the next weeks the idea refused to exit my mind. Jonathan enthused about the idea of our making a movie because he believed a film documenting my struggle to prove that *The Vatican Boys* had been ripped off could be a powerful tool in advancing our cause of uncovering the crime – even if our current potential litigation funders dropped out.

I was initially more interested in making sure everything we discovered preparing our legal claim was recorded for posterity. Those same reasons would later impel me to write this book. But at that moment the prospect of people watching a documentary that cogently tells the story was enough for me. I had not been permitted a jury trial in the United States because of the machinations of Dan Brown's attorneys. But through a movie the whole world could be my jury – as I now hope it will via this book.

I had not seen my old friend Don Moorhouse in ten years. Don was a well-known business figure in the Western Massachusetts area and besides being a local radio personality had written a movie called *Cathedral Pines*. We were due a catch up and this seemed the perfect opportunity.

The site of our reunion was fitting. We met in the Barnes & Noble bookstore coffee shop in the Holyoke mall where this story started. I hoped it was where we would progress at last into a triumphant final act.

'Long time, no see,' I said as I found Don sitting at a table.

'It's been a while, Jack. You're looking well.'

I wasn't feeling it, but was happy to take the compliment. 'You too,' I replied. 'Listen, Don, what I told you on the phone is only a small portion of what I've been dealing with. Let me explain.'

In an hour I had brought Don up to speed. He listened closely as I took him through everything that had erupted in the last few years.

'That's quite a yarn,' he said, once I had finished. 'You're right, Jack – it has the making of an interesting film.'

'You want to make it?'

Don grinned. He had always been up for a challenge. 'Yeah, sure,' he said. 'When do we begin?'

Over the next three months Don and I scripted a documentary

we called *The Plagiarist* and decided how to progress it. We hit upon the idea of dramatizing sequences from *The Vatican Boys* which we would then show alongside equivalent sequences from to *The Da Vinci Code* movie which would convey how clearly the two novels aligned.

Soon David Horgan and his son Cory joined us in the production. Like Don, I knew David from years back. Besides having notable friends in the film industry, he had directed a wide variety of movie projects. Cory was a brilliant young camera operator, studying film in Boston.

By late summer we had produced enough footage to put together a trailer. I did a number of interview segments and we also talked to others who had been involved in the US lawsuits. We also secured many of Dan Brown's own interviews which are available on the internet. Once all this was compiled, we set about producing four scenes from *The Vatican Boys* which were clearly mirrored in *The Da Vinci Code* movie.

The most visually compelling shots were made at a beautiful Holyoke Church where we hired an actor to play my Opus Dei assassin Jeremy, searching the floor of the church for an ancient stone. We then set it side by side with the scene from *The Da Vinci Code* where Brown's Opus Dei assassin Silas searches the floor of a church for his own ancient stone. There could be no doubt that one story aped the other.

The effect was even more striking when we hired an actress to play Catherine Turrell from *The Vatican Boys*, and filmed her hunting for the clue hidden behind the slit in the back of the painting of Christ just as Sophie does in *The Da Vinci Code*. It is remarkable to see the same character performing the same roles.

Another crucial scene that we replicated was the meeting between the leaders of the Catholic Church and the head of Opus Dei at a church-owned property outside the Vatican. In this sequence a bishop discusses how the Vatican bank's money relates to the relic at the centre of the story. In both my story and Brown's, this character, at the Pope's direction, has control over the Vatican's finances.

'It's persuasive,' said Don as we watched the footage. 'But it needs gravitas; some outside authority underpinning it. Jack, we need an expert's opinion. Without it we're too easily dismissed. We can make this movie as thrilling as we like. But without a compelling analysis underpinning it how do we make folks believe? People know movies can deceive as well as inform. They'll see these scenes we're recreating and they'll start to believe you. But unless we give them the reassurance of an expert's opinion, it could come across as smoke and mirrors. Once the documentary's over, they'll move on. We need that authoritative analysis to give it a lasting impact.'

Don was right. Movies could be compelling, but could also be fleeting. I wanted to convince the world of an important truth, not titillate them for ninety minutes and only for the subject matter of the film then to be forgotten. A robust and independent literary analysis which proved that Dan Brown had plagiarized my book was vital.

At the end of that afternoon we left the old Holyoke church with both a great deal accomplished and much yet to do. Don, David and Cory were to put together a trailer from the existing footage. My task was to find a reputable literary expert willing to be drawn into our drama and have the courage come down on the side of the truth and against the mighty forces of Dan Brown and Penguin Random House.

I did not know it then but I was about to encounter an analytical mind which could explore the two books differently from how they had been done previously. Someone who by looking at the case from a unique angle could provide fresh evidence that *The Vatican Boys* and *The Da Vinci Code* were inextricably intertwined.

I was about to enter the world of 'fictional facts'.

12

Fictional Facts

Fall had endowed New Hampshire with its unique beauty. All around the trees were turning from green and gold to vibrant russets and red.

The drive from Holyoke to the small town of Rindge is a pleasant 90-minute ride along country roads. But somehow the deeply forested trails reminded me of the years of struggle since that night in the Barnes & Noble bookstore, and the thick undergrowth and dead-end trails I had been hacking my way through since.

This time I hoped it was different. This trail led to the literary scholar Alan Perlman; and, though I did not know it yet, this was to be my most promising expedition yet.

I had first come across Alan while searching the internet for a reputable expert in the field of copyright infringement in literature. His brief, according to his website, was actually much broader. But the testimonials of those he had worked with who ranged across the legal and academic profession was enough to convince me that he might be the man to assess my claim with the authority we needed. Today I was going to meet him for a short consultation at which we could sound each other out and decide if there was any profit in progressing the association. I did not have high hopes; the last twenty years had stamped those out of me. But there remained a flicker of expectation inside me, and I had promised Don we would find an authoritative expert for our documentary. At this stage it did not feel as if I had anything to lose.

Alan was obviously a scholar of high renown. After receiving his doctorate from the University of Chicago he had practised forensic linguistics since 1979. As well as being a highly sought-after corporate speechwriter for powerful CEOs he had become a court certified expert witness in linguistics. His unusual range of academic and practical experience meant he was highly regarded as an expert in determining the authorship of potentially forged documents, and cases of plagiarism and copyright infringement. He had given his first expert testimony in a 1979 case about whether lyrics by the English rock band The Who had been plagiarized, and had not looked back since.

I found Alan to be an impressive figure, but our first meeting was largely devoted to sizing each other up. After I had told him something of what we had been trying to prove he took me through the techniques he had developed to detect plagiarism. Alan was attracted to linguistics as an undergraduate because he believed that language was the organizing principle for everything else, and understanding language would help him assimilate new information from many fields. Linguistics also gave him the ability to analyse and interpret documents, and, in this case, to assess the likelihood of plagiarism in which he has some 50 years of experience as a student, professor, and forensic linguist. All this time he has maintained a 'gold standard' of plagiarism. Can it be proved that original ideas and/or phraseology were lifted and passed off as the author's own? Those were the criteria he would apply to my claims.

Alan was willing to make a provisional study of the novels and the catalogue of convergences I had prepared. I spent that

Christmas and New Year anxiously waiting, and in February 2019, returned to Rindge to discover where his thoughts lay.

'Jack,' said Alan as we sat down at his kitchen table, 'I've read what you prepared. I can see what you describe as the same sequence of your characters and events occurring in his text.'

I sat upright. 'That's good news, isn't it?'

But Alan, veteran of so many courtrooms and of standing firm in areas of ambiguity, remained impassive. 'Perhaps, perhaps not,' he continued. 'International plagiarism laws are neither consistent nor clear regarding this type of copying. There's already been resistance to accepting this line of evidence as conclusive in your lawsuits, hasn't there?'

'A friend of mine named Howard put it into perspective for me,' I said. Howard was the skilled assistant district attorney who assisted Gary Ensor in my first lawsuit. 'He says that when he tries to convince a jury to convict a criminal he begins with one piece of evidence and then adds more pieces until there's no doubt the criminal committed the crime. His argument when he offers the first piece of evidence is, "if you consider this alone, it may not be sufficient enough to convict this person. But then there's this ...", and he presents another piece of evidence. Then he tells the jury, "If you add this, the proof builds. But maybe even these two pieces aren't enough to convince you." Then he presents another, saying, "if you add this one, there's a stronger basis for you to accept the guilt of the accused." He goes on like this until he's presented his entire case, building arguments until the evidence to convict is overwhelming.'

'Precisely,' Alan replied. 'So you understand that the structural arguments are powerful – but not in themselves conclusive.'

'We're looking for the substantial part,' I said, and referred him to the extensive catalogue of copying we had already documented. 'It's in there somewhere. We just need to know which element, or group of elements, it is. What do you suggest?'

Alan had evidently been musing on it for some time. 'It will be expensive,' he warned me. 'I have to dissect these chapters line by line, looking for specific frames.'

He had already told me something of the things he did. Forensic linguistics is a rich and complex field, applying linguistic principles to legal proceedings. Even then, I was warned, it is an inexact science. Even an expert like Alan could not guarantee a particular outcome.

Even so we had come this far. I wanted both the documentary to take flight and for the truth to be established in a court of law.

'Let's do it,' I said, and in doing so ventured my fate on Mr Perlman's literary forensics.

The seasons passed by that year in a strange haze as the ordinary patterns of life reasserted themselves and I waited for Alan's expert analysis. As Thanksgiving approached our documentary filming was in hiatus, though Don and Cory were both itching to get back to the project just as soon as our professional forensic opinion arrived.

When the call finally came I was caught unawares. 'Jack,' Alan's deep voice rumbled down the line, 'You should come up here as soon as possible. I've found things in your book and his that I can't find anywhere else.'

Two hours later I was sitting at Alan's kitchen table listening to what he had discovered.

'I made a list,' Alan said, laying a page on the table. 'It's compelling, Jack.'

I began to read:

1. The Opus Dei was involved in shady financial activities with the Vatican Bank.
2. The Opus Dei gave the Vatican Bank a billion, or billions, of dollars.
3. It was only because of this financial munificence to the Vatican Bank that the Opus Dei was made a personal prelature by Pope John Paul II.

I looked up at Alan, my brow furrowing as I tried to discern the significance of these elements he had drawn out of my novel. As I did so Alan read out the fourth and final line on the paper: 'Only because of their relationship with the Vatican Bank was the founder of Opus Dei, Josemaria Escrivá, fast-tracked to sainthood. It usually takes centuries but took only seventeen years in your book, and twenty years in Brown's.' He paused. 'Do you see what I'm getting at yet, Jack?'

Initially I was not certain that I did. Opus Dei was central to both stories but my deployment of it could not be protected by copyright because it is a real institution. Even the fact that John Paul II had made it a personal prelature – a kind of Catholic institution under the governance of the Vatican's Congregation for Bishops – is recorded fact. There were uncanny similarities in our use of Opus Dei in the novels, but Alan seemed to be hinting at some greater significance.

Next Alan showed me further information he had unearthed. 'I've looked at all the responses Opus Dei released after *The Da Vinci Code* was published. They rebut everything Brown says about them in *The Da Vinci Code*. But Brown's so-called research has already been found wanting. Look back at *The Holy Blood and the Holy Grail* trial – all of that material he'd "researched" and hadn't verified, about the origin and history of the Priory of Sion. He thought it was all historically accurate, not realising that the Priory is in fact a hoax. Well, now think about Opus Dei.'

Now I saw what Alan was driving at. It hit me like a bolt from the blue. 'The Opus Dei is real,' I said. 'So are its connections to the Vatican. But as for the rest; its connection to the Vatican bank, the shadowy finances in 1982, the "real" reason why the Opus Dei was made a personal prelature, the "real" reason Josemaria Escrivá was fast-tracked to sainthood. They're all my inventions to make my story work. It's what I've been doing since my first novel, researching my history as closely as I can, then weaving my own imagination into it.'

'I couldn't find references to these things anywhere – not in any of the online resources reference and historical material I consulted. The only two places they exist, as far as I can see, are in *The Vatican Boys* and *The Da Vinci Code*.'

'It's all my fiction. It's not real history at all.'

'Dan Brown portrays all these four inventions of yours as real fact in his book.'

'And there's only one place in the world Brown could have got them.'

Alan had dug a little further. 'In the real world,' he said, 'the Pope doesn't have direct control over the Vatican Bank.' I nodded. That too was a departure from history in *The Vatican Boys* where I had adjusted historical events to suit my creative aims. 'Yet in both your book and his, the Pope is described as being able to access funds from the bank directly. In your book, you have the chief secretary to the Pope being the one in charge of the Vatican Bank's reserves – and you make it clear that, in 1982, Pope John Paul II was aware that all of this shady Opus Dei financial activity was occurring all around him.'

It was all just more of my fictions.

'And yet it's right here, in *The Da Vinci Code* as well,' Alan went on. 'It appears that Dan Brown thought that so far as these issues are concerned you were documenting *genuine* history.'

I do not know why I had not appreciated the significance of these things until then. It looked so simple. Where I had made adjustments to the history of Opus Dei the better to fit the story, Dan Brown had thought they were true facts.

I already knew that he was not a diligent researcher, and this only seemed to prove it. He had cherry-picked my 'fictional facts' and passed them off as his 'facts' because he had not done the research himself. Why should he if he thought I had done it for him, especially if he had sent around a delegate in 1999 to pick my brains who might well have come away from the meeting with the impression that given the depth of my research every historical element of my book could be taken as fact.

'Here's the thing, Jack,' Alan went on. 'The plots of both books rely heavily upon the proposition that these events – the financial wrangling between Opus Dei and the Vatican, and how money is controlled inside the Vatican itself – actually took place. It serves as the basis for the assertion that the Opus Dei is a sinister organisation doing illegal things, and that both the Pope himself and his chief secretary are heavily involved in it. The end game is for the Opus Dei to use its Vatican Bank connections with its suspiciously-supplied financial resources to get hold of the relic so it can enhance its power within the Catholic Church.'

'Yes,' I stuttered, 'that's … *The Vatican Boys*' fictional plot-line. Alan, I made it all up.'

'Well, it's an essential part of Brown's story too. Without being able to use the departures from history that you threaded through *The Vatican Boys* – your original and specific fictional material – his plot disintegrates.'

'Incredible,' I said. 'My fictional facts have caught him out.'

Until this moment I had not appreciated that some of the apparently minor details of how Dan Brown's version of the Opus Dei mirrored my own had much more significance than the broader convergences. It would not be easy for an attorney defending someone like Dan Brown to convince a court that two authors had independently inserted the same 'fictional facts' into recorded history for the very same purpose. How, I wondered, could Brown possibly get out of this one?

'I couldn't find these things anywhere else,' Alan repeated. 'There are thousands of pages written about the history of the Opus Dei, across a multitude of books. But it's clear there are only two places these pieces of "historical" information are found. And that's in *The Vatican Boys* and *The Da Vinci Code*.'

'And my book came six years earlier.'

Alan smiled.

We've got him, I thought. We've *finally* got him.

'Alan,' I said, 'we have to film this. This all needs to be captured in the documentary.'

'Okay,' Alan responded, lightly. 'What type of outfit should I wear?'

Fictional Facts. The words sound almost absurd side by side. In a sense they are a contradiction in terms. But here was proof, hard and undeniable, that contrary to their denials Dan and Blythe Brown had used my novel as one of their 'resources' while they were writing *The Da Vinci Code*. The adoption of my 'fictional facts' as real facts even travelled into the arguments that were used against me in my US case.

Here is an example of how two of my fictional facts were even adopted as such even by the attorneys representing Dan Brown and Penguin Random House. Here is a paragraph from *The Vatican Boys*:

> "'The Rumasa organization was a business consortium which owned about 20 banks and hundreds of other businesses all over Europe. It went belly up in 1983." She paused for a moment for Julien to take it all in. "The head of the Rumasa was a man by the name of Josemaria Ruiz-Mateos. And guess what? Ruiz-Mateos arranged bogus loans to be made from a half-dozen of his banks to the IOR just before they went under. This illegal business was approved by Archbishop Zagranski himself. The monies all of the bankers loaned to the IOR, in other words the Vatican, were quite substantial. If you add up the totals, the sums are billions of dollars.'"

Here is a sentence from the "Reply" document which was put before Judge Ponsor by Dan Brown and his publishers' lawyers:

> 'Brown merely references the actual historical fact that the Opus Dei lent the Vatican Bank money in 1982 when the

Vatican Bank was in bankruptcy.' (in exchange for Pope John
Paul II granting Opus Dei the status of a personal prelature).

The problem for Legal Team Brown is that as a matter of historical
fact the Opus Dei did not lend the Vatican Bank money and it has
never approached bankruptcy. These were 'fictional facts' that
appear in Dan Brown's book, and which only appear in one other
place – a book which he claims to not have even have heard of
before he wrote *The Da Vinci Code*.

As I reflected on what Alan had discovered my mind went to the
judgment of Judge Robert Patterson Jr in the case JK Rowling had
brought against RDR Books, who had published their unofficial
Harry Potter Lexicon. Patterson had written, 'Invented facts
constitute creative expression protected by copyright.' Well, surely
that applied to my claim? My invented facts were my own creative
expression and so were protected by copyright, and were right there,
scattered throughout Dan Brown's pages.

It had been nearly fifteen years since that night in the Barnes &
Noble bookstore where my life had been upended. My drive to see
the crime exposed had waxed and waned across those years as the
fortunes of my cause ebbed and flowed.

But the old fire was back. It is hard to put into words the cocktail
of emotions I was feeling as I sat down again with the two books
and Alan Perlman's discoveries on a list beside me. For the first
time it felt as if I had the evidence I needed, not just to prove my
case to a lay person's standard but also in a court of law, evidence
which at least proved that Dan Brown had plundered my creative
treasure trove.

What was more, I thought, where there was smoke, there was also fire. So before I booked my flights to London to reconvene with Jonathan and present him with this new angle on the case, I immersed myself again in my well-worn copies of *The Vatican Boys* and *The Da Vinci Code* because I did not believe that the 'fictional facts' that Alan Perlman had discovered were the only such instances.

One last push and I was certain that justice would be ours.

13

The Silent Witness

How strange it felt returning to London in December 2019 to meet again with Jonathan and set out on the next stage of this journey. I landed on a grey London day, returning to the familiar streets of Blackfriars and the Victoria Embankment though this time not with a heavy heart. This time I did so with the wind blowing strongly in my sails, certain that – after long months where everything seemed stalled – we were about to make progress.

On Thursday, December 5th, Jonathan and I got together at the Apex Temple Court Hotel.

'I have it,' I told him. 'I've found the elusive "substantial part."'

I had already informed Jonathan there had been significant developments in my quest for evidence that could prove to a court that the plagiarism had taken place, but I had not been willing to commit it to email. This was not only for the sense of occasion it brought our meeting, though I admit that the storyteller in me preferred the drama of the face-to-face encounter to a dry exchange of emails. Perhaps it is difficult to understand but over the past years I had also become slightly paranoid about the forces that opposed me, powerful, moneyed organisations whose vested interest was in keeping the truth hidden, the very phenomenon I had written about in *The Vatican Boys*. The way I had been roundly dismissed by the US legal system when the correlation between the two texts was so evident had propelled me to some dark places, and I had become anxious about the prospect of what I had unearthed being discovered and dark forces unleashed. I had never forgotten that feeling of being in a courtroom confronted by the might of Dan Brown, Random House, and Sony, pitted against their inexhaustible resources and aggressive lawyers.

'We've been stalled in the last eight months,' I began – though Jonathan hardly needed telling. He had already confided to me that our very own David vs Goliath story was beginning to wear him out. I knew the feeling. 'When Nick and Andrew told us we didn't have the evidence to file the High Court lawsuit, I knew I had to shift gear. I have located a scholar from New Hampshire who looks at plagiarism differently. He's a forensic linguistic expert called Alan Perlman who reviews copying claims in his own unique manner.'

'How does he do it?'

'He developed his techniques inspecting copies of the Torah, becoming an expert in mapping how meanings changed in different translations and brought those skills into forensic analysis. He started interrogating *The Vatican Boys* and *The Da Vinci Code* in a way we hadn't considered.'

'And what did he find?'

'Jonathan, there are original elements in my book that only crop up in one other place – the pages of *The Da Vinci Code*.' I paused to let the idea sink in. 'The reason that these bits of information don't exist anywhere else is because *I made them up*. It's been part of my modus operandi ever since *The Diary of William Goffe* to build a story combining things that actually happened with fictional elements of my own. *The Vatican Boys* needed the Opus Dei to be a much more sinister, controlling, powerful organisation than they are in the real world. So in the service of my story I made up various facts about them and how they interacted with the Catholic Church. It's those "fictional facts" that Alan zoned in on when he analysed the two texts.'

I paused to allow Jonathan time to take this in.

'What you're saying ties unique features of *The Da Vinci Code* to unique features in *The Vatican Boys* that you had presented as facts, but in fact were figments of your imagination?'

'And it doesn't leave room for any other explanation,' I went on. 'Dan Brown clearly used *The Vatican Boys* as his primary resource. He imported the fictional information I'd made up about the Opus Dei into *The Da Vinci Code* because he thought it was all historical fact.' I paused. 'And it's been established in the law that "invented facts constitute creative expression protected by copyright." That's part of the JK Rowling judgment and Dan Brown is absolutely in violation of it.'

'He's more than that,' said Jonathan. 'There's every chance this leaves him open to a charge of Contempt of Court as well.'

'Contempt of Court?'

'It goes back to *The Holy Blood and the Holy Grail* trial. As I explained in the consultation with counsel, in his witness statement Dan Brown lists all of the books he says he used for research in writing *The Da Vinci Code*. Everything's supposed to be covered there. It's where he admits that Leigh and Baigent's book was one of his literary sources. The problem for Dan Brown is that he didn't admit to using *The Vatican Boys* as a literary source. If what you're saying is true, he deliberately misled the court. That could lead to serious trouble for him in the UK justice system, leaving aside problems he may face in the US. How clearly can you show it?'

I produced another set of papers I had brought out with me and laid them out on the table between us. The print-outs were direct copies of sections of *The Da Vinci Code*, lined up against sections of *The Vatican Boys*. 'Each chapter contains very specific information related to the history of Opus Dei. I don't think the most blinkered judge could dismiss it.'

The first section was taken from Chapter 7 of *The Da Vinci Code* where Dan Brown introduces Manuel Aringarosa, as the head of Opus Dei, a man whose 'ascension to grace was jump-started in 1982 when Pope John Paul II unexpectedly elevated them to a "personal prelature of the Pope," officially sanctioning all of their practices.'

The same section states that Opus Dei's elevation had come in the same year that it had transferred a billion dollars to the Vatican Bank to save it from bankruptcy. Then, 'in a second manoeuvre that raised eyebrows, the Pope placed the founder of Opus Dei on the "fast track" for sainthood, accelerating an often century-long waiting period for canonization to a mere twenty years.'

Once Jonathan had finished reading, I said, 'It's a founding premise of Dan Brown's plot. The same information is repeated and emphasised in Chapters 41 and 100 of his book. This idea that the Opus Dei bailed out the Vatican Bank and that, in return, the head of Opus Dei was fast-tracked to sainthood is threaded through *The Da Vinci Code*. The problem is, it isn't historical fact at all. It's a series of fictions that I formulated for the plot of *The Vatican Boys*. Alan Perlman showed me all the places where the real-life Opus Dei has rebutted it, as you would expect since I made it up. Dan Brown presented it as 'Fact' because he thought he was piggybacking on my research. In reality he was piggybacking on my imagination.'

Jonathan looked up.

'It's been staring right at us,' I said. 'The chronology and significance of these 1982 events is exactly the same in both books. I made it all up, Jonathan, which I can prove because it doesn't exist anywhere else. Dan Brown copied it from *The Vatican Boys* into *The Da Vinci Code*, thinking it was all documented, historical fact. It's the smoking gun we need. It proves he both had "access" to my novel and plundered it.'

'This really is remarkable,' Jonathan replied after a moment to reflect.

'If you recall the trial about *The Holy Blood and the Holy Grail*, Dan Brown said his wife Blythe was instrumental in the research. Justice Smith said, "Blythe Brown provided the material for the [Langdon/Teabing] lectures with *HBHG* in her hands." Well, there's every chance she did it with *The Vatican Boys* as well. Even the locations in the two stories contain my fictions presented as facts.'

Jonathan was looking at me intently. 'There's more, isn't there?'

I nodded. 'After Alan revealed all this to me, I went back to the novels myself. Almost everything Brown infers about the Opus Dei is derived from my novel. He doesn't just use the facts I created. He uses them in *precisely* the same order.'

I could see I really had Jonathan's attention.

'It's what Judge Robert Patterson Jr said in the JK Rowling judgment. Invented facts constitute creative expression protected by law – and they can create a skeleton that holds a story together. Well, that's what this is too, Jonathan. Brown takes my invented facts and, because he threads them through his story in the same order I do in mine, they become one of the structural foundations of his book. His characters and plot can't develop in the way they do unless he uses my fictional facts in the same order that I did.'

I directed Jonathan's attention back to the page.

'What am I looking at?'

'It's my analysis of the plot structure that my Opus Dei facts build up; the one which is at the heart of *The Da Vinci Code* as well. See ...' And I took Jonathan through it, step by step. 'Once a nun answers the question, yes, she knows who the Opus Dei Bishop is. She says he is the head of Opus Dei. He is powerful with the IOR – that's the Vatican Bank. In 1982, the Opus Dei was unexpectedly made a personal prelature through the help and approval of Pope John Paul II because of their large donations to the Vatican Bank. The Opus Dei itself has flat out rebutted this – again, as you would expect because I made it up, just as it rebutted the idea that they gave the Vatican Bank billions of dollars to bail it out of bankruptcy – and with good reason, because I made that up too. The Vatican Bank wasn't even having financial problems in 1982. Then there's the proposition that Pope John Paul II officially sanctioned all of the Opus Dei's practises and that, because of its financial backing, it was granted favours by the Pope himself, bringing him under suspicion of impropriety. Fiction, Jonathan, which I invented, and which Brown then passed off as fact in his book.'

Jonathan looked pensive. I paused for a minute to let him reflect, and then went on.

'And so it goes on, because the Opus Dei didn't even have a billion dollars to throw around in 1982 – and it's doubtful they do now. It's just another figment of my imagination. But every element of it appears in the same order in both plots, chapter by chapter.' I paused. 'What do you think? Does it meet the established criteria for copyright infringement at your High Court?'

Jonathan mused on a moment. 'In my mind, yes, it would seem so.'

'So what's our next move?'

'Avoiding Summary Judgment; the equivalent to the fate that befell your US case is still our first goal if we start legal proceedings, although, with this new evidence, and subject to the views of our barristers, hopefully it will not be too much of a problem. That leads to two scenarios, one of which is that they offer to pay up. If they don't, we got to trial and Dan Brown is compelled finally to explain why there is such a staggering array of commonalities between his book and yours if he never read it before writing *The Da Vinci Code*. This time, because of the criticism of her absence in the first trial, Blythe's going to have to give evidence at any such trial, or the judge is unlikely to believe a word that Dan Brown says – though they may not do so anyway. Then there's the small matter of perjury.'

Jonathan paused, and I could see fight flashing in his eyes. 'I think we need to pick up the pace again, Jack. There are other litigation funders that might be interested in this project. We seem to have the evidence we need, but we also need to have funding in place so Team Brown know they cannot out-cost us in any legal battle. I have good connections in the broadcast and print media. In the next few months we should be able to bring them on board. We'll have to get a favourable opinion from our barristers. Then hopefully we should get our funding and be on our way.' Jonathan was swaying in his chair planning his strategy. Then with a broad smile he said, 'Let's see Dan Brown lie his way out of this one.'

We sat in silence, enjoying the moment. It was coming. It was on the horizon. Finally, the truth would come out.

14

Two Writers

This book began with two writers setting out to fulfill their dream of thrilling the world with stories drawn from their imaginations and expressed in lovingly crafted novels. It ends with those same two writers from similarly unexceptional beginnings arriving at very different destinations. One blazed his way into riches, fame, and a place in the history of world literature on the back of the imagination, work and skills of others. The other has retained his integrity, and occupies a genteel but modest obscurity.

In early 2020, just as Jonathan and I were chronicling how my 'fictional facts' had journeyed from *The Vatican Boys* to *The Da Vinci Code*, the world lurched into an unprecedented global disaster as Covid-19 rampaged across the planet. As the international shutdown began it seemed my quest to expose the truth was defeated or at least long delayed. We had our evidence, but still needed litigation funders in place and for that we needed the positive opinion of specialist barristers. This cost time and money, two resources which were running short after nearly two decades of struggle.

But I am a writer and I believe in the power of words.

A couple of years ago while we were still trying to jump through the hoops to bring a UK legal claim Jonathan introduced me to an independent British publisher, Silvertail Books, run by Humfrey Hunter, who had eschewed the world of corporate publishing and was brave enough to publish material which corporate publishing would not, such as books critical of the aggressive and litigious Church of Scientology, which Jonathan had 'legalled' for him – just as he has this one.

I found Humfrey to be a warm and intelligent man who became convinced by degrees, just as Jonathan had, of the truth of my story. He read both books and saw all the reasons why I was sure that Dan Brown's best seller was an iteration of my book. This is the email that he sent to Jonathan: 'I can see why you have confidence in winning this case. It is quite gobsmacking. I don't think I have ever come across anything so blatant. The copying is simultaneously lazy in terms of the widespread lifting, and thus also very faithful to the original source. I was reading it on the tube and found myself several times involuntarily exclaiming "oh my god", at what I was reading. I kept wondering what he must have been thinking when he was doing it. It's hard to see what his defence can be.'

Initially Silvertail Books was just to re-issue *The Vatican Boys*. But Humfrey also offered me the opportunity to get this story out into the world in the form of a book. So it was, becalmed and incarcerated by Covid 19, I began writing a memoir which would start with my earliest days as a writer through to the discovery of Dan Brown's literary fraud and my quest to see justice done.

Like the documentary we had started but lacked the funds to complete, the memoir would serve a dual purpose. With good fortune, and Humfrey's expertise and courage, it might provide the financial means both to finish the documentary and secure our day in court. But even more important than that, I wanted the book to be a lasting testament to the truth that it contains which is so precious to me.

That memoir is the one you are holding in your hands right now, a modest account of one writer's life, a trenchant piece of investigative journalism and, I hope, an engaging work of non-fiction. Thank you so much for reading it, and if you have come away from these pages believing what is written in them about *The Vatican Boys* and *The Da Vinci Code*, that is more than enough for me. The other writer might have acquired wealth, fame and adulation. But that is not what I got into writing for. I did so to touch people's hearts and minds with my words, and that is what I sincerely hope I have done with this book.

And the world keeps turning. Dan Brown's life has taken another tumultuous spin – and there is a chance that as a result, more may be revealed about how *The Da Vinci Code* came to be written. In 2019 Dan and Blythe Brown announced their divorce after twenty-one years of marriage. By the summer of 2020, the divorce proceedings had reached such an acrimonious pitch that details of their claims and counter-claims against each other court the attention of the media and were the focus of articles from the *Daily Mail* to the *New York Times*.

In the summer of 2020 Blythe Brown launched a furious lawsuit against her former husband, claiming – amongst other things – that he had misrepresented his assets at the time of the divorce, and had lived a life of deceit and extra-marital affairs. Dan Brown, in turn, describes in his counter-claim how their marriage had become increasingly dysfunctional since the vast success of *The Da Vinci Code*, and that the influx of wealth that came with the novel proved to be the beginning of the end of their union.

The bitter legal proceedings between Dan and Blythe Brown have cast interesting light on the creative process behind the novels. Blythe claims that Dan Brown withheld from her the information that a television series, *Langdon*, based upon the character Robert Langdon (though actually on my creation, Stephen Hathaway) was in development, and that she was instrumental in creating Robert Langdon because of the significant role she played in writing Dan Brown's novels; especially *The Da Vinci Code*.

This is paragraph 22 of Blythe Brown's complaint: 'Blythe was the driving force and the one who developed the premise of the critical concepts, historical emphases, and complex plot twists of the now famous novel. So immersed was Blythe in their joint project that she left her job in order to devote herself full time to the research that produced the intricate blend of historical fact and fiction that became the hallmark of the book's success and that captivated readers around the world.'

From my perspective the most crucial aspect of these proceedings is that both Dan and Blythe Brown have separately asserted that together they were responsible for creation of *The Da Vinci Code*. In effect, they have declared that they were jointly responsible for lifting elements of my own novel and seeding them in *The Da Vinci Code*.

If my day in court ever comes, and Dan and Blythe Brown have to testify as to the genesis of their record-setting novel, it will be an explosive moment. If the threats of a defamation claim which emerge from correspondence sent by Dan Brown's publishers Penguin Random House are carried out then the opportunity for a court determination will arise that way. Both Dan Brown and his publishers have been told that this book will accuse him of being both a plagiarist and a liar, allegations which have been described as 'seriously defamatory'. Okay, so sue me if that's right. That way everyone will find out who is right and wrong in this.

This story is not finished yet. Perhaps someday I will look back on the writing of this memoir as a stepping-stone along the way, one of the many leaps we were forced to take to get our day in court. But for now these pages stand as testimony to the journey I have been on and as the receptacle for evidence that even if it never goes before a judge, will convince the world that Dan Brown's status as a mega-star author is undeserved.

Riches come and go, and as Dan Brown has discovered, they can be one of the most destructive forces on earth. But truth endures, and even if my day in court never comes, I will forever be grateful and proud that in writing this book I have played my part in exposing this *Da Vinci Fraud*.

15

You the Jury

One of the consistent features of my quest to reveal the truth about how *The Da Vinci Code* came to be written is that everyone who has looked into the facts has come to the same conclusion as I have. The only exceptions appear to be Dan Brown, his publishers, Sony Pictures, their lawyers, and Judge Michael Ponsor.

You remember how in Chapter 6 Judge Ponsor was persuaded by the attorneys acting for Dan Brown, his publishers and Sony Pictures that there were no substantial similarities between the two books, with the result that he refused me my constitutional rights both to jury trial and to enjoy the fruits of my literary labour. Now you will understand why my US attorneys and I were so shocked by that decision.

Leaving aside the legal niceties, the thing that I wanted the jury to do was to find that in writing *The Da Vinci Code*, Dan Brown had plagiarized my book. By that I meant that contrary to his denials, he had in fact read my book, and in writing his he had produced his own plagiarized version of it, mixing in elements of *The Holy Blood and the Holy Grail*. If you take both those elements out of *The Da Vinci Code* there is precious little left.

But a jury is only 12 people. The thing that excites me about this book is that it allows me to invite the whole world to be my jury. You, the reader, are free to make up your own mind, to decide whether I am right about there having been an immense *Da Vinci Fraud* in the form of *The Da Vinci Code* – or if I am wrong.

If I am right then a number of things must follow. Dan Brown has spent around twenty years lying about how he came to write his most successful book; lying to his publishers and readers, and to Sony Pictures, Tom Hanks and all those that watched *The Da Vinci Code* film. He has lied to the English and American courts, and in the case of the English court, he is guilty both of two criminal offences, Perjury and Contempt of Court. He should therefore share the fate of other perjurers and be sentenced to jail. Instead, he has gained immense wealth and fame under false pretences.

Since by reading this book you have taken your place as a member of a unique world jury, I have given over the rest of this final chapter to Jonathan, who is a lawyer, while I am a writer. Jonathan has prepared what would be his opening speech in a jury trial to determine if Dan Brown did indeed plagiarize my book in writing *The Da Vinci Code*. Whether you find in my favour or not, and regardless of whether or not at some future time you decide to re-read *The Da Vinci Code* with copies of *The Vatican Boys* and this book open alongside it, I am truly grateful that you have come this far with me.

Note that in Jonathan's speech, I am called the 'Plaintiff' in the US, and the 'Claimant' in Great Britain. Dan Brown and Penguin Random House are called 'the Defendants' in both jurisdictions. Some of the evidence set out in this book was compiled for the US claim, and some in preparation for the UK legal action against Dan Brown and Penguin Random House. We have also compiled important new evidence as part of the process of writing this book. Jonathan has also done his best fairly to summarise the arguments that were set out by Dan Brown's UK attorneys in response to his letter setting out my claim, which is a yet more comprehensive and detailed analysis of my plagiarism claim that was used in the US proceedings. As we have explained, the evidence that was advanced by the Defendants in the US proceedings was also fatally tainted by false assertions made on behalf of Dan Brown and Penguin Random House by their lawyers. You will find the letter that Jonathan wrote to Penguin Random House's UK headquarters and its accompanying schedules in the appendices.

So, imagine you and the rest of the jury have been sworn in and have elected your chairperson. The clerk has ordered, 'Silence in court,' the judge has taken his seat, and the clerk has announced the parties to the case that you are about to hear tried before you: Jack Dunn as Plaintiff, and Dan Brown and Penguin Random House as Defendants. Jonathan, as my lead counsel, has taken to his feet to address you, and your opportunity to make up your own mind about the origin of *The Da Vinci Code* and to deliver your verdict has arrived.

Now, over to Jonathan …

***

Ladies and Gentlemen of the Jury,

I represent Jack Dunn in this case, whose stark claim is no less than that in writing **The Da Vinci Code** Dan Brown stole the plot, characters, themes and locations of his book **The Vatican Boys**.

The issue before you is therefore one of plagiarism, for which the dictionary definition is: "The practice of taking someone else's work or ideas and passing them off as one's own." The question that you are asked to determine is whether in writing **The Da Vinci Code**

185

Dan Brown plagiarized Jack Dunn's book, **The Vatican Boys**; and whether, apart from sections of Dan Brown's book which were taken from another book called **The Holy Blood and the Holy Grail**, much of the content of **The Da Vinci Code** has been taken from **The Vatican Boys**.

THE CASE FOR THE PLAINTIFF

My submissions are in five parts:

1. <u>Timing</u>;
2. <u>Access</u>;
3. <u>Convergences</u>;
4. <u>Fictional facts</u>;
5. <u>Statistics</u>.

<u>Timing</u>

Jack Dunn began writing **The Vatican Boys** in 1990, and after <u>six years</u> of painstaking research completed it in 1996. It was published in 1997.

Dan Brown had his 'big idea' to write **the Da Vinci Code** in around 2000. He completed the synopsis in 2001. He apparently wrote the first half of his book in a mere <u>eleven months</u> between January 2001 and March 2002. **The Da Vinci Code** was completed sometime in late 2002 and published in March 2003.

It is difficult to imagine that Dan Brown was able to write a book in about fourteen months which he claims was the product of thorough and original research, which in terms of historical content overlaps substantially with a book that took six years to write because of the amount of research that was required to complete it.

Access

Dan Brown flatly denies ever having had 'access' to **The Vatican Boys**; which translates in lay terms as his denying that he ever read it or even heard of it, prior to writing **The Da Vinci Code**.

Jack Dunn's book was published in 1997 and was sold by local booksellers in and around New England. In 1997 Dan Brown was living about 90 minutes from Jack Dunn. His first book **Digital Fortress** published in 1998 was sold in the same local bookstores as Jack Dunn's book. Both writers were at the time 'local authors' with their books being sold mostly in New England bookstores.

The Vatican Boys was sold in the Lord Jeffrey bookstore in Amherst, Massachusetts, where Dan Brown both lived and went to college. When Dan Brown talks about selling at local bookstores it is likely that he sold it in Amherst where **The Vatican Boys** was also sold. Dan Brown was trying to sell his books at the very same bookstores where **The Vatican Boys** was being sold. Dan Brown did at least one book signing of **The Da Vinci Code** in this Amherst bookstore, where Jack Dunn had also signed books.

Dan Brown credits the Water Street Bookstore 'for tracking down so many of my research books.' Jack Dunn's book was being sold at this same time in the Water Street Bookstore. Dan Brown was therefore using a local bookstore to source writing material which sold Jack's book – the subject matter of which is nearly identical to that of Dan Brown's book. Since Jack and his work were well-known to the staff, it seems most unlikely that they would not have sent his book to Dan Brown; unless of course Dan Brown had already secured a copy.

Dan Brown says he had no intention of writing **The Da Vinci Code** before 1998, which is the very year after Jack's book went on sale in the very bookshop that Dan Brown used for his research.

Convergences

We believe that there are several hundred (between 400 and 500) examples of the same material appearing in **The Da Vinci Code** which also appears in its predecessor, **The Vatican Boys**. For the sake of argument, shall we say there is only half that. You can imagine the infinitesimal statistical likelihood of those being a product of chance – an issue to which I will return.

You can read a non-exhaustive list of those commonalities in the two schedules that accompany my claim letter to Penguin Random House's London office, a copy of which the usher will hand you now. Time constraints do not permit me to do this issue justice in this my address, so I will just give you three examples.

EXAMPLE ONE
This scene appears both in **The Da Vinci Code** and
The Vatican Boys

1. Mercenary takes control of Central Male Character;
2. Mercenary has a gun;
3. Main Male Character is lying on the floor injured and in pain;
4. Main Female Character sitting or propped up against a 'couch'/divan;
5. A Main Character has an 'injured right ankle';
6. Scholar is talking to Mercenary as the other characters listen to them;
7. Mercenary holds a gun to the head of one of his captives;
8. Mercenary 'lowers his gun';
9. Mercenary is injured and in pain,

10. Scholar captures Mercenary;
11. Opus Dei sent Mercenary after the Relic the Scholar has control of in the room;
12. A 'miracle' happens;
13. The same 'Four Characters' (the same in both books) are present in the Scene(s) at the same time – The Central Male Character, the Central Female Character, the Scholar and the Mercenary;
14. Mercenary is distraught and feeling helpless;
15. Three Main Characters (Main Male Character, Main Female Character and Scholar) regain (are in) control of the Relic as the scene ends.

EXAMPLE TWO
In the first 60 pages these characters are introduced in both books in a similar order:

The Vatican Boys

1. Mason murdered – Roberto Calvi
2. Blackfriars Bridge (capital city landmark)
3. Jose Maria Escriva – Founder of Opus Dei
4. Stephen Hathaway – Main Male Character, 40ish attractive, intelligent, blue eyes
5. Catherine Turrell – Main Female Character, beautiful, classy, French, upper-class, 35 years old, good with numbers and knows the Knight Banker who has the secret in his private bank from a party at her family's French country estate, 10 years ago

6. Jeremy Willoughby – Mercenary hired by head of Opus Dei

The Da Vinci Code

1. Knight/Mason murdered – Jacques Saunière
2. The Louvre (capital city landmark)
3. Jose Maria Escriva – Founder of Opus Dei
4. Robert Langdon – Main Male Character 40ish attractive, intelligent, blue eyes
5. Sophie Neveu – Main Female Character, beautiful, classy, French, upper-class, 32 years old, good with numbers and knows the Knight Banker who has the secret in his private bank from a party at her family's French country estate, 10 years ago.
6. Silas – Mercenary hired by head of Opus Dei

EXAMPLE THREE
Theological and historical convergences (theology and relics)
in BOTH books:

1. Scroll – (Aleppo Codex in *The Vatican Boys*, in Cryptex in *The Da Vinci Code*)
2. Dead Sea Scrolls
3. Hebrew Writing
4. Papyrus
5. Rolled in a round jar
6. Poem written on it in Reverse
7. Protected by a jar in *The Vatican Boys*, and by a glass cylinder protects in *The Da Vinci Code*

8.   Related to Bible Teachings
9.   Conflicts/Church's teachings
10. Vatican suppresses truth
11. 1st class relic (Turin Shroud in *The Vatican Boys*, Holy Grail in *The Da Vinci Code* but **originally** Turin Shroud)
12. Blood of Christ/Turin Shroud in *The Vatican Boys*, Blood of Christ/Holy Grail but **originally** Turin Shroud in *The Da Vinci Code*
13. Questions Christ's Divinity
14. Holy Cloths are Relics in *The Vatican Boys*, bloodline is related to the Relic in *The Da Vinci Code*
15. Theological controversy

Fictional facts and factual errors

We believe that this is the most cogent evidence that Dan Brown plagiarized Jack Dunn's book when he wrote **The Da Vinci Code**. There are seven 'fictional facts' (including one which is the product of an error) that Jack Dunn invented for **The Vatican Boys**, which are then presented in **The Da Vinci Code** as real facts; and which (so far as we know) appear in no other literature other than these two books.

1.   The papal secretary;
2.   The billion-dollar payment by Opus Dei to the Vatican bank;
3.   The Vatican bank was effectively bankrupt at the time;
4.   This payment secures the early beatification of Opus Dei's founder;
5.   The Opus Dei was involved in shady financial activities with the Vatican Bank;

6. It was only because of this financial munificence to the Vatican Bank that the Opus Dei was made a personal prelature by Pope John Paul II;

7. The Vatican conclave said to have taken place in the 1990's;

<u>The papal secretary</u>

The first factual error in **The Vatican Boys** which has been adopted by Dan Brown in **The Da Vinci Code** concerns a senior Vatican official. Jeremy Willoughby (**The Vatican Boys**) and Silas (**The Da Vinci Code**) are both assassins hired directly or indirectly by the 'Chief Secretary to the Pope' to secure the religious secret which is at the centre of both books.

In fact, there was no such post in the Vatican as 'Chief Secretary to the Pope'. The allusion in **The Vatican Boys** to the Chief Secretary to the Pope as the sponsor for the mercenary assassin was a mistake on Jack's part, which then re-appeared in **The Da Vinci Code** with the Secretariat providing the Vatican Banks money to get the relic.

<u>The billion-dollar payment, to the 'bankrupt' Vatican Bank, allied to the early beatification of the founder of Opus Dei</u>

These are three closely related 'fictional facts' from **The Vatican Boys** that all found their way into **The Da Vinci Code**. All three are central to the plots of both books, and yet none has any basis in fact.

<u>The fictional papal Vatican conclave</u>

A papal Vatican conclave in the late 1990's is featured in both books.

This is another of Jack Dunn's 'fictional facts' that re-appears in **The Da Vinci Code**. In fact, there was no such conclave.

Statistics

In the United Kingdom, the test that you are asked to apply is 'the balance of probabilities'. In the US, the usual test appears to be the 'preponderance of the evidence'. I believe that, in practical terms, the two tests are a little different because they produce the same result. But I am going to ask you to use the English test because it is easier for a lay person to apply.

When dealing with an issue such as 'convergences' there is inevitably scope for argument. In this case, in the US in particular, it was argued for the Defendants that the analysis of convergences which was relied on by Mr Dunn was exaggerated. We say that even if it was – which we do not accept – only a proportion of it needs to be correct to prove plagiarism.

We believe that any bona fide evaluation of the numerous elements that comprise the fictional architecture and structure of the story in **The Vatican Boys**, and a comparison of the same elements in **The Da Vinci Code** proves beyond any doubt that Dan Brown heavily plagiarized **The Vatican Boys** in writing **The Da Vinci Code**. These are the primary common elements/themes:

1. Story Convergences;
2. The Relics and convergences of their use; in both stories they are both 'First Class Relics', and to do with Jesus' blood;
3. The synopsis for **The Da Vinci Code** featured the exact same relic, the Turin Shroud;

We say that cumulatively these common features of **The Vatican Boys** and the subsequent **The Da Vinci Code** – whether or not these may in part comprise 'stock' elements – render the likelihood of **The Da Vinci Code** having been created independently of **The Vatican Boys** well beyond mathematical calculation.

The evidence of 'convergences', both in terms of their detail and chronological use, is overwhelming; and the instances numerous. We therefore asked an eminent statistician to apply well-established statistical principles to establish the likelihood of those 'convergences' occurring by chance. The results are staggering.

This is how our statistical expert put it: 'If there are <u>six</u> elements in a sequence, the probability that they will be arranged in a specific order is 120 to 1.'

As she explained it, that means if the numerical probability that two, college-educated, American, male authors born between 1950 and 1960 read the same books or magazines and decided to express the story components in the same order, the odds are 120 to 1.

If you apply the same formula to just <u>seven</u> elements in a sequence, you get to 5,040 to 1. For eight elements in a sequence, the figure goes up to 40,320 to 1. It would be very hard, on any analysis, to argue that there were not at least eight independent elements in the same sequence which find their place in both **The Vatican Boys** and **The Da Vinci Code**. We have established a much larger number of such instances.

Those figures, determinative though they are, do not take account of the additional 'fictional facts' element. If you add to those figures the likelihood of two authors producing from their own imagination a series of seven identical 'fictional facts', then you start to add so many noughts that you are well into the realms of the tens of millions to one chance.

THE CASE FOR THE DEFENDANTS

Since the Defendants have elected not to have a jury trial, they are not here represented. I will therefore do my best to present their Defence as I believe they would, based on the arguments that they have advanced such documents as they have put forward in response to Jack Dunn's claim. Their arguments fall into seven categories:

1. <u>Dan Brown has not only not read **The Vatican Boys**, but prior to Jack Dunn raising his copyright claims, he had not even heard of it.</u>
2. <u>Dan Brown is a 'reputable author' against whom no such allegation is credible.</u>
3. <u>The common elements are 'stock' ones which can be found in many such novels.</u>

4. (By inference) those alleged similarities are merely coincidental, and not the result of plagiarism or copying.
5. The 'fictional facts' argument is contrived and does not prove either copying or plagiarism.
6. That allegations of copying against Dan Brown have been tried both in the UK and the US, and in both cases have been rejected.
7. In the UK copyright case Dan Brown set out in detail his evidence of the sources for his book **The Da Vinci Code**, and **The Vatican Boys** does not appear in that list.

I should say at the outset, in fairness to Dan Brown and his publishers, the correspondence that has been generated by the lawyers representing them has focused primarily on the issue of copying and not plagiarism, as have the legal proceedings. It is however clear from the documents by which the Defendants argue their case that in addition to denying copying, Dan Brown also denies plagiarizing **The Vatican Boys** when writing **The Da Vinci Code**; not least because Dan Brown vigorously denies having had "access" to **The Vatican Boys** before writing his book.

Plagiarism is neither a criminal wrong, nor a civil wrong; it is only a moral wrong. It is the point where merely being influenced by an earlier work crosses over into your having re-versioned it and passed it off as your own. You, the Jury, are not being asked to apply the tricky legal tests around breach of copyright. Your task is solely to determine the question as to whether Dan Brown acted in a morally reprehensible way by plagiarizing **The Vatican Boys** in his book **The Da Vinci Code**, and thereby passing off the skill, labour, and imagination of Jack Dunn as his own.

Dan Brown has never read The Vatican Boys

This submission was made by the Defendants in the hearing before Judge Ponsor. There are probably only two people who know whether this is true or not, Dan and Blythe Brown, both of whom have accused each other of lying in their divorce proceedings. To be fair to Dan Brown it is always hard to prove a negative. However, it is for you to decide if you believe that claim or not based on the evidence before you.

Dan Brown is a 'reputable' author

The in-house lawyer at Penguin Random House responded to being informed of the imminent prospect of the publication of this book as follows: "I was somewhat surprised, therefore, to read that you are proposing to publish a book where the author seems to be intending to make seriously defamatory allegations of copying against a successful and reputable author..."

In my response I wrote that by reason of the findings against him by Mr Justice Peter Smith who found that more use of **The Holy Blood and the Holy Grail** had been made than Dan Brown had admitted, that some of Dan Brown's sworn evidence was not credible, and that at least of it was being made up, the claim made by Penguin Random House that Dan Brown should be regarded a 'reputable author' was hard to sustain.

The convergences are merely stock elements of a thriller

This is how the argument was put in the letter from Dan Brown's UK attorneys (Carpmaels & Ransford) which they sent to me on 12 October 2017: "The supposed similarities consist of:
  • Ideas, themes and narrative strands which are commonplace

in thrillers of the kind exemplified by [the two books] and are not protectable under UK copyright law – for example, popular mythology surrounding Christianity such as the Holy Grail and the bloodline of Jesus, or fictious power struggles within the Catholic Church.

- **Scènes à faire** which are obligatory for a novel centred around such ideas, themes and narrative strands – such as the Vatican (the seat of the Catholic Church), major cities such as London and Paris, and more specific locations such as Fleet Street, London, which feature in novels for the imaginary they readily convey to ordinary readers.
- Organisations taken from real life – for example, Opus Dei."

We say however that even if that letter is right about the nature of the overlapping material, which we say it is not, then such a plethora of such convergences still requires an explanation; and that mere chance is ruled out by means of a simple mathematic assessment of probability. These paragraphs offer no explanation for the adoption by Dan Brown of a series of fictions found only in **The Vatican Boys**. The far more likely, and only other credible explanation, is that Dan Brown's book plagiarizes the one written by Jack Dunn.

Any alleged similarities are coincidental

The list of 'convergences' which was sent to Penguin Ransom House in my claim letter was compendious. It is simply not credible for Dan Brown or Penguin Random House's lawyers to dismiss them as 'coincidental', as must be their contention as the only alternative to plagiarism. The simple application of statistics to incontrovertible facts makes it a very hard case to substantiate that one author has not plagiarized a predecessor.

The 'fictional facts' arguments are contrived, and prove neither copying nor plagiarism

We do not agree, and Dan Brown's lawyers have conspicuously failed to offer any explanation for the emergence of seven 'facts' that are presented as such in **The Da Vinci Code**, but which are in fact nothing of the sort. They appear to have no other credible source than **The Vatican Boys**.

The cases won by Dan Brown in the US and UK

The Defendants rely on the Ponsor judgment which includes this: 'Having now read both novels carefully, the Court is obliged to conclude, with the greatest possible respect to [Mr Dunn], that no ordinary reader could conceivably find any substantial similarity between the books, let alone encounter an overlap sufficiently extensive that it "rendered the work so similar that the later work presented a wrongful appropriation of expression."'

Jack Dunn was first alerted to the fact that his book had been plagiarized by Dan Brown by numerous 'ordinary readers' of both books, all of whom were independently convinced that the content of Jack Dunn's book had been stolen wholesale and inserted between the covers of **The Da Vinci Code**. The same letter quotes this section of the same judgment: 'It is well settled that "facts" cannot be copyrighted. As the Second Circuit has noted, "the scope of copyrighting historical accounts is narrow indeed, bracing no more than the author's original expression of particular facts and theories already in the public domain" ... this limitation has particular relevance to the facts of this case, given both books' reliance on church history, on the existence of an actual entity, Opus Dei, and on certain contemporary locale.'

However, Judge Ponsor delivered his judgment before the 'fictional facts' evidence had been identified. He may have found differently if he had known that no fewer than seven key facts that are presented as such in the **Da Vinci Code** and on which its plot is based are in reality figments of Jack Dunn's imagination.

The same letter goes on to comment that Jack Dunn, 'Relies on purported "similarities" which, in substance, amount to little more than differing artistic treatment of historical facts as well as popular historical myths ...'

We say firstly that this does not take account of the re-use by Dan Brown of no fewer than seven 'facts' that were made up by Jack Dunn. Secondly one of the striking points that emerge from a comparative study of the two books is that the 'artistic treatment' of the 'historical facts' is remarkably similar, as is the choice of those 'historical facts', and the order in which they appear.

In the UK case Dan Brown set out in detail his evidence of the sources for his book The Da Vinci Code, and The Vatican Boys does not appear in that list

This same letter cites some elements of the judgment of Mr Justice Peter Smith, in support of the claim that Dan Brown's 'partial bibliography was an accurate reflection of the sum of books to which Mr Brown made reference when devising the Synopsis', and that nothing in the disclosure 'gave the judge any reason to conclude otherwise'. (emphasis added)

As Smith J observes, Dan Brown's bibliography was only 'partial', and the judge was only looking in his judgment at the parts of **The Da Vinci Code** which overlapped with elements of **The Holy Blood and the Holy Grail**. The sole issue before him was whether in writing those parts of **The Da Vinci Code** Dan Brown had lifted parts of **The Holy Blood and the Holy Grail** to a sufficient extent to amount to copyright infringement. Our answer is that Smith J was not in a position to make any finding about a book which was not relevant to the issue that he was trying, and did not appear in the evidence which was before him; and that consequently the quoted sections of Smith J's judgment are therefore of no assistance to the Defendants.

There are however sections of the judgment of Mr Justice Peter Smith which cast serious doubt on the veracity of Dan Brown's sworn testimony in that case. Consequently, you may think the election of the Defendant's to rely on it is something of an own goal. The Defendants cannot pick and choose. Smith J did not believe Dan Brown's denial that he had copied the work of other authors.

Smith J's judgment also effectively concludes that Dan Brown's failure to call his wife to give evidence was a device to deny the court key evidence which was adverse to his case; in other words Dan Brown was withholding evidence from the court which contradicted his own testimony. It is reasonable to assume that this will not have been the only such instance.

If in fact Dan Brown had drawn most of the content of **The Da Vinci Code** from **The Vatican Boys**, it is hardly likely that a copy of Jack's book would be in the list of Dan Brown's sources, any more than it would appear in his disclosure/discovery documents. A judge cannot really make a finding of fact about a book that he has never seen.

CONCLUSION

There you have it, ladies and gentlemen. We call no evidence from any literary experts because we are confident that you, as the 'ordinary reader', which is the test in the United States for copyright infringement, are more than capable of making up your own minds about whether the later book is a plagiarized version of its predecessor.

Thank you for your time and attention, ladies and gentlemen of the jury. When you feel that you are ready to deliver your verdict, you are invited to visit www.thedavincifraud.com for more updates, or follow us on Twitter via @thedavincifraud or @silvertailbooks. Please feel free to get in touch.

Appendices

The following three documents are the correspondence sent by my lawyer, Jonathan Coad, to Penguin Random House (Penguin and Random House merged in 2013) in September 2017. The first document, Appendix I, is Jonathan's letter to Penguin Random House's legal department. Appendices II and III are the addenda which accompanied that letter. Appendix II (which is titled Schedule One) is a comprehensive analysis of the common elements between *The Vatican Boys* and *The Da Vinci Code*. Appendix III (which is titled Schedule Two) analyses the following elements common to both books: the fictional papal secretary, billion-dollar bribe for the beatification of the head of Opus Dei, and non-existent Vatican conclaves. All three documents have been reproduced in their entirety because we felt it was important to include as much information as possible.

Please note that we have tried to keep the documents as close to their original format as possible, believing this to be important for you as readers, but as a result the layout on the page might not be ideal for reading purposes, especially as an ebook, and I apologise for this.

Appendix I

14 September 2017

Dear Sirs,

Re: Jack Dunn and The Da Vinci Code

A.   Introduction

1. We act for the author Jack Dunn.
2. Jack Dunn is the owner of the subsisting copyright in a book written by him called **The Vatican Boys** ("TVB") and published in 1997, which he wrote after many months of research and writing.
3. In 2003 you published a book written by Dan Brown, **The Da Vinci Code** ("TDC"), which contains so many striking similarities to TVB that there can be no alternative explanation that in writing TDC Dan Brown and his wife (who appears in effect to have been his co-author) copied a substantial part of TVB. It is Mr. Dunn's case that in writing/publishing TDC Dan Brown and Random House have infringed Mr. Dunn's copyright subsisting in TVB.
4. It was not our client who initially identified the extent to which TDC plagiarises TVB. Our client's attention was originally drawn to TDC as an infringing copy of his book because literary friends and critics alike who had previously read TVB told him that TDC was *"his book"*.
5. Having compared the books, this is conclusion is unsurprising. There are hundreds of similarities between

TVB and TDC which comprise copying portions of TVB in the form of storylines, plots, characters, historical information, scenes, themes, and even factual errors which have been appropriated from TVB by Mr and/or Mrs Brown in writing TDC.

6. We set out many of those instances the first schedule to this letter (**Schedule One**), but we do not believe them to be exhaustive because each time that further analysis is undertaken between the two books, additional similarities emerge.

7. At **Schedule Two** appended to this letter, we set out three factual errors which our made when writing TVB which were faithfully repeated by Mr Brown in TDC. We also enclose with this letter two analyses which both individually and collectively prove that our client's book was copied in the creation of TDC:

    i.   The Narrative Analysis

          a) This structural/comparative analysis which shows the degree to which TDC follows the same narrative structure as TVB ("the Narrative Analysis"). The Narrative Analysis is in the form of a flow chart which shows copying in sequences that list page numbers in both books of the copying as they occur. As the Narrative Analysis shows, the sequence in which the components of the storyline of TVB are used is closely replicated in TDC.

          b) The Narrative Analysis shows that in

addition to copying the sequence in which the characters, ideas and components of TVB are deployed Dan Brown (and/or his wife) also copied TVB's narrative structure in writing TDC. The Narrative Analysis sets out the "flows" of the characters, the story, the histories, the movements of all the ideas and entities necessary to develop the plots, themes and story movements in the books, TDC closely replicating in all of these respects the framework and content of TVB.

ii.   <u>The Key Elements Analysis</u>

     a)   This analysis identifies forty-one key elements of TVB which are reproduced in TDC ("the Key Elements Analysis").

     b)   As you will see from pages 42 and 43 of the Key Elements Analysis the ten key plot elements of TVB are shown not only to be reproduced in TDC but in precisely the same order.

B.   The substantial investment made by our client in skill and labour in writing TVB

1.   Our client began the process of writing TVB by conducting research into the historical components of the story for the novel. To begin this process he went to Jerusalem in 1996 to see the Dead Sea Scrolls Museum where many of the documents relating to the famous scrolls found in Qumran.

2. On entering the building, he read; "***The Israel Museum has been home to the Dead Sea Scrolls since its opening in 1965. The light-sensitive scrolls are housed and exhibited in the Shrine of the Book, designed by Armand Bartos and Frederic Kiesler, whose signature dome evokes the lids of the jars in which the scrolls were found***".

3. Seeing the 'rolled papyrus scrolls in the glass jars' our client began to be inspired with ideas for the writing project which became TVB. Their detailed historical explanations along with that of the Apocrypha gave him the inspiration which lead to the formation a central part of the central TVB story. Our client also walked the *Via Dolorosa* (Path of Sorrows), the Way of the Cross, which was the path on Jesus Christ was led to the place of His crucifixion.

4. This led our client to the Church of the Holy Sepulcher. In it were altars where Golgotha was located and a tomb area where Jesus was taken after He had been crucified. Our client thought that the pursuit by rival characters in a thriller of some hugely significant historical object that the Catholic Church was hiding because it apparently contradicted something that it was teaching factually, would make an exciting component to the story.

5. When our client returned to his home to Western Massachusetts in the United States, he began researching what was a little-known organization at the time, the Opus Dei. He bought a non-fiction book written by a journalist named Penny Lernoux called ***People of God*** in which she explained what a controversial and strange organization the Catholic sect was within the church.

6. Our client then decided to create a story around this organization and somehow to link it with secrets the Catholic Church had been keeping for centuries in its archives. He researched the Turin Shroud; a holy relic linked to the Blood of Jesus Christ (just as the Holy Grail). He decided to use it as a secret being sought by the characters he created as his book's cast of characters; some who were in the high echelons of Opus Dei. He reasoned this would make a strong impression on readers about fundamental theological truths being hidden from Catholic believers by the leadership of the church.

7. Part of what our client learned in his research about the Opus Dei involved the Vatican Bank, Institute for Works of Religion (IOR), and the Roberto Calvi affair. Calvi was found hanging in London in 1982 under suspicious circumstances with the suicide or murder yet unsolved by the police that had to do with the Freemasons and was linked to a group of Knights of the Catholic Church. It seemed to our client there was a lot of dubious activity around the Vatican Bank; secret money and people hiding theological truths in order to preserve the power of the Catholic Church.

8. So it was that our client decided to create twists and chases in the story to structure or weave all of this together as the nuts and bolts of the narrative to create the central plotlines for TVB. A man being murdered for a secret he knows that could destroy the Catholic Church would begin the story, the secret his original characters were looking for involved the Opus Dei, the Masons and Knights, and

the relic was being sought to gain power. Our client then just needed to link everything together with a plot device that was original and intriguing.

9. Our client decided to achieve this by deploying a numerical code and password that would secure the characters the secret, and that it would be hidden at a Knight's private bank because his research of the Roberto Calvi affair revealed to him that this is what the Masons, Knights and Opus Dei were doing; setting up private banks as receptacles for the vast sums of money which Opus Dei was accumulating using its power and influence within the Catholic Church.

10. The Opus Dei is central to the story of TVB, (and TDC). After learning about it our client travelled to London to do more research. He wanted to see Blackfriars Bridge where Roberto Calvi was found hanging and wanted to document city landmarks that he could use in writing the story.

11. During his UK research trip our client found out that Opus Dei had one central location in London, near the river Thames, Ranelagh Gardens and Chelsea Bridge Road. He went into the compound and walked up to the front door of the main building. He was greeted there by a young female Opus Dei numerary, an initiate, who showed him around the building explaining everything about Opus Dei and its founder Monsignor José Maria Escrivá. She also gave him a substantial quantity of literature about the organization.

12. Our client then spent a number of hours there reading everything he could about the controversial cult. He

decided then that he wanted to use the Opus Dei compound to be a part of the location for the story and did this when he wrote the narrative. While in London he documented his route there from other parts of the city by landing at the airport and seeing landmarks and city sights including Blackfriars Bridge.

13. While our client was expending a considerable amount of skill and labour in writing the narrative for TVB he created the Chief Secretary to the Pope (a fictional character of his own making which was then appropriated by Mr and Mrs Brown), and made him the Head of the Opus Dei who is in control of the Vatican Bank and its money. He linked this fictional character with the Roberto Calvi Affair and connected all them together as part of the TVB plot. In TVB these characters do shady Catholic Church and Vatican Bank banking business together (as also re-produced in TDC).

14. In creating the Head of the Opus Dei who is the Chief Secretary to the Pope, he joined him up, specifically he hires a lone mercenary to help him find the secret the Mason figure was murdered for that begins the story, the narrative (same as in TDC).This two-person union of these two original characters begins to form the plots so the historical information questioning the Catholic Church's teachings about Jesus Christ can be introduced, including a relic associated with the Blood of Jesus Christ being a secret sought by them to gain power and control in the church.

15. The Roberto Calvi murder by a secret brotherhood sets the

stage in both books to begin the story by linking this character (Jacques Sauniere in TDC) to the relic or secret missing and the Head of the Opus Dei knowing all about Catholic Church secrets. The relic which apparently shows that the church is hiding inconvenient truths is being sought only by members of the Catholic Church but also by this Head of the Opus Dei and his hired lone mercenary.

16. To compete with them in the race to discover the key historical and theological secrets which comprise the very high stakes at issue our client created a 35ish French female, whose family has a French Country Estate. He teamed her up with an American 40ish male who knows about the Opus Dei, the Knights and the secrets of the Catholic Church. He can solve clues and codes and joins the female to fight the Head of the Opus Dei and his mercenary for the secret.

17. Once our client had structured all of this and had everything in position to continue the chase scenes, he transitioned the story moving everything specifically from Paris to London. The beginning of the second half of TVB narrative was written using the information our client gathered on his trip to London (and others to Paris) bringing the central characters together in London; and finally, at the Opus Dei compound for a climax to the story.

18. When our client was in London researching the murder of Roberto Calvi which took place under Blackfriars Bridge and the location of the Opus Dei he hand-wrote notes, documenting what he saw as far as streets and possible

locations for the action of the narrative in London. He chose Fleet Street out of hundreds of locations as the entry point of his original characters for the transition of the story from Paris to London.

19. In his book our client describes what he saw and read about along the street as far as sights, sounds, and specific images which stood out to him that he wanted to use in his narrative; like Blackfriars Bridge, the gargoyles, the fire of London in 1666, Westminster, prestigious museums, Victoria Embankment.

20. These were all images to create visions of London in the readers' mind about where the characters were and why they were there. In TDC the last part of the story narrative transitions from France to London and the TVB same TDC copied characters arrive on Fleet Street.

21. There are also similar descriptions in TDC as are in TVB as to the sights, Blackfriars Bridge, gargoyles, the Fire of London in 1666, Westminster, prestigious museums, Victoria Embankment. Just like in TVB, the same copied TVB characters in TDC go to Opus Dei compound for the climax of the story.

C. **The comparative analyses between TVB and TDC**

1. The detailed evaluations of the fictional structure of the story in TVB that we have conducted, and a comparison of the same elements common elements/themes show a remarkable degree of similarity between TVB and TDC:

i.   Story Commonalities;

ii.   The Relics – Use and Commonalities of Use – The Relics in both stories are 'First Class Relics' – those ones associated directly with Jesus Christ's life;

iii.   Character Commonalities;

iv.   Text Commonalities;

v.   Single Scene Commonalities;

vi.   Scene Components' Commonalities;

vii.   Historical Commonalities;

viii. Storyline Commonalities;

ix.   The Epilogues: Commonalities – The Ideas and Descriptions to end the Story.

2. Taken together and cumulatively these common elements of TVB and the later TDC place the likelihood of TDC having been created independently of TVB is way beyond mathematical calculation. These similarities shift the evidential burden to you author Mr Brown and his wife to explain them other than by their being the product of the systematic copying of our client's book.

3. Looking at the remarkable number of similarities between TVB and TDC it would seem that Dan Brown and his wife did not just take parts of TVB and use them to write the story in TDC. They duplicated a large part of the intellectual creation of TVB; narrative structure, scene and chapter by scene and chapter, character by character, themes and plots by themes and plots; and not only this.

4. Both stories are told in much the same sequence and use

exactly the same flows of ideas and the same cast of types/characters interacting in the same manner together, in the same order of appearance, and telling the same information to move the stories plots along; i.e. plot copying.

5.   All of the characters in both books are almost identical in the manner in which they are introduced and deployed from the beginning of the story to the end. A number of important characters and their roles telling the story are identical. Each character has similar personalities in both stories. Each character is removed from both stories at the same points in each story.

D. The cogent geographical evidence that Dan Brown had access to TVB

1.   Jack Dunn lived in Granby Massachusetts in Western Massachusetts from 1990 – 2003 and then since in other towns and cities in Western Massachusetts. He published TVB in 1997 and it was sold by local booksellers in and around New England and one of the first books to be sold on the Internet and by Amazon.

2.   In 1997 Dan Brown was living in Portsmouth New Hampshire about one and a half hours journey from Jack Dunn's home in Granby. His first book Digital Fortress published in 1998 was sold in the same local bookstores as Jack Dunn's book TVB. Both writers were at the time 'local authors' with their books being sold mostly in New England at local bookstores.

3. TVB was sold in Lord Jeffrey bookstore in Amherst, where Dan Brown went to college, so when he talks about selling his books at local bookstores it is likely that he sold it in Amherst. Our client can confirm TVB was sold in Amherst because his editor and first publisher, Modern Memoirs, is located in Amherst.

4. It follows then that while he was trying to sell his earlier books such as Digital Fortress Dan Brown was frequenting the very bookstores where TVB was being sold. Here are some relevant excerpts from Dan Brown's Witness Statement in the Leigh and Baigent trial:

    66. Unfortunately, when the book came out (Digital Fortress), my print run was slashed down to 12,000 copies with virtually no publicity at all. I was once again on my own and despite enthusiastic reviews, the novel sold poorly. Blythe and I were heartbroken as we had put so much work into this book. Once again, we took matters into our own hands, booking our own signings, booking our own radio shows, and <u>selling books out of our car at local events</u>.

    68. This was not an easy time financially. I remember that we were forced to literally sell books out of our car at low profile publishing events. The store where we buy most of our books, <u>The Water Street Bookstore in Exeter New Hampshire, was hand selling my books</u>, but the superstores still did not even know my name." (emphasis added)

5. Our client's book was being sold at this same time in the Water Street Bookstore in Exeter New Hampshire, which

is now selling the sequel to TVB. We know therefore that Dan Brown was using a local bookstore to source writing material which sold our client's book – the subject-matter of which is identical to that of Dan Brown's book.

6. In the acknowledgment page of TDC Dan Brown says this; "*My gratitude also to the <u>Water Street Bookstore</u> for tracking down so many of my research books...*" (emphasis added). TVB would have been an obvious choice as a research book for TDC.

7. TVB is replete with historical and theological material which has found its way into TDC; including three factual errors. It was on also sale in that shop at the time when Dan Brown was writing TDC; and the shop was engaged by Dan Brown to track down books which had as their subject matter the very same material as is in TVB.

8. According to Dan Brown's own evidence in the UK Action (as defined below) there was no intention on his part to write TVB before 1998; the year after TDC was published in the area where he lived, and sold in the bookshop where he drew his research material from.

E.   The UK copyright claim concerning TDC ("the UK Action")

1. In 2005/6 Michael Baigent and Richard Leigh sued your publishing house claiming that TDC "*appropriated the architecture*" of their non-fiction book, **The Holy Blood and The Holy Grail**, which was published in 1982 also by you publishing house. The UK Action failed at first

instance; a decision that was upheld on appeal.

2. There was a striking absentee from the trial of the UK Action; namely Dan Brown's wife Blythe who plainly played a major part in the writing of DVC, and yet was not tendered as a witness. This omission did not escape the attention of the court which drew adverse inferences from her absence as a consequence of the substantial part that she plainly played in the writing of TDC, which the court concluded was prompted by the fact that she would not have supported Mr Brown's version of events as delivered to the court in defense of the claim.

3. According to both the trial judge and the Court of Appeal, while dismissing the copyright claim concerning TDC, Dan Brown had misled the court in some of his evidence to the court about how he came to write TDC. It was also found that Dan Brown did appropriate elements of *The Holy Blood and the Holy Grail* in writing TDC.

4. It follows then that in any trial of this action both Mr and Mrs Brown would be obliged to give evidence, and the evidence of Mr Brown will suffer the severe impediment of both being from a tainted source, and having already been found to have appropriated material from other authors without acknowledging that in his own book.

F.   Infopaq International A/S v Danske Dagblades Forening

1. We have set out at paragraph **B** above the substantial care

and skill deployed by our client in writing TVB, and accordingly that TVB comprises the expression of his intellectual creation.

2. We have set out at paragraph **C** above and in the appendices and schedules to this letter the remarkable extent to which our client's work has been appropriated by Mr and Mrs Brown without his permission.

3. According to principles established in <u>Infopaq International A/S v Danske Dagblades Forening</u> ("Infopaq"), which we summarize below by means of the leading textbooks, the appropriation by Mr and Mrs Brown of our client's expression of his intellectual creation in writing TDC comprises a substantial infringement of his copyright in TVB:

    i.   According to ***Copinger and Skone James*** 3-21; *"Following <u>Infopaq</u>,...the focus is on whether a part that has been reproduced contains elements that are the expression of the intellectual creation of the author of the work."*

    ii.   ***Copinger*** 7-05; *"...copyright is infringed* [by anyone who without license does the restricted acts in respect of] *...any part which contains elements which are the expression of the intellectual creation of the author of the book."*

    iii.   ***Copinger*** 7-46; (<u>from Infopac</u>); the key issue is *"whether the part contains elements of the author's own intellectual creation". "...if a part which has been identified, it seems that the*

218

part must be dissected from the rest of the claimant's work and examined for elements of intellectual creation." "...the test is not whether the part in question is novel or striking or commonplace. The focus is on the expression of intellectual creation alone."

iv. ***Laddie Prescott and Vittoria***; *3.135; "In Infopaq the ECJ said that parts of a work enjoyed protection under the Copyright Directive provided that they contain elements which were expression of the creation of the author of the work and suggested that the concept of acts covered by the right of reproduction should be construed broadly."*

4. The European Court of Justice has confirmed that the storing and printing out of mere 11-word extracts from newspaper articles could constitute *"reproduction in part"* under Article 2 of Directive 2001/29 (on the harmonization of certain aspects of copyright and related rights in the information society). In this case the reproduction by Mr and Mrs Brown of our client's literary work has been massively more substantial and comprehensive.

G.   Conclusion

1. There are parts of TDC which so closely replicate TVB that the impression is created that Mr and Mrs Brown wrote their book with our client's book open next to them. It is

however the copying by Mr Brown of elements of TVB which contain factual errors however removes any doubt that copying took place.

2. If on enquiry of Mr Brown you are nonetheless satisfied firstly that despite the adverse findings of the court concerning Mr Brown's credibility in the UK Action he can credibly explain the plethora of similarities between TVB and TDC other than by a process of plagiarism then we request that those explanations be set out in the form of a detailed response to this letter. Given these similarities, the evidential burden shifts to you, and Mr and Mrs Brown, to explain how the plethora of similarities with TVB that have appeared in TDC, other than by a systematic process of copying.

3. In the absence of any such credible explanation being sent by <u>4pm on 13 October</u> we require you to do the following:

   i.   Admit liability for the copying of our client's work, which we accept has been undertaken unwittingly by you;

   ii.   Agree to there being an account of profits or an enquiry into damages (at our client's election);

   iii.   Undertake to indemnify our client for his reasonable legal costs in this matter.

4. In the absence of either a credible explanation sourced from Mr and Mrs Brown for the plethora of similarities between TVB and TDC, or the stipulations set out at paragraph **G**3 above being complied with, you may proceed on the basis that proceedings for copyright

infringement will be issued and served either at your offices or at a firm of solicitors of your election.

Yours faithfully,
Jonathan Coad

Appendix II

Schedule One

The plethora of common elements between TVB and TDC

1. The common elements between the first major Scenes in the first Parts of TVB and TDC

    i. Through the first 60–80 pages of both books the entities, events, characters, descriptions and information are introduced in a both a similar manner and similar order:

       a) Opus Dei is closely related to the Vatican – TVB – Back Cover, the pivotal role that the Opus Dei Organization played in their lives and the insidious influence of its corrupt priests on the Vatican, TDC Fact Page, *"The Vatican prelature Opus Dei is a deeply devout sect that has been the topic of recent controversy due to brainwashing, coercion and a dangerous practice known as corporeal mortification".*

       b) The Guardian of a secret- Roberto Calvi is murdered at a Famous City Landmark – Blackfriars Bridge (London) TVB – Introduction Page – The Guardian of a secret- Jacques Sauniere is murdered at a

Famous City Landmark (Paris) – The Louvre; TDC Page 3-5.

c) *"Precious Object"* – *"sacred treasure so carefully hidden"* (kept secret) passed on – ancient secret dating back to 49 A.D and *'Calvi dying with a secret'.* TVB Page 3-5, TDC *"secret treasure"* *"I must pass on the secret"* TDC Page 5 *"most powerful secrets ever kept"* – Sauniere.

d) Others in the Brotherhood mentioned, TVB Introduction page. Others in the Brotherhood mentioned – TDC Page 4 – There are '4' members of 'The Brotherhood' in each book who *"guard the secret"* – Roberto Calvi, Sindona, Ruiz-Mateos and the Venetian keep the *"secret"* in TVB – Jacques Sauniere and the other three other men killed in TDC are the keepers of the *"secret"*.

e) The first time we see Catherine Turrell, *"she awakes"* in strange surroundings. *"Catherine awoke,"* TVB page 11. The first time we see Robert Langdon *"he awakes"* in strange surroundings, *"Robert Langdon awoke slowly,"*; TDC page 7.

f) Catherine Turrell looks at herself in the mirror; *"When she looked in the mirror the haggard face she saw there was almost unknown to her, she felt physically light*

and emotionally heavy"; TVB Page 13, TVB
– Langdon looks at himself in the mirror,
*"He gazed into the full-length mirror, the
man staring back at him was a stranger-
tousled and weary" "His usually sharp
blue eyes looked hazy and drawn tonight"*;
TDC, page 8.

2. The commonalities of just one scene
    ii.   The First Major Scene in the Second Part of the
    books is set out at pages 179-188 in TVB and
    pages 275-288 of TDC. These are the common
    elements:
    a) Mercenary takes control of Central Male
       Character;
    b) Mercenary has a gun;
    c) Main Male Character is lying on the floor
       injured and in pain;
    d) Main Female Character sitting or propped
       up against a 'couch' (divan);
    e) A Main Character has an *'injured right
       ankle'*;
    f) Scholar is talking to Mercenary as the other
       characters listen to them;
    g) Mercenary holds a gun to the head of one of
       his captives;
    h) Mercenary *"lowers his gun"*;
    i) Mercenary is in pain, injured
    j) Scholar captures Mercenary

224

k) Opus Dei sent Mercenary after the Relic the Scholar has control of in the room.

l) A "*miracle*" is introduced as a happening (Happens to Jeremy (Mercenary) – Silas (Mercenary) prays for one, and in hours he will get one – one will happen.

m) Out of all of the characters in the books, the same 'Four Characters' (the same in both books) are present in the Scene(s) at the same time – The Central Male Character, the Central Female Character, the Scholar and the Mercenary

n) Mercenary is distraught and feeling helpless

o) Three Main Characters (Main Male Character, Main Female Character and Scholar) regain (are in) control of the Relic as the scene ends

3. The Key with a Cross on One End features in both TVB and TDC

   i.   The cover of TVB shows the Vatican Seal – with the keys in the middle of the symbol – with a cross at one end of the Key. The use of a Key with a Cross on one end that is associated with the Catholic Church or a group associated with the Catholic Church (Priory of Sion) is taken from TVB and used in TDC.

   ii.   The key described in TDC with a Fleur-de-Lys

on it; *"The identity of the living Priory members is kept extremely secret"*, Langdon said, *"but the P.S. Fleur-de-Lys that you saw as a child are proof. It could only be related to the Priory."* Langdon pulled the heavy key from his pocket again. *"Langdon had realized that this key in addition to having the Priory seal embossed on it, possessed a more subtle tie to the Priory of Sion. The equal arm cruciform was symbolic of balance and harmony but also of the Knights Templar. Everyone had seen the painting of the Knights Templar wearing the tunics emblazoned with a red equal-armed cross. Granted, the arms of the Templar cross were slightly flared at the ends, but they were still of equal length."* – *"A square cross just like the one on this key."* On page 168 of TDC the association is made between the key and the Holy Grail, Langdon *"fantasized about what they might find. **The Holy Grail.**"*

4. The extraordinary degree to which TDC mirrors the theological and historical themes of TVB
   i. Introduction of Opus Dei Founder Jose Maria Escrivá, TVB Page 14. TDC – Introduction of Opus Dei Founder Jose Maria Escrivá, page 28
   ii. Introduction of Opus Dei Mercenary – Jeremy – TVB – Page 7. Introduction of Opus Dei Mercenary – Silas- Page 12-13

iii.   Introduction of a Relic TVB – *"precious object"* *"relic passed on"* – page 3-4 Introduction of a Relic TDC, page 13 – *"the legendary keystone"* (relic)

iv.   Peter Zagranski (Chief Secretary to Pope) is introduced (the head of Opus Dei), TVB page 7. Bishop Manuel Aringarosa is introduced, (the head of Opus Dei), TDC page 28.

v.   Escrivá had made Opus Dei an ultra-conservative Catholic Organization, TVB page 5. Jose Maria Escrivá promoted a return to conservative Catholic values TDC page 28, and use of exactly the same word; *"ultraconservative – Christian secret society."* TDC page 29.

vi.   Opus Dei was *"founded at a small church in Spain, in 1928"* and is a personal prelature of the Pope, TVB page 5. Opus Dei *"founded in 1928 by the Spanish priest"* and is a personal prelature of the Pope, TDC page 28-30.

vii.   Escrivá and his philosophies controversial, TVB Page 6. Escrivá and his philosophies are controversial, TDC page 29.

viii.   Escrivá's book introduced, The Cronica, TVB page 46. Escrivá's book introduced, The Way, in TDC, page 14.

ix.   Escrivá's beatification is questionable and Opus Dei's financial influence over the church is suspicious. TVB page 5-7. Opus Dei's, *"intricate worldwide financial empire exercised considerable influence on the church*". It was for this reason that, "*the beatification was taking place a mere seventeen years after his death,*" and signified some of the "*greatest changes in procedure ever to take place in Western religious history.*" See also- TVB page 78, "*In 1928 with the approval and help of Pope John Paul II, Opus Dei was made a personal prelature.*" On page 130 of TVB "*the IOR was given "billions of Dollars by the bankers.*" And TVB page 127, "*without the financial support of the Opus Dei, the Catholic Church would have been broke.*" TDC page 40-41- "*the Pope placed the founder of Opus Dei on the "fast track" to sainthood, accelerating the often century long waiting period for canonization to a mere twenty years.*" And, "*Suspiciously Opus Dei's elevation to a prelature occurred in the same year (1982) the Opus Dei wealthy sect allegedly transferred one billion dollars into the Vatican's IOR Institute for Religious Works commonly known as the Vatican Bank, bailing it out of an embarrassing bankruptcy.*" TDC page 40-41 – Use of the year 1982 – Money transfers (one billion dollars) to the IOR by Opus Dei in TDC.

x. On page 29 of TDC "*Opus Dei had taken root in Spain before Franco's regime*". The Franco government is mentioned in TVB on page 78, *"Opus Dei "attracted members from the right wing pro-Catholic Franco government".*

xi. Opus Dei has, *"an intricate worldwide financial empire exercising considerable influence on the church",* TVB page 5 (the same phrase is used), TDC page 29, *"most financially secure Catholic organization in the world".*

xii. Opus Dei is being opposed by another entity, Opus Dei forms *"new secret military order,"* TVB page 6-7, *"There had been reports that Escrivá sympathized with Adolph Hitler",* (scandals), TVB page 6 and *"Opus Dei is being opposed by a force infinitely more powerful than the media,"*- and *"They know not the war they have begun,"* Aringarosa says, TDC page 30. References to the *"military"* and *"war"* – when talking about the church. Then Brown makes mention of the media's opinions of Opus Dei, *"The media always gravitated towards scandal, and Opus Dei, like most large organizations, had within its membership, a few misguided souls who cast a shadow over the entire group,"* TDC page 29.

xiii. TVB brings together Freemasonry, the Knights Templar, church secrets and a hugely significant Christian relic (The Turin Shroud). At pages 202-203 of TDC Dan Brown describes and connects the Masons (Priory) and the

Knights – the keystones (Secrets) and The Holy Grail (Relic) – the Secret that is being protected.

xiv. In both TVB and TDC all the characters and the plots move around to the finding of a secret relic that a Brotherhood possesses, that is linked to the blood of Jesus Christ.

xv. In TVB and TDC the secret is kept in a Knight's safety deposit box in a private bank managed by the Knight who is helping others in a Brotherhood to guard a secret that is important to many people and organizations of the Catholic Church.

xvi. In TVB the Dead Sea Scrolls are described as glass jars or cylinders with a papyrus scroll rolled up inside it. In TDC what everyone is looking for is a "*Cryptex*" – It is a box containing a glass cylinder with a papyrus scroll rolled up inside it.

xvii. In both books the rolled scroll of papyrus has an ancient poem written on it.

xviii. The key to open the box involves the circular moving of letters on it that must be put into proper sequences (order) to spell a specific 5 letter word password. In TVB it is a number sequence code that needs to be deciphered and put into sequence and a five-letter password IBIZA. In TDC the five-letter password is SOFIA. In both TDC and TVB the passwords are linked directly to an earlier feature the major female character's life.

xix.   Five-letter words are used as the password to get the secret out of "*a Knights bank*" with the password code figured out by the lead male character while he is in London.

xx.   In TVB the number code of two parts is used – Page 171, "*The account number combinations went together too easily; the first two and the last two digits of each were exactly the same.*" TDC Page 60-61, "*This is the Fibonacci sequence,*" she declared, (Sophie) – (it's a number sequence clue to get the secret, same as in TVB), "*A progression in which each term is equal to the sum of the two preceding terms.*" TDC – Page 97- "*The scrambled Fibonacci sequence is a clue. The numbers are a hint as to how to decipher the rest of the message.*" TDC – page 67 – number code is 13-3-2-21-1-1-8-5. The last two numbers are equal to the first number. In TVB and TDC the same combination of numbers is used to decipher clues to get at the secret. It's a number combination of the same '*two parts*', last two and first two specifically.

xxi.   The TVB secret kept in a Knight's Private Bank, Page 169-170 – "*Michael had withdrawn her money from his banks*"... Page 157-160, "*The Knights of Malta*" ... Catherine had met Michael

Macheras (Knight banker) at a party at her family's French country estate…, Page 160 – *"he told her that accounts could be set up in her name at his Cyprus bank"*. The same as in TDC, the secret is kept at a Knight's private bank. TDC – Page 176-191, Andre Vernet, The Depository Bank of Zurich.

xxii.   In TVB the Knight Private Banker Catherine met at a Party at her family's French Country estate, TVB page 159 – *"There had been one exception. It had been at her father's birthday party 10 years ago at the family estate just outside Monaco…home on term break"* her father is hosting a party. *"When she first saw Michael Macheras."* In TDC the Knight Private banker who Sophie saw at party at her family's French country estate, TDC page 140 -141, *"Sophie had witnessed proof of that ten years ago. Returning for spring break, she goes to the (family's) vacation chateau in Normandy"*… her grandfather is *"hosting a party."* TDC- Page 183 – *"The woman before him was as unexpected a visitor as Vernet had ever had. "I'm sorry, do we know each other?"* Sophie asked.

xxiii.   *"It's a simplistic cryptographic joke."* TVB Page 171- it is a code number sequence based upon the number 2; *"the first two and the last two digits of each set were exactly the same,"* and

"*the password, too was ludicrously simple.*"
Similar phrase used to describe "*the number code', 'simplistic joke' and 'ludicrously simple'* –
TDC page 61.

xxiv. TVB – Page 171-172 "*The password, too, was ludicrously simple*". It is a *five letter* word, 'IBIZA'. TDC – Page 200 "*We require a password,*" ... "*This cryptex has five lettered dials.*" In TDC Page 303- 321, the password is the five letter word, SOFIA. In both TVB and TDC the five-letter passwords are linked to Catherine or Sophie' life.

xxv. In TDC, page 304, "*Hebrew alphabet... is found throughout the Kabala and the Dead Sea Scrolls*"... "*The mystical teachings of the Kabala drew heavily on anagrams rearranging the letters of Hebrew words to derive new meanings*"– Hebrew words on a scroll, like the Dead Sea Scrolls in TVB on Page 50.

xxvi. In the TVB and TDC a glass cylinder inside containing a scroll – a leaf of papyrus that is an ancient document that is critical to religious beliefs. The 'idea' of a papyrus scroll being used for this purpose to describe religious beliefs is written in TVB beginning with the descriptions of the Dead Sea Scrolls on page 50. In TDC – the Holy Grail – the Divinity of Christ or the Bloodline.

xxvii. In the TVB and TDC solving the riddle (Poem) of the scroll found inside the cryptex involves the figuring out of a code message written backwards (Hebrew scroll writing). Scroll writing is backwards. In TVB everything moves in the same manner towards a *"secret"* "treasure" and a Codex (Aleppo) is described that *"is the earliest known Hebrew manuscript"* (the writing is backwards).

xxviii. In the TVB and TDC the importance of the Dead Sea Scrolls and the Aleppo Codex is explained – and the Prophesy of future military struggles is described. The concept of a Prophesy also appears in TDC.

xxix.   In the TVB and TDC, four main members of the Brotherhood are described; members of the Priory or the Knights Templar. TVB has four Bankers who are Knights/Masons and members of a Brotherhood. The Knights Templar or reference to the Priory – are the Knights of Malta in TVB.

xxx.   In the TVB and TDC the Grand Master is mentioned – in the Introduction Page of TVB referring to a brotherhood – linked to Roberto Calvi's (Introduction – Mason man murdered) murder the Masons and later to the Knights. In TDC page 171, *"my grandfather was one of them?"* (Jacques Sauniere – Prologue – Mason man murdered). Page 218, *"my grandfather"* and *"the brotherhood,"* page 264, *"Even if your grandfather were the Priory Grand Master [Knight's – Masons]."*

xxxi. In TVB you need two things to open the safety deposit box where the treasure is – a personal account number and the password. In TDC you need two things to open the safety deposit box where the treasure is, a key (the crucifix) as a personal account number (10 – digit number sequence code) and the five-letter password that opens the Cryptex.

xxxii. In the TVB and TDC to get the treasure (the proof of a secret) it is the lead figures who figure it all out; Stephen Hathaway and Catherine Turrell in TVB, and Robert Langdon and Sophie Neveu in TDC.

xxxiii. In the TVB and TDC – The scrolls are found in round jars or cylinders. The Aleppo Codex is introduced in the beginning of TVB. It is *"the earliest known Hebrew manuscript. The one here in Israel contains 295 of the original 487 leaves,"* (papyrus). The Scrolls described along with the Codex are rolled mostly on round cylinders and are papyrus scrolls. The scrolls are described on TVB Page 50 – 52, (Hebrew) and *"psalms like poems"* a partial text of the book of Isaiah, and an apocalyptic work about a future military struggle. The chapter describes in detail the finding of the Dead Sea Scrolls and other scrolls and gives a considerable amount of information about many papyrus and leather scrolls that have been found in the last century. In the beginning explanations of the finding of the famous Dead Sea Scrolls in 1947 it is written in TVB that *"the scrolls had been found in jars (round cylinders) to protect them from the humidity, a practice which was described in the Bible and the Apocrypha"*. *"The discovery of the seven Dead Sea Scrolls in 1947 in a cave near Qumran'. Qumran was known for being terribly arid."* Arid conditions will destroy papyrus scrolls. TVB, Page 51- Aleppo Codex is the earliest known Hebrew manuscript. In TDC the papyrus (Hebrew) scroll in the second cryptex box that opens with the word APPLE. In it is a Hebrew manuscript in a *round glass cylinder* to protect it from the vinegar that will destroy it. All of the scrolls (Hebrew) in both TVB and TDC refer to Hebrew documents- psalm like poems – that need to be deciphered – to tell the reader a riddle, leading them somewhere or giving them information. The Apocrypha or Gnostic Gospels are mentioned in TVB on Page 50. In TDC on Page 234 and Page 245 a similar description... *"The Dead Sea Scrolls were found in the 1950's hidden in a cave near Qumran'*, in the Judean desert. And, of course, the Coptic Scrolls in 1945 at Nag

Hammadi." Identical descriptions to the Dead Sea Scrolls found in Qumran and the Apocrypha, Coptic Scrolls or Gnostic Gospels found in Nag Hammadi are in TVB on Pages 50-51 and in TDC on Page 234.

xxxiv. In fact, more accurately, if Dan Brown had done his own research instead of merely copying TVB text into TDC, he would have written this; *"The Dead Sea Scrolls were actually found in <u>Wadi Qumran</u>, <u>in the Qumran Caves</u> — 19 kilometers from the ancient West Bank city of Jericho"*.

xxxv. In the TVB and TDC the same 'idea' to create the 'central entity' of a story exists, the 'core idea' of the 'relic' (scroll) is the one of the most important elements of both stories. The search for this object begins the search for the Holy Grail, to prove both that the Bloodline exists and that Jesus Christ is not Divine. Without the scroll there is no quest. In TVB the quest begins with everyone searching for a core object – the Holy Cloth TURIN SHROUD that develops the plots and themes of the story to show that Jesus Christ is Divine. In TDC the quest begins with a search for the HOLY GRAIL to show that Jesus Chris is Not Divine.

xxxvi. TVB – Page 166 – *"To publish evidence strongly questioning the validity of church teachings... like Jesus being alive when He was taken to His burial chamber... The lords of*

Rome... buried everything (conflicting doctrines and findings) deep in the Vatican archives with volumes off other information that contradicted their teachings,"; *"the reports had been suppressed by the Vatican."* TDC also in explaining the Bloodline Theory, which is based on the proposition that Christ was alive when taken from His burial chamber, describes conflicting Scriptures and Concepts of the Catholic Church; Christianity involving the APOCRYPHA, Gnostic Gospels and *"gospels that don't match up with the gospels in the Bible"*, TDC Page 245-246. See also TDC – Page 234-235- *"Church's desire to suppress these documents comes from a sincere belief in their established view of Christ. The Vatican is made up of deeply pious men who truly believe these contrary documents could only be false testimony."*

xxxvii. The Dead Sea Scrolls and the Apocrypha described in TVB at page 50, along with the Turin Shroud descriptions on TVB page 164-167 regarding the possible *Blood of Christ* being found in the Turin Shroud form the basis of an apparent conflict in evidence that puts the teachings of The Catholic Church and Christianity in question about the Divinity of Christ. The Blood if Christ and a missing relic (secret) and conflicts in church doctrines is very similar to the Bloodline Theory as developed in TDV by Dan Brown with his by introducing missing parts of the real history of the church (Apocrypha) regarding among other things the concept of Jesus Christ and His Divinity – concepts and teachings directly related to the *Blood of Christ* and the introduction of a secret relic that will prove He was not Divine – the Holy Grail.

xxxviii. There is a distinctive series of links common to both TVB and TDC between missing documents, secrets, the Apocrypha, rolled Hebrew papyrus scrolls, teachings related to the Bible, the Blood of Christ, His Divinity, the doctrines of The Catholic Church and Christianity; which turns on the finding of a relic and the proving or disproving of Catholic/Christian teachings.

xxxix. Reference is also made to conflicting gospels and any evidence that conflicts with the Catholic Church linking all of this with one of the Central Themes and a Main Entity and the Divinity of Christ. TVB page 166, "*The whole belief system of the Catholic religion rested upon Jesus dying on the cross that terrible Friday and then being resurrected and mystically ascending into heaven. Although scholars had rejected the (Turin) Shroud's authenticity, their findings presented* conflicting arguments about the actual circumstances which surrounded the death of Jesus Christ." And, "to publish evidence strongly questioning the validity of church teachings was not considered to be in the best interest of the church and the reports had been suppressed by the Vatican." On page 234 of TDC Brown writes – Teabing said, "The Dead Sea Scrolls were found in the 1950's hidden in a cave near Qumran in the Judean Desert. Then Teabing continues, "Of course, the Vatican, in keeping with their tradition of misinformation, tried very hard to suppress the release of these scrolls. And, why wouldn't they? The scrolls highlight glaring historical discrepancies and fabrications, clearly confirming that the modern Bible was compiled and edited by men who possessed political agenda – to promote the divinity of the man Jesus Christ and use His influence to solidify their own power base." Brown writes on page 235; Teabing countered, "is that almost everything our fathers taught about us about Christ is false. As are the stories about the Holy Grail." This directly links the Dead Sea Scrolls descriptions in TDC on page 234 and conflicting doctrines of the Vatican on the same page to Brown's major entity and theme- the Holy Grail and The Bloodline and the Divinity of Christ on page 235. Out of the thousands, hundreds of thousands, of artifacts that have been found that conflict with the teachings of the Catholic Church, that is suppresses things that threaten it, in both TVB and TDC the Dead Sea Scrolls, the Apocrypha (Nag Hammadi), Coptic Scrolls of Nag Hammadi, or Gnostic Gospels are the significant historical findings to justify that the Catholic Church is suspicious.

xl.   In TVB on page 166 the documents and arguments are *"conflicting"*. In TDC at page 235 they are described as *"contrary"*.

xli.   In the TVB and TDC – the (same-age) *"Scholar"* (the characters serve the same purposes) is the one giving the reader all of this vital information. In TVB the Scholar is Father Rovarik and in TDC the Scholar is Teabing.

5. <u>The Communalities comprised by Relics (both their presence and use) and theological controversy</u>

i.   The relics in both books are 'First Class Relics' (out of 3 classes of holy relics) because they are associated directly with Jesus Christ's life.

ii.   The relic is introduced, *"The holy relic added credibility (power) to the rightness of his (Escrivá's – Opus Dei) mission and the holiness of his life"*, TVB page 7; and the keystone (relic) will be secured TDC page 54, *"How powerful that will make the Opus Dei"*.

iii.   All of these entities and their relationship to each other appear in both books, TVB and TDC. All of the major entities are parts of the Structure – Architecture – of TVB- a book of Fiction published in 1997. All of these major entities were copied (appear) in TDC – another book of Fiction published in 2003.

Theology/relic in TVB	Theology/relic in TDC
1. Scroll – (Aleppo Codex)	Scroll – (In Cryptex)
2. Dead Sea Scrolls	Dead Sea Scrolls
3. Hebrew Writing	Hebrew Writing
4. Papyrus	Papyrus
5. Rolled in a round jar	Rolled in a round glass cylinder
6. Poem written on it in Reverse	Poem written on it in Reverse
7. Jar protects it	Glass cylinder protects it
8. Related to Bible Teachings	Related to Bible Teachings
9. Conflicts/Church's teachings	Conflicts/Church's teachings
10. Vatican hides Truth	Vatican suppresses Truth
11. 1st class relic (Turin Shroud)	1st class relic (Holy Grail)
12. Blood of Christ/ Turin Shroud	Blood of Christ/Holy Grail
13. Questions Christ's Divinity	Questions Christ's Divinity
14. Holy Cloths are Relics	Bloodline is related to the Relic
15. Theological controversy	Theological controversy

9.   Character Commonalities: The Specific Characters and Use- Descriptions, Personalities, Positions and Roles

i.   The similarity between the characters (and their interactions) which makes up TVB and TDC is astonishing, and extends not only to the major characters but also the minor players in the narrative.

ii.   Major Characters in the two books are:

a) Roberto Calvi is replicated by Jacques Sauniere (Powerful Influential Moneymen, Knight) 60ish, murdered to begin the story.

b) Stephen Hathaway is replicated by Robert Langdon; both handsome, bachelors, in their forties, highly intelligent and erudite puzzle solvers. Stephen Hathaway a bachelor is forty –something, and has a *"commanding appearance. He is a vital attractive man with dark hair and intense blue eyes".* *"As always he had an engaging smile on his face the kind women love."* He is attractive to females. Women flirt with him – TVB page- 27-28. Langdon a forty – something confirmed bachelor is attractive to females. Flirting, a student introduces Langdon and says, *"Although Professor Langdon might not be considered hunk-handsome like some of our younger awardees, this forty-something academic has more than his share of scholarly allure"* – he is attractive. The female continues – his captivating presence is described by his female students, as *"chocolate for the ears,"* TDC page 9.

Stephen Hathaway has *"intense blue eyes"* in TVB page 27 and Robert Langdon has *"sharp blue eyes"* TDC page 9.

c) Catherine Turrell is replicated by Sophie Neveu; beautiful, wealthy French ladies, number analysts who are caught in the middle of a web of corruption in the Catholic Church, both 30-something women seeking help from the lead male character, with sexual tension developing between them and the lead male characters; They are both single, Catherine Turrell is an intelligent beautiful French woman, *"thirty five years old, five feet eleven and blond, classic features, deep set blue eyes, elegant demeanour of upper- class privilege, that causes men and women to stare at her"*; TVB page 10. Sophie Neveu is an intelligent thirty- two years old beautiful French woman, an *"unembellished beauty"*, classy and upper class, with the demeanour that *"drew men's eyes away from their work"*, (they stare), TDC page 49-50. Catherine has disturbing dreams, TVB, page 10. Sophie had images that awoken her countless times when she was a little girl; and *"But, as in her dream, the pictures evaporated into oblivion,"* TDC, page 76. Catherine, *"didn't wake up trembling"*, after a dream,

TVB page 20, and Sophie is described after listening to a message on her answering machine, "*In that fleeting instant, Sophie saw images from the dream that awoken her countless times,*" and "*Sophie stood trembling for what seemed like minutes,*" TDC page 76. (The word 'trembling' describes emotions and physical reactions to dreams).

d) Jeremy Willoughby is replicated by Silas; both are mercenaries with "skills for hire" and they are the only assassin hired by the Chief Secretary to the Pope to get the secret. As we set out below it is highly significant that the allusion in TVB to the Chief Secretary to the Pope as the sponsor for mercenary assassin was a mistake on our client's part which was then copied into TDC, as there is/was no Chief secretary to the Pope at this time.

e) Karl Rovarik is replicated by Leigh Teabing; both father figures and senior theological scholars;

f) Peter Zagranski is replicated by Manuel Aringaraso; both characterised as the head of Opus Dei;

g) Michael Macheras is replicated by Andre Vernet; they are both elegant, crafty, international Knight bankers, (Knights of

Malta/Knights Templar);

h) Rovarik is the Scholar/Teacher; and Teabing is the Scholar/Teacher;

i) Jose Maria Escrivá – Founder of Opus Dei – features in both books

j) The Pope features in both books;

k) The members of The Opus Dei feature in both books;

l) The Knights of Malta/The Knights Templar- (Priory of Sion) feature in both books;

iii. The Minor Characters:

a) Fashe in TDC is replicated by Ruiz in TVB;

b) Remy in TDC is replicated by Father Timothy in TVB;

c) Jamie Cole in TVB is replicated by Sophie's brother in TDC;

d) Every character in TVB has a counterpart in TDC, and the only characters of any substance in both books are those identified above.

10. Text Commonalities – non-exhaustive listing

i. All of the characters, their personalities, the entities, information, and movements in the stories to develop the plots and themes of the books are the same;

ii. TVB and TDC take place in the same locations; Paris, London and Rome;

iii. The first description of Paris in TVB is at page 149, *"The world of the 1990's seemed to be moving on fast forward and the turmoil taking place everywhere was insane, but removing oneself from the madness was almost impossible."* In TDC; *"the Citroen navigated the chaos with authority."* TDC- Page 148, *"The world has gone mad"*;

iv. To begin both books, Roberto Calvi is murdered in TVB – Jacques Sauniere is murdered in TDC. Both are related to the corruption in the high echelons of Catholic Church, a secret brotherhood and to a secret missing that threatens the Catholic Church and Christian faith;

v. Both men are murdered by a Masonic organization linked to the Catholic Church;

vi. Both men are Knights and/or Masons;

vii. The Grand Master is mentioned (Masons); Introduction page TVB and linked to Roberto Calvi's murder and on page 12 TDC – The Grand Master – relating to Sauniere's murder;

viii. Opus Dei promotes self-abuse using cilices (celices) and whipping ropes – breaks skin, causes bleeding, self-flagellation – in both TVB and TDC – details which do not appear in 'usual descriptions' of Opus Dei;

ix. In both TVB and TDC a secret relic is missing which linked to the blood of Jesus Christ. "The secret must be passed on";

x.   A *"billion dollars"* was given to the IOR (Vatican Bank) by the Opus Dei;

xi.   Opus Dei is a described as a conservative religious organization founded in Spain in 1928 by Jose Maria Escrivá;

xii.   In both TVB and TDC Escrivá is referred to the author of a book, *'The Way'*, or *'El Camino'*.

xiii.   In both TVB and TDC Escrivá is described as being *'fast-tracked'* to sainthood in violation of established church procedures and protocols, the words used in this part of the books also being similar;

xiv.   In both TVB and TDC Escrivá's organization was made a personal prelature of the Pope in 1982 the same year that the money was given to the church;

xv.   In both TVB and TDC Opus Dei is described as demanding absolute and unquestioning obedience from its adherents and promoting violent self -abuse including the use of cilices (celices);

xvi.   In both TVB and TDC the head of the Opus Dei is a sinister Cardinal (Zagranski/Bishop Aringarosa) who knows and condones all about all of these practices;

xvii.   In both books the main male character of the story (Stephen Hathaway in TVB and Robert Langdon) is introduced as searching for something and trying to solve a historic Christian mystery which has major theological significance;

xviii.   In both TVB and TDC two specific entities are introduced both associated with the Catholic Church, the Opus Dei and the Knights Brotherhood and both organizations are searching for a relic that is vital both to their power base within in the church and even to their very survival;

xix.   In both TVB and TDC the history and hierarchy of the Catholic Church is the main setting for the narrative, and its members are searching for the *first class relic* linked to the Blood of Jesus Christ which is at the center of the story;

xx.   A mercenary (Jeremy Willoughby in TVB and Silas in TDC) is an assassin working for the Head of the Opus Dei who is both murdering individuals perceived as a threat to Opus Dei and looking for the missing relic;

xxi.   The main female character (Catherine Turrell in TVB and Sophie Neveu in TDC) are both French, upper class, in their 30's, beautiful and both of their families have French country estates;

xxii.   In both TVB and TDC the lead females are portrayed rebellious members of a very wealthy French families;

xxiii.   In TVB Bishop Ruiz is an Opus Dei Member

working with Zagranski, and in TDC Fache the policeman is performing the same role;

xxiv. In both TVB and TDC the main male and female characters work out that a code for number sequences is used in the search for more clues that uses the number 2 as its basis;

xxv. In both TVB and TDC the code is a progression in which the last two numbers are the same as the first two or add up to be;

xxvi. In both TVB and TDC the code is 'simplistic'/'simple';

xxvii. In both TVB and TDC a group of nuns is introduced who are defiant to the Opus Dei;

xxviii. In both TVB and TDC a cross/crucifix is given to the central female character;

xxix. In both TVB and TDC while the Central Female and male characters decide what to do as they are being chased by a number of people;

xxx. In both TVB and TDC the lead male and female characters are trying to solve a cipher puzzle as part of a quest to find a religious secret/relic;

xxxi. In both TVB and TDC Cardinal the corrupt senior Catholic cleric (Zagranski and Bishop Aringarosa) go to the Pope's residence because the issues under discussion (i.e. the relics or Opus Dei money) cannot be talked about at the Vatican;

xxxii. In both TVB and TDC The Cardinal and the Bishop's goal is to get the relic for the Opus Dei to solidify their power over the entire Roman Catholic church;

xxxiii. The Knights of Malta in TVB and in TDC the Priory of Sion or The Knights Templar are introduced whose origins date back to 11th Century Jerusalem;

xxxiv. The main male character deciphers the code, *"the first two and the last two digits of each set were exactly the same."* It is extraordinary that out of all of the numbers to choose from the number '2' is used for the number sequences of the code in both books;

xxxv. In both TVB and TDC -The Knights Templar are described as having been founded in the 11th Century and as a secret society within the Catholic Church, and whose original goal was to protect or not protect pilgrims;

xxxvi. The Knights of Malta or Knights Templar had then evolved into a group whose members looked to curate and/or retrieve hidden documents/religious artifacts, or as powerful financiers that exercised great power within the Catholic Church;

xxxvii. The Knight's history is one which sees them engaged at different times in both godly and ungodly activities;

xxxviii. In both TVB and TDC membership in the Knights is limited to 'particular family lines' or 'bloodlines' – although exceptions are made for men and women who have achieved a high level of financial or political power;

xxxix. Members of the Knights enjoy access both to the upper echelons of Catholic Church hierarchy and elite international financial groups;

xl. In both TVB and TDC The Knights' member's lists are described as being kept secret;

xli. In both TVB and TDC a highly significant relic is introduced (the Turin Shroud in TVB and The Holy Grail in TDC) that contains evidence that the blood of Jesus Christ which is linked to the relic shows that Christ was not dead when He was taken down from the Cross, which in turn is portrayed as casting doubt on a central tenet of the Catholic Church/Christian Faith – Jesus Christ's divinity;

xlii. In both TVB and TDC the possibility that Jesus Christ may not have been not dead when he was taken down from the cross is potentially explosive evidence that a fundamental element of the teachings of the Catholic Church is not correct;

xliii. In both TVB and TDC both this places in jeopardy all of the teachings and doctrines of the Catholic Church and comprises credible evidence that Jesus Christ was neither resurrected from the dead nor Divine;

xliv. Jeremy Willoughby (TVB) and Silas (TCD) are

both lone murderous mercenaries working for the Opus Dei who are sent after the relic;

xlv.   In TVB Bishop Juan Carlos Ruiz is introduced as the helper of the head of the Opus Dei. The Policeman Fache is introduced in TDC for the same purpose;

xlvi.   In TVB Stephen Hathaway and Catherine Turrell are trying to work out how to access a safety deposit box in a Knight's Private bank. Robert Langdon and Sophie Neveu do the same in TDC;

xlvii.   Stephen and Catherine (TVB) are searching for clues to solve a puzzle. Robert and Sophie (TDC) are doing the same;

xlviii.   Karl Rovarik joins the main characters in Paris (TVB). In TDC at this point in the story all of the equivalent characters are in Paris;

xlix.   Catherine (TVB) and Sophie (TDC) are both given crucifixes;

l.   In TVB the lead characters head to London. In TDC the lead characters head to London;

li.   In TVB Rovarik has a relic and he gives a description of it to Catherine and Stephen. In TDC Teabing describes the Holy Grail relic to Robert and Sophie;

lii.   A Private Bank where the treasure is kept is introduced in both books;

liii.I   n both TVB and TDC a mysterious Banker is introduced who is a member of a Brotherhood of Knights;

liv.   In TVB the Banker – a Knight was a friend of Catherine's father. In TDC the Banker – a Knight was a friend of Sophie's grandfather;

lv.   In TVB a meeting of Catholic Church priests in held in Rome where Peter Zagranshi the '*Chief Secretary to the Pope and Head of Opus Dei*' meets with other men in a "*poorly lit room with a long table*" for the purpose of discussing the ways of recovering the relic that is in Rovarik's possession. A meeting is held in TDC with Opus Dei head Aringarosa that is described in the same way as the one in TVB;

lvi.   In London Stephen and Catherine access the bank account using number sequences that will let them into accounts using an '*account number*' which involves the combination of number sequences a combination of the number 2 and a password (TVB). In TDC Robert and Sophie access the bank account using a combination of the number 2 and a password Key.

lvii.   In TVB the key to the treasure is hidden in the piece of microfilm they retrieved from the '*art object*' the '*horse's right eyeball*' (orb) cut out of its socket on Martha's Vineyard containing numbers provided by the banker. In TDC a clue – an orb – serves the same function leading the characters to the treasure;

lviii.   In TVB Catherine met the Banker at her

Father's birthday party at the 'Family's French Country Estate'. Sophie encountered the Banker at a party at her Family's (grandfathers) French Country Estate;

lix.   Using the information provided the banker Stephen and Catherine find the treasure (TVB). With the help of the banker Robert and Sophie find and get the treasure (TDC);

lx.   In both TVB and TDC the treasure everyone is looking for is in the '*Knight's Bank*';

lxi.   In both TVB and TDC the murderous mercenary (Jeremy/Silas) is chasing the main characters. They are all trying to get hold of the relic;

lxii.   In TDC Robert and Sophie try to figure out how to open the cryptex cylinder they have with a scroll in it written on Papyrus paper. In TVB the Dead Sea Scrolls and the Aleppo Codex are written on papyrus paper;

lxiii.   In both TVB and TDC the Dead Sea Scrolls are described in the same manner;

lxiv.   In TVB Catherine described the relationship of her father to the banker. In TDC Sophie explains to Robert the relationship of her grandfather to the Knights;

lxv.   In both TVB and TDC Apocryphal books of the bible are described;

lxvi.   In both TVB and TDC the missing books conflict with orthodox Catholic church teachings;

lxvii.   In both TVB and TDC the mercenary
          (Jeremy/Silas) is depicted as getting closer to
          and stalking the main characters once the
          treasure is found;

lxviii.   In TVB Stephen and Catherine are in
          possession of the treasure and Catherine is
          directing the actions; In TDC Robert and
          Sophie are in possession of the relic and Sophie
          is directing their movements;

lxix.   In TVB the scholar Rovarik knows all about the
          relic and its history. In TDC Leigh Teabing is
          introduced who is a scholar who knows all
          about the relic and its history;

lxx.   In both TVB and TDC the scholar takes control
          of the action and explains everything he knows
          about the relic;

lxxi.   In both TVB and TDC the scholar discusses the
          tenets and history of the Christian faith and the
          power of the Catholic Church;

lxxii.   In both TVB and TDC, the Dead Sea Scrolls are
          introduced to build the themes of Church
          history and theological controversy;

lxxiii.   In both TVB and TDC the Dead Sea Scrolls and
          their significance is explained and related to the
          teachings of the Catholic Church;

lxxiv.   In both TVB and TDC much of the information
          and teachings of the Catholic Church are
          characterized as questionable;

lxxv.   In both TVB and TDC doubt is cast on the

teaching of the Roman Catholic Church that Christ died on the Cross, and by extension on Christian claims that he rose from the dead;

lxxvi. The Scholar explains the significance of the blood of Christ and the relic. In TVB the relic is the Turin Shroud, in TDC the Holy Grail;

lxxvii. In TVB Zagranski (Opus Dei) is searching for the relic to control the church and make himself and Opus Dei powerful. In TDC Aringarosa (Opus Dei) is trying to get the relic so he can control the church and make Opus Dei powerful;

lxxviii. In both TVB and TDC all of the characters and organizations that are important and necessary to develop the themes and plots of the story are described in the same sequences;

lxxix. In both TVB and TDC the lead characters both play the same roles and perform many of the same functions;

lxxx. In both TVB and TDC all of the characters' roles have been determined and all of the functions of the religious groups and other entities introduced into the story have been presented by introducing them in sequence and combination with the necessary supporting historical documentations and the other information required to explain their participations in the story;

lxxxi. In TVB in possession of the treasure Stephen rejoins Catherine and Father Rovarik who has the relic Opus Dei is looking for after taking a flight in where through the aircraft's window he *"watched a series of thick white clouds pass over the wings of the aircraft."* In TDC Teabing, Sophie and Robert have the relic that the Opus Dei is after and Aringarosa is on his way in looking out the window of the airplane;

lxxxii. Jeremy (TVB) reappears sick, wondering why everyone has betrayed him. Silas (TDC) is portrayed as being sick and felling betrayed;

lxxxiii. In TVB Rovarik explains the significance of the Turin Shroud and the blood found in it comprising evidence of Christ's survival of the crucifixion (i.e. that he was alive when placed in the tomb). In TDC, Teabing introduces the concept that the Holy Grail is not a relic, but is in fact *"Mary Magdalene, the mother of the royal bloodline of Jesus Christ"*, which bloodline is created by a sexual liaison between Christ and Mary Magdalene which it is said occurred after Christ's survival of the Crucifixion or Christ was not dead when he was taken down from the Cross (TVB- Page 167);

lxxxiv. In both TVB and TDC it is suggested that the Catholic Church has covered up this seismic evidence information because of fears that it would undermine central elements of its teaching concerning the death and resurrection of Jesus Christ;

lxxxv.   In TVB (Gypsies) in a circus (Magical World) practicing their arts are featured, and Disney's magic world is featured in TDC;

lxxxvi. In both TVB and TDC the Vatican tries to get rid of everyone or anything that threatens them;

lxxxvii. In both TVB and TDC historical evidence is recounted that there has been conflict and violence since the time of Christ between the Vatican, the Knights and anyone else who possessed or said anything that put into question the church's doctrines and the church teachings; especially those concerning one of the fundamental beliefs of the Catholic Church, that Jesus Christ died on the Cross and rose from the dead;

lxxxviii. In TVB the four bankers who had stolen from the Catholic Church were eliminated by the church. In TDC the four Masters of the Priory were killed by the church;

lxxxix. In both TVB and TDC the scholar says that if the church gets hold of the relic or any documents that are harmful to the church it will destroy it all;

xc.   In both TVB and TDC the mercenary appears and after taking control of the main male character (Robert) by "*a crushing blow to the head*" who is now, "*groaning on the floor*". In TVB Catherine answers a knock at the door and Stephen disoriented, '*falls to the floor*'.

xci.   In TVB after breaking into Catherine's apartment Jeremy has them – *"propped up against the couch"*, and *"bound with cord."* In TDC Silas who has a gun has Teabing and Sophie tied up in a rope and *"propped up against a divan"*;

xcii.   In TVB Stephen 'injures *his right ankle'*. In TDC Silas is described as having an '*injured right ankle'*;

xciii.   IN TVB Jeremy has a gun. In TDC Silas has a gun;

xciv.   In both TDC and TVB the mercenary (Jeremy/Silas) holds the gun to the head of one of his captives;

xcv.   In TVB scene Rovarik is described as defiant. In TDC scene Teabing is described as defiant;

xcvi.   In both TVB and TDC a discussion takes place with just the Scholar and the mercenary;

xcvii.   In TVB Zagranski is on his way in, (Opus Dei) after the relic. In TDC Aringarosa is on his way in, (Opus Dei) after the relic;

xcviii.   After tricking him Rovarik captures Jeremy and takes control and the relic is kept safe (TVB). After tricking him Teabing captures Silas and takes control and the relic is kept safe (TDC);

xcix.   In both TVB and TDC all of the main characters end up being all together in one place with the relic;

c.   In TVB all of this action takes place in London

and a small private airport is featured. Cardinal Carmen Hernandez's kidnapping and conveyance to a private airport is on pages 87-88 in TVB. In TDC the characters head to a small private airport where a private plane will take them to London;

ci.   In both TVB and TDC a miracle takes place in London;

cii.   In TVB Hernandez is forced down between the seats of the car, *"grunting like a pig"* because he has been tied up. In TDC Silas is described as *"coughing, breathing through his nostrils,"* because he was bound up and his mouth was taped;

ciii.   *"One of his people infiltrated the Opus Dei group,"* TVB – page 185. "The brotherhood was infiltrated," TDC page 295;

civ.   Carousels are featured in both TVB and TDC;

cv.   Descriptions of what the characters *"see"* or *"look at"* the same point in both stories in London as Fleet Street is used as a major point of entry for the characters into London in the stories in both books. In both stories when the characters look at their surroundings, they 'see' dragons and demons.

    a) TVB Page 155; *"Fearsome dragons guard the entrances to Old London, hellish demons perched on tall pedestals said to stop evils from entering the city. The most prominent one is on Fleet Street,"* On page 156, Catherine, *"she looked up to see the dragon on its Fleet Street perch. Seeing it reminded her of the nightmares, the ones in which a gorgon haunted and hunted her on a bridge."*

b) TDC page 337, *"Fleet Street? There's a crypt on Fleet Street?"* – TDC page 347 there are descriptions in the Temple Church; *"Langdon was feeling gooseflesh too as they stepped into the circular chamber His eye traced the curvature of the chambers pale stone perimeter, taking in the carvings of gargoyles, demons, monsters and pained human faces all staring inward."*

6. <u>The use of both historical and theological elements in the same sequence to craft the narrative in both of the books</u>

   i.   The narrative centres around corruption with the Roman Catholic Church driven by a desire to wield power and acquire wealth.

   ii.   The narrative architecture comprises the Vatican, senior elements of the Catholic Church, a powerful and shady organisation within the Roman Catholic Church whose tentacles extend into its highest echelons and to the Vatican itself.

   iii. A main Character of both books has *"an*

unusual role" at a Vatican "*conclave*".
Significantly both books feature a fictitious
conclave which occurs in the late 1990's.

iv. A central feature is the movement known as
Opus Dei, which is a rich powerful Roman
Catholic organization which exercises power
within the Vatican and throughout the Roman
Catholic Church worldwide.

v. Opus Dei has many followers around the globe
who practice celibacy; give all of their money to
the organization.

vi. Opus Dei demands absolute and unconditional
obedience from its members.

vii. Opus Dei is immensely rich because of
donations made by its wealthy members and
other organizations, entities, companies, banks,
families and poor members.

viii. Opus Dei is very powerful in the Roman
Catholic Church and directs many of its agendas
because of its financial investments in the
Church.

ix. Opus Dei is a Pope John Paul II Vatican
Personal Prelature which is known as a deeply
devout sect that is highly controversial.

x. Opus Dei was made a personal prelature by
Pope John Paul II in 1982. Personal prelature is
an institutional structure of the Roman Catholic
Church which comprises a prelate, clergy and
laity who undertake specific pastoral activities.

xi. This process was made possible under the new framework introduced in Vatican II.

xii. Opus Dei gave the Vatican IOR (Institute for Religious Works); a division of the Vatican Bank, one billion or more dollars in 1982- the same year the Pope made them a 'personal prelature'.

xiii. The Vatican was almost bankrupt when Opus Dei donated this money, bailing it out of embarrassing financial problems

xiv. Opus Dei has a worldwide financial network which involves a series of secretive banks.

xv. Opus Dei has financial relationships with numerous banks and bankers.

xvi. Opus Dei is the most financially powerful Catholic Organization in the world and its members occupy senior positions within the Roman Catholic Church.

xvii. Opus Dei is described as being *"ultra-conservative"*.

xviii. Opus Dei is highly controversial because of its excessive practices, secretive nature, immense wealth and great power.

xix. Opus Dei is associated with organizations that are suspected of illegal activities.

xx. Opus Dei's aims are in conflict with those of some other senior Catholic Church officials and members.

xxi. Opus Dei's ill treatment of women and the

opposition of women to that treatment is described.

xxii.   Opus Dei's lack of respect for women applies especially to nuns, and their consequential opposition to Opus Dei is described.

xxiii.   A Mother Superior *"despised the Opus Dei, its goals, it methods and its philosophy of power. The way its priests treated women was an abomination."* (Page 106 of TVB). Sister Sandrine; *"Opus Dei had always made her uneasy"*, and *"their views on women were medieval at best."* (page 41 of TDC).

xxiv.   Opus Dei practices self-abuse and the use of the cilice (celice) – a device to inflict pain are described. Adherents also use heavy ropes to torture themselves and others. The abuse breaks skin and is bloody.

xxv.   Josemaria Escrivá founded Opus Dei in Spain in 1928, three months after his ordination.

xxvi.   He then built it up to be very powerful both politically and financially in the Catholic Church.

xxvii.   The main goal of Opus Dei members is to spread the teachings of Josemaria Escrivá as described in his books The Way, El Camino and The Cronica.

xxviii. Many scandals have been associated with Josemaria Escrivá and the Opus Dei.

xxix.   Jose Maria Escrivá is described as is a

controversial figure whose theology and
teachings are questionable.

xxx.   Descriptions of Jose Maria Escrivá's founding
and the building up the organization of Opus
Dei are given – by the end of the 1940's the
movement had prospered and grown strong,
financially and politically in Spain.

xxxi.   Opus Dei/Escrivá had a relationship with the
Franco Government in Spain.

xxxii.   Jose Maria Escrivá's book is introduced.

xxxiii.   Escrivá died in 1975.

xxxiv.   Escrivá is being beatified in less than 20 years
after his death.

xxxv.   Escrivá's beatification and his being elevated to
sainthood was being 'speed tracked' in 1992.

xxxvi.   This is process that usually takes decades or
even centuries was completed in less than
twenty years.

xxxvii.   Escrivá's beatification was contested by many
Catholic Church members because of his
reputations, teachings and practices.

xxxviii. Many of the Catholic Church's rules regarding
the elevation to Sainthood are being
overlooked in the beatification of Escrivá,
which appears to be the result of Opus Dei
using its influence in the Roman Catholic
Church.

xxxix.   The current head of Opus Dei is introduced; a
Catholic Cardinal/Bishop who directs the

operations of the Opus Dei and finds the relic around which both books are written.

xl. A significant man who holds secrets that pose a risk to the Roman Catholic Church is murdered at a famous city landmark – a criminal act in which Opus Dei is implicated.

xli. A secret of potentially huge is significance which the murdered man possessed must now be both secured and passed on.

xlii. A fundamental element of the church's teachings about Jesus is threatened by this secret.

xliii. The secret revolves around a relic of the highest significance.

xliv. Control of the relic and the secret that it holds is the key both to immense power within the church and access to huge wealth.

xlv. The secret/relic are therefore a magnet to corrupt elements of the Roman Catholic Church.

xlvi. Two groups both associated with the Catholic Church are competing for the possession of the relic.

xlvii. The power or an influence that the relic/secret is perceived as carrying is sought by corrupt elements of the powerful Opus Dei organization.

xlviii. An Opus Dei mercenary is sent by a Cardinal or Bishop of The Catholic Church, 'the Head of the Opus Dei' to find the relic.

xlix. The mercenary's actions are being directed by this Head of the Opus Dei.

l. The Opus Dei mercenary is willing to commit murder to secure the secret and the power represented by the relic.

7. Story Commonalities – the climax to both books

i. Many elements are taken from TVB when in TDC the four main Characters, Langdon, Sophie, Teabing and Silas fly to London on Teabing's private plane.

ii. *"Cat and Mouse Game"* TVB, page 43; *"Cat and Mouse Game"* TDC page 293.

iii. The horned devils that are on page 155 of TVB are the same as the descriptions of the horned devils at page 316 of TDC.

iv. In TVB the password is a five – letter word, *'Ibiza'* – a geographical location; the word being thought up, by a Knight. In TDC the password is a five-letter word *'Sofia'*; the word being thought up by a Knight.

v. After not being seen for a while the bankers appear at the same point in both books; Michael Macheras in TVB and Andre Vernet in TDC.

vi. The description of the weather in London as the characters enter the city in TVB on page 83-84 and in TDC page 328 is the same. It is early morning, a misty, foggy morning (dawn) and with *"drizzle"*.

vii.   In TVB on page 155; *"hellish demons perched on tall pedestals (headstones) said to stop demons from entering the city"*. In TDC on page 316; A *"horned devil known as Satan"* appearing in and the devil or Baphomet *"must be what the poem is referring to – A headstone praised by Templars,"*

viii.   Everyone goes directly to Fleet Street in both books where the rest of the books' 'stories' begin; page 155 in TVB and page 337 in TDC. Chapter 82 of TDC begins, Fleet Street? Langdon asked."

ix.   In the Introduction page of TVB a Knight was killed in London as described in TVB, killed by the church, hung under Blackfriars Bridge, which comes off Fleet St. Roberto Calvi, the banker, did something to incur the wrath of the church, to make them do this to him, to kill him. All the lead characters in TDC are on Fleet Street looking at a tomb, a crypt the sites, the hellish demons- thinking about what the images could mean, Langdon and Teabing figure out that the codes, the poem means *"that a knight is buried in London"*, Langdon reads *"In London lies a knight a Pope interred,"* the poem is referring to a knight a Pope had killed.

x.   The whole story of TVB begins at Blackfriars Bridge with a Knight being hung under it. At page 338 of TDC Teabing says, *"This knight obviously did something that incurred the Holy wrath of the church."* And, on Page 339 Remy calls over his shoulder; *"You said Fleet Street is near Blackfriars Bridge?"* Teabing answers, *"Yes take the Victoria Embankment."*

xi. As set out in the opening of TVB, Roberto Calvi was a Knight (Mason), and he was killed -by the Catholic Church for stealing Hundreds of Millions of Dollars from the church. He incurred their wrath (Opus Dei). They murdered him. The knight in TDC incurred the wrath of the church. At page 125 of TVB Catherine says, "Roberto Calvi was a man Carmen (Cardinal) did a lot of business with," and Sister Julien says, *"Wasn't he the guy found hanging under Blackfriars Bridge in London?"* Catherine answers, *"Yes,"* and describes how Calvi could have "implicated the Opus Dei and many other members of the Catholic Church" in *"illegitimate financial deals"*, (incurred their wrath). So they killed him. In TDC Teabing and Langdon figure out a knight was killed in London, one who incurred the wrath of the Catholic Church (the church kills him).

xii. At page 189 of TVB; *"Father Rovarik and Catherine got off and walked in the direction of the bridge. But they didn't go over it. They turned right instead onto the Embankment and*

270

went west." Blackfriars Bridge and the Victoria Embankment are mentioned on page 339 of TDC.

xiii. In the next section once the characters of both books are seen as being aware of their surroundings by descriptions of London the following occurs in both books.

a) The '*Old City of London*' is described

b) The fire of London in 1666 is mentioned

c) A brief discussion of architecture of the area is given

d) The characters are in the historic district of London

e) The characters move out of the historic district of London

xiv. At this point in the story in TVB Rovarik performs a miracle on Jeremy using the relic (holy cloth). In TDC the lead characters enter the Temple Church to search for the Holy Grail. Outside Remy (the manservant of Teabing) shows that he is an Opus Dei operative, sets Silas free and a miracle occurs.

xv. In TVB by page 188-189, Rovarik has "*freed Jeremy*" from the curse (miracle), and he is in control of the relic and the action taking place. By page 366 in TDC, Remy, Silas and Teabing are moving away from the Old City of London leaving Langdon and Sophie behind in the Temple Church after Remy "*frees*

Silas"(miracle) – and he is in control of the relic and Teabing and the action taking place.

xvi. TVB at page 189; "*The rain was pounding down hard on the Thames River as the double-decker bus took a sharp right turn at Ranelagh Gardens and came to a stop on Chelsea Bridge Road. Father Rovarik and Catherine got off and walked in the direction of the bridge. But they didn't go over it. They turned right instead onto the Embankment and went west. Their destination wasn't on the other side of the river. It was on this side, two blocks away in the Embankment Gardens. They were going to Dawliffe Hall and Shelley House, the offices of the Opus Dei where Catherine had worked.*" In TDC on page 383 the same characters move in the same way to the Opus Dei House. In TDC, "*London's Opus Dei Centre is a modest brick building a 5 Orme Court, overlooking the North Walk at Kensington Gardens... Despite the <u>rain</u> Remy had dropped him off a short distance away,*" despite the rain Remy had dropped him (Silas) off a short distance away in order to keep the limousine off the main streets. Silas, Catherine and Rovarik are dropped off, and they all walk only a short distance to Opus Dei House.

xvii. In TVB on page 190-191, Catherine and Father Rovarik entered the compound through a set of bent and rusted black gates and go directly to Shelly House. *"Catherine was counting her paces as she climbed the granite steps up to the front doors."* In TDC on page 383 Silas, *"moving across a small courtyard to the front door."*

xviii.   In both TVB and TDC the characters enter a *"minimalist foyer."*

xix.   In both TVB and TDC the characters who enter the building are greeted by a member of the Opus Dei organization when they go into the building. Someone who – *"hears the bell ring"* in TVB – and hears *"a muted electronic chime"* in TDC.

xx.   In TVB on page 191 and in TDC the word *'bell'* is used in the exact same place and someone hearing it comes to greet the person(s) who rang it.

xxi.   TVB on page 119; *"the screeching sea gulls from the docks below nor the whistling wind."* On page 385 TDC; *"The stormy weather had brought instead seagulls from the ocean. The lawns were covered with them – hundreds of white bodies all facing in the same direction, patiently waiting out the damp wind."* (all emphasis added)

xxii.   Two men meet in both books in a square of London, a famous Park is mentioned with birds in it and the weather described. The men in both books are members of the Opus Dei and one is a high-ranking member of the Opus Dei, in TVB it is Cardinal Hernandez, In TDC it is the Teacher.

xxiii. In TVB the reason Jeremy gives up is that he has been poisoned and Rovarik has what he thinks is the 'antidote'. In TDC (on page 386) Remy after serving the Teacher is poisoned and killed by him. In both cases a character is eliminated by being poisoned.

xxiv. In TVB the scene takes place in a famous landmark -Trafalgar Square – that is not crowded. In TDC the scene takes place in a famous landmark, Saint James' Park – that is not crowded. It is raining and foggy in both places. Two men are talking and there are large numbers of birds around them.

xxv. Once the character is eliminated, the action reverts to the search for the relic. In TVB by pages 196-197 Rovarik has the relic and he and Catherine are in the Opus Dei House and Zagranski and Ruiz are headed there looking for them and the relic. In pages 388-392 in TDC with The Teacher and Bishop Aringarosa both in London headed to the Opus Dei House where Silas is and Langdon and Sophie looking for clues to tell them where it is.

xxvi. In TVB the mercenary Jeremy was 'employed' by Zagranski and in TDC the mercenary Silas was 'employed' by Aringarosa – both priests are the heads of Opus Dei).

xxvii.   On page of 197 of TVB the Sicilian bodyguards crash into the Opus Dei House. On page 393 of TDC the police crash into the Opus Dei House. Both the police and the bodyguards are working for the Opus Dei and are looking 'in the Opus Dei House for the same characters in both books.

xxviii.   After healing Jeremy Rovarik is only interested in Stephen and Catherine (TVB).After killing Remy the Teacher goes looking for, "*Only two people now remain. Langdon and Neveu.*" (TDC).

xxix.   TVB Zagranski and Ruiz arrive at the Opus Dei House looking for Rovarik who has the relic. In TDC (page 394) once Silas eludes the police, he injures Aringarsosa who has arrived at the Opus Dei House looking for him and the relic.

xxx.   In TVB after Rovarik and Catherine escape from Zagranski and Ruiz at the Opus Dei house they are re-united with Stephen – page 199. In pages 201 –206 there are discussions between the 'three people' teamed up again – about the Church and its wrong doings. By the end of the Chapter 28 the only thing Stephen is interested in is "*getting Catherine out of this.*" In TDC there is a debate about what to do about the wrongdoing in the church. "*The three of us together.*" Teabing, Sophie and Robert are going to team up again. And, Robert is only interested in "*getting Sophie out of here alive*".

xxxi. By page 199 of TVB the themes, plots, plot points, character movements, scenes, locations, and the story being told, everything is identical to the equivalent part of TDC; right down to there being birds and rain and fog in a major scene described in both books and everyone meeting in parks and headed to the Opus Dei house in London where all hell breaks loose in both books. As of page 409 in TDC most of the same themes, plots, plot points, character movements, scenes, locations, and the story being told are fully developed.

xxxii. On page 186 of TVB, "*It's an old herbal remedy for unwanted interferences, Jeremy. The concoction affects the central nervous system. One dose produces severe changes in the body's cellular chemistries. The long-term effects are degenerative-and deadly.*" Jeremy is poisoned. In TDC Teabing he poisons Remy with a "*powder*". The poisoning happens at the same exact place in both books. Jeremy (TVB) like Silas (TDC) is removed from the story.

xxxiii. At page 100 in TVB; '*May God forgive you for what you are doing.*" On page 418 of TDC the Bishop says; "*Forgiveness is God's greatest gift.*"

xxxiv.   The descriptions of Rovarik to Catherine and Stephen in TVB as he tells them about everything when they are in Monte Carlo beginning on page 201 are paralleled in TDC.

xxxv.   In TVB we learn on page that Jeremy has gone mad. In Chapter 102 of TDC -Silas dies. Both mercenary characters are removed from the storyline of each book at the same point.

xxxvi.   In TVB (page 209) the characters set up the Galilee Fund to pay back the victims of the bank frauds using the money they recovered. It serves a purpose and is explained in detail how the repayments will be arranged and why they are being done – to get Catherine free of the men chasing her. At page 429 of TDC Bishop Aringarosa is given the millions of dollars in bearer bonds back that the Bishop was using to buy the Holy Grail. The Bishop being remorseful elects to disperse the money among the victims of the activities of the Opus Dei. In both cases the storylines have restitution payments and the ideas appear at the same points in both books.

xxxvii.   In TVB the movement of the Story first takes Rovarik, Stephen and Catherine to Monte Carlo on pages 201-210 where the three discuss the relevancy of the cloth that Rovarik has, he says, *"According to prophesy, a day will come when the two pieces of cloth will be brought to the actual place of Christ's death and placed over the sacred rock at the altar of Golgotha in the Church of the Holy Sepulchre – (under the church). At that time, something fabulous will happen."*

xxxviii. In TVB (pages 208 and 209) descriptions are given of the finding of the two cloths and their relevance to all that is happening in the story. A detailed description is given of the relationship between the cloths, Jesus Christ and the Holy City of Jerusalem. The two holy cloths guarded the entrance to the cave. The Holy Grail is described as being in a 'massive subterranean chamber' in TDC.

xxxix. There are two holy cloths in TVB. In TDC there is a *"second rosewood box- an exact duplicate of the one Langdon has"*. At the same place in TDC's narrative we are told there are 2 identical boxes that are significant just like there are 2 identical holy cloths in TVB. Both are *'essential'* to understand the treasure or complete the theme and plot of the story.

xl. In both books the Holy Places are described as being known for centuries as a place where the relics might be or where something existed to bring seekers of 'the truth' or the relic 'to'. In TVB on page 141, the Monastery is described; *"For hundreds of years, the monastery where she was had sheltered nuns, monks, and other spiritual travellers looking for peace and eternal truths.*" In TDC on page 432-433 Rosslyn Chapel is described by Brown, "*For centuries, this stone chapel had echoed with whispers of the Holy Grail's presence.*" (emphases added)

xli. Alice's restaurant features in TVB at page 178. Alice in Wonderland is referred to at page 432 of TDC. Both "Alice" references occur the same points in the stories which also replicate each other in the book.

xlii. In both books the Central Female Character is removed from the story before the final ending. She just fades away. Sophie is happy with her new 'family' and Catherine will to return to the nuns in Canada (her new family) where she will be happy.

xliii. In both books the Central Male character is still active at the end of the story. Langdon returns to Paris. Stephen makes a deal in exchange for his testimony.

8. <u>The communalities between the role of two elderly women introduced near the end of both books</u>

i. In both books elderly women assume control of the flow of the narrative. Each of them is protecting secrets that are centuries old, and each is confident that others will help them to do it.

ii.   In TVB an old woman is the keeper of one of the cloths; the *"keeper of a secret"*. In TDC Sophie is reunited with her Grandmother who has the second box (jewellery box).

iii.   The Old Woman in TVB is the Grandmother in TDC and they are both important to the story because they are both the *"keepers of a secret"*, and provide information that is necessary to understand the narrative. The feelings ascribed to the Old Woman (TVB) and those of Sophie (TDC) are remarkably similar.

iv.   The introduction of an elderly woman in TDC coming at the same time in the narrative as the Old Woman in TVC is of itself remarkable. The two old women serve the same purposes; have the same functions as characters. They help fill in the missing pieces and set up the ending of the Story. And, without this essential character, there would be no ending, illustrating the absolute importance of this character to both books.

v.   However, there are numerous other similarities in the roles which these mirror characters play:

    a) TVB – the old Gypsy woman is respected as a truth seeker, an elder with powers (control). She is delicate and full of wisdom. She had one of the holy cloths that 'is' a relic. TDC – Sophie's Grandmother heads the Rosslyn Trust – i.e. she is powerful. She has one of the boxes that is a relic.

b) The relic they both have (had) has been passed down through generations.

c) Both of the old ladies know all about everything that is going on.

d) Both women are remembering – thinking about events or people from their past when we first see them in the story – they are both in pain or crying and the things they are thinking about make them sad.

e) In both stories as the scene progress the sadness of the women turns to joy.

f) At the end of the scene both old women are feeling confident and hopeful that the 'truth' will finally be told, and consequently they are at peace.

g) Both Old Women live in a Holy Place. The Old Gypsy Woman is in a Holy Monastery in the mountains of Tibet that is related to a Brotherhood and 'the relic'; and the Grandmother is at Rosslyn Chapel, in the mountains near Edinburgh, Scotland which is a famous Holy Place related to the Knights (Brotherhood) and 'the relic'.

h) Both Old Woman are half of a 'team' guarding the secret and a relic; Rovarik and his sister – The Old Gypsy Woman, and Jacques Sauniere and his wife – The Grandmother.

vi.   In TVB (page 143) the Old Gypsy woman brought the holy cloth 'to Escrivá', some years before, when he was in power at the Vatican, before he died in 1975. On page 442 of TDC the Grandmother has helped keep 'the secret' for 28 years. It is clear from the narrative this would be about the time Escrivá died. The publishing date of TDC is 2003-28 years; i.e.1975 – the year of Escrivá's death.

vii.   In TVB the Old Gypsy woman sets the stage for the ending by thinking about the Holy Cloth being 'safe' and "*It was comforting for her to know that others still believed, lived, and worked to protect eternal truths and wisdom. Centuries ago, her ancestors had helped the holy one find His way to this holy place. <u>One day,</u> she thought, all that He had prophesied here would come to pass.*" In TDC on page 447 after reading the papyrus scroll and its hidden meaning, the Grandmother is the one who figures out the puzzle of the Holy Grail. She becomes the prime mover of the story by showing and telling Langdon what is going on. When she is through she warns him, "*<u>One day</u> it will dawn on you.*"

9.   <u>The Structural Similarities in the endings of both books</u>

i.   In TVB two old people have been identified as being in charge of 'keeping the secret' and in charge of a relic that is linked to Josemaria Escrivá, Father Karl Rovarik and his sister, the Old Gypsy Woman in the mountains of Tibet (Grandmother of the Brotherhood). By the end of the main part of the book the relics are safe. No evil entities (organizations) have captured them – as was the fear for most of the book. The relics are still in their care. There is still hope that the secrets will continue to be protected, will live on. When the book ends the relic is with Rovarik – one of the keepers. In TDC two old people have been identified as being in charge of 'keeping the secret' and in charge of the relic for the last 28 years (since the death of Josemaria Escrivá in 1975), Jacques Sauniere and his wife who is now called Marie Chauvel or the (Grandmother of the Brotherhood- Priory). By the end of the main part of the book the relics are safe. No evil entities (organizations) have captured them – as was the fear for most of the book. The relics are still in their care. There is still hope that the secrets will continue to be protected, will live on. When the book ends the 'relic' is with the Grandmother-one of the keepers.

ii.   In both TVB and TDC at the end point in both books, the characters separate and the 'Keeper of the Secret – keeps the Relic' but not before passing a secret on!

iii.   In TDC on page 449 – before the Epilogue begins, Sophie summarizes what the whole story of TDC has been all about. Sophie, "*her tone turned serious,*" says she will meet Langdon in Florence provided there are, "*No museums, no churches, no tombs, no art, no relics.*" This line summarises what both TDC and TVB are all about.

10. <u>The Epilogues: Commonalities – TVB (page 225), TDC (pages 451-454)</u>

      i.   In TVB its – two holy cloths coming together- two separate entities – joined together that complete the theme. See page 225. Two entities – both the same, identical copies – come together. In TDC the answer to the riddle is right in front of Langdon on page 454 – and it is in two pieces – joined together. He is at the site of the Holy Grail.

      ii.   In TVB – page 209- "According to prophecy (legend), a day will come when the two pieces of cloth will be brought to the actual place of Christ's death and placed over the sacred rock at the altar of Golgotha in the Church of the Holy Sepulchre. *(Joined together). At that time something fabulous will happen." (Christ will come again – His Divinity (A Theme is proven). In TDC the two entities have to come together to find the Holy Grail – The Chalice above. The

Blade below. Two (holy relics) pyramids are described – two pyramids -The Chalice above. The Blade below, – joined together they lead to the site of the remains of a Holy Woman, Mary Magdalene. For a moment Langdon thought, *"he heard a woman's voice... the wisdom of the ages... whispering up from the chasms of the earth."* The two pyramids join together to lead Langdon to the Holy Grail, to Mary Magdalene. The Theme is the Divinity (or lack of) Jesus Christ. Two entities (pyramids) are necessary to be joined together, so that the Holy Grail can be found and the major Theme of TDC established and proven.

iii.   TVB page 225, *"Listening to the pounding avalanches outside the monastery, two monks removed the second* [two parts] *holy cloth from beneath the golden urn that held the revered Gypsy woman's ashes"*. TDC -The quest for the Holy Grail is the quest to kneel before the bones of Mary Magdalene.

iv.   TVB – They folded it, bowed respectfully to the Buddha there and left the room. TDC – With a sudden upwelling of reverence, Robert Langdon fell to his knees. Reverence in both TVB and TDC.

v.   TVB – A long, dimly lit hallway led them to a series of underground caves. TDC – At the end of the tunnel, he emerged into a large chamber.

TDC – Illuminated in the soft lights of the deserted entresol (cave) Dimly lit – Soft lights – similarities – descriptions of an underground tunnel's light used in both TVB and TDC.

vi.   TVB – *"As they walked, the younger monk asked his companion, when do you think they will be ready for this cloth?... Some now, some never, he said, but they will all experience its power soon... He is coming back, with their help or without it. As they softly padded their way towards the deep caverns, they chanted only one word. Soon."* TDC – *"For a moment, he thought he heard a woman's voice... the wisdom of the ages... whispering up from the chasms of the earth"*. Voices- Chanting – the words- thoughts- of Jesus Christ and Mary Magdalene being spoken or heard – the themes – TVB – He is coming! TDC – She is heard!

vii.   TVB -The monks are underground, two holy cloths are mentioned that will be 'joined together' (one is at a high place and one below), they are at the site of a golden urn, (holy site) which contains the remains (ashes) of a Holy Woman, the revered Gypsy woman, and before they leave the holy site – they bowed respectively- Reverence. As the stories of both books end, we are at the site of the remains of a revered Holy Woman, underground in a cave – passing through a dimly lit tunnel and the last

286

images we see or hear are of voices or chanting – signalling the return of someone who is related to the stories being told combined with the significance and purposes of the two relics and – a holy woman. And the thoughts of the characters in both stories are about someone who is below them. Even though they are underground, in both stories the characters are – thinking about things or someone who is below them.

Appendix III

Schedule Two

The fictional papal secretary, billion-dollar bribe for the beatification of the head of Opus Dei, and non-existent Vatican conclaves common to both TVB and TDC

1. <u>The three communalities that prove that copying took place</u>
   i. The inclusion in one copyright work of an element which is in the earlier rival work which denotes an error then explaining the re-appearance of that error in the subsequent work other than by it being the product of copying is virtually impossible.
   ii. This has happened not once, but at least three time in this case;
      a) <u>The papal secretary,</u>
      b) <u>The billion-dollar payment by Opus Dei to the hard-up Vatican secure the beatification of its founder, and</u>
      c) <u>The Vatican conclave supposed to have taken place in the 1990's.</u>

2. <u>The non-existent papal secretary in TVB and TDC</u>
   i. The first factual error in TVB which has been picked up by Dan Brown in TDC concerns a senior Vatican official. Jeremy Willoughby (TVB) and Silas (TDC) are both mercenaries

with "*skills for hire*" and they are the only assassin hired by the "*Chief Secretary to the Pope*" to get the secret.

ii.   In fact there was no such post in the Vatican as "*Chief Secretary to the Pope*". The allusion in TVB to the Chief Secretary to the Pope as the sponsor for the mercenary assassin was a mistake on our client's part which was then copied into TDC.

iii.   The TVB account:

    a) The Chief Secretary (first secretary) to the Pope of the Catholic Church is an original character title created by Jack in TVB. However in reality in the 1990's there was no Chief Secretary or first secretary to the Pope, Pope John Paul II in the Catholic Church. In reality there was no "*Head of the Opus Dei*" that was a member of the Catholic Church hierarchy.

    b) In TVB the function of this character is that he is a high-ranking Archbishop in the hierarchy of the Catholic Church, the head of the Opus Dei brotherhood, and the head of the Vatican Bank monies, the IOR (Institute for the Works of Religion). It is he who controls the money in the church and does shady financial deals with scandalous people with the co-operation of other members of the church's hierarchy.

c) In TVB on page 7 he is introduced, "*Seeing, this the priests sent for Peter Zagranski, the chief secretary to the pope, who had personally seen the relic on several occasions.*"

d) TVB Page 125, "*the Banco Ambrosiano affair. I think it was about <u>1982</u>.*"

e) TVB page 130, "*Do you know who Archbishop Perter Zagranski is, Julien?*" Catherine asked. She replies; "*Yes he's the first secretary to Pope John Paul II.*" "*Zagranski has succeeded him (Escrivá) as the head of the Opus Dei organization. He's been in charge of it for the last 15 years. He's also been the director of the IOR for the last 13 years.*"

f) TVB page 130-132, "*Ruiz-Mateos arranged bogus loans made from a half-dozen of his banks to the IOR just before they went under. This illegal business was approved by Archbishop Zagranski himself. The monies all of the bankers loaned to the IOR, in other words the Vatican, were quite substantial. If you add up the totals, the sums are <u>billions</u> of dollars.*"

g) "*They wanted it because the church had money problems,*" Catherine says. "*The church had financial problems,*" Stephen says. "*As the director of the IOR, he (Chief*

Secretary) was in control of the church's money," Catherine says.

h) The clandestine Meeting of high-ranking Catholic Church hierarchy at a privately – owned Catholic Church in Rome property is on. Chapter XX, page 145-147, *"Palace of the Vatican ...Papal apartments magnificent buildings of Bernini...In five minutes he* (Zagranski-Chief Secretary) *walked up two flights of stairs of the church – owned property".* He is meeting with his confidante and other Opus Dei men of high rank in the church. *"Besides Cardinal Hernandez (being kidnapped) a substantial amount of money..."*

iv. The TDC account:

a) TDC copies the title and function Chief *"First Secretary"* to the Pope, Pope John Paul II, and the *"Head of the Opus Dei".*

b) TDC Page 40, *"Perhaps you know him? Manuel Aringarosa?" "The head of the Opus Dei?" "Of course I know of him. Who in the church doesn't?"* Sister Sandrine says giving a description of the Opus Dei that is the same as in TVB on page 5-5 and page 78 and page 130-132.

c) TDC, page 40, *"In 1982 Pope John Paul II unexpectedly elevated them to a "personal prelature of the Pope". "Suspiciously, Opus*

Dei's elevation occurred the same year the wealthy sect allegedly had transferred almost one <u>billion</u> in the Vatican's Institute for Religious Works – commonly known as the Vatican Bank – bailing it out of an embarrassing bankruptcy..." Escrivá is fast-tracked for sainthood same as in TVB, page 6.

d) TDC page 173, Bishop Aringarosa the head of the Opus Dei goes to the Catholic Church – owned property Meeting in Rome, "*Castel Gandolfo... "Welcome Bishop*," a man's voice said from across the room. The *Secretariat Vaticana*, overlord of all legal matters within Vatican City. The other two were high-ranking Italian cardinals. (Chief Secretary to the Pope and the Head of the Opus Dei meet to discuss matter related to the Vatican Bank).

e) "The funds are exactly as I requested?" (Covert monies are given to the Head of the Opus Dei by the secretarius to the Pope who controls the Vatican Bank.)

f) "*The secretarius nodded, "Large denomination bearer bonds drawn on the Vatican Bank. Negotiable as cash anywhere in the world.*" The secretarius is in charge of the Vatican Bank's – IOR money.

g) "*Aringarosa defended. "Opus Dei is a personal prelature of Vatican City, and His*

Holiness can disperse monies however he sees fit." Aringarosa eyed the sheet before him. *It bore the Papal Seal.* "*This is identical to the copy you sent me?*"

h) TDC page 415 -416, Meeting inside Castle Gandolfo changed Head of Opus Dei Aringarosa's life, "*But only three people were present.*"

i) "*The Vatican secretarius. Obese. Dour.*"

j) "*Secretarius?*" *Aringarosa said, puzzled.* "*As you are aware.*" *The secretarius said,* "*His holiness and other in Rome have been concerned lately with the political fallout from Opus Dei's more controversial practices.*" "*I want to assure you,*" *the secretarius added quickly,* "*that His Holiness does not seek to change anything about the way you run your ministry.*" "*Bishop, I am not sure how to say this delicately, so I will state it directly. Two days ago, the Secretariat Council voted unanimously to revoke the Vatican's sanction of Opus Dei.*" "*His Holiness agrees and we are already drawing up the legal papers.*" "*His Holiness has become uneasy...*" *Aringarosa shot to his feet,* "*As His Holiness if Opus Dei was an embarrassment in 1982 when we helped the Vatican Bank.*" "*The Vatican will always be* grateful for that," the secretarius said, his tone appeasing, "and yet there are those who still believe your financial munificence in 1982 is the only reason you were granted prelature status in the first place."

v.   In a book called **The Truth about Da Vinci** that was written as study about what in TDC is fictional and what is factual this is the relevant section:

> **Secretariat Vaticana**
> Fictitious Roman Catholic official in **The Da Vinci Code** who exercises control over the pope's financial and legal matters (173, 415). Somewhat similar in type to the Vatican's Secretary of State, who has no control over the finances of the pope or of the Roman Catholic Church.

3. <u>The billion-dollar payment fiction allied to the beatification of the founder of Opus Dei</u>

i.   TVB

a) In TVB page 5-7; Escrivá's beatification is characterized as questionable and Opus Dei's financial influence over the church as suspicious. Opus Dei's, "*intricate worldwide financial empire exercised considerable influence on the church*". It was for this reason that, "the beatification was taking place a mere seventeen years after his death, and signified some of the "greatest changes in procedure ever to take place in Western religious history."

b) See also- TVB page 78, "*In 1928 with the approval and help of Pope John Paul II, Opus Dei was made a personal prelature.*"

c) On page 130 of TVB the IOR was given "*billions of Dollars by the bankers.*"

d) And TVB page 127, "*without the financial support of the Opus Dei, the Catholic Church would have been broke.*"

   ii.   TDC

a) TDC page 40-41- "*the Pope placed the founder of Opus Dei on the 'fast track' to sainthood, accelerating the often century long waiting period for canonization to a mere twenty years.*" And, "*Suspiciously Opus Dei's elevation to a prelature occurred in the same year (1982) the Opus Dei wealthy sect allegedly transferred one billion dollars into the Vatican's IOR Institute for Religious Works commonly known as the Vatican Bank, bailing it out of an embarrassing bankruptcy.*"

b) TDC page 40-41 – Use of the year 1982 – Money transfers (one billion dollars) to the IOR by Opus Dei in TDC.

4. The fictional Vatican conclave

   i.   There is also a Vatican conclave in the late

1990's featured in both books – which both purport to have been the based on the Catholic Church's real identity and activities – despite the fact that there was in fact no such conclave

ii.   TVB – Page 5-7; *"Pope John Paul II, resplendent in white and gold vestments, was sweating profusely as he stood before the hastily constructed altar in St. Peter's Square. Nevertheless he ignored the sweltering heat and dutifully conferred the rites of beatification upon Josemaria Escrivá de Balaguer."* The ceremony is described as controversial. The ceremony was the centrepiece of a conclave (late 1990's) of Opus Dei officials to set the organization's future agenda and to plan tactics to strengthen its financial position in the church.

iii.   TDC – Page 148; *"Five months ago, the Vatican had phoned to request Aringarosa's presence in Rome... Aringarosa had no choice but to accept the invitation. Not a fan of the current papal administration, Aringarosa, like most conservative clergy, had watched with grave concern as the new Pope settled into his first year in office. An unprecedented liberal, His Holiness had secured the papacy through one of the most controversial and unusual conclaves in Vatican history"* (late 1990's).

Acknowledgments

Jack Dunn

In life we are all presented with challenges and have to make choices and moral decisions to have a code with which to live. The ones we decide upon determine the course of our lives to fulfil our destinies. Along the road in my life, I have had the help of many wonderful people to decide what path I would take. To name everyone who supported me would be impossible. But my friends know who they are and I cannot thank them enough, whether they are dead or alive.

As always, I am thankful for my family, especially my daughter Kim and my grandchildren, Liam, Rory, and Ainsley and their father Andy Rose.

I would be remiss if I did not name a few people who have been there for me in the last twenty years; Don and Jean Brunelle, Marty Dunn, Terry Ashe, Tom Kenefick, Thom Hays, Barry and Fletcher Poret, Mike Williams, Sam and Alberta Pizzi, Bill Wegrzyn, Benjamin and Kathleen Kilbourne, Claus and Anita Agerskov, Tim and Donna Zielinski, Mike Dominov, Dave Rodriguez, and Elisandro Cuevas to name only a few.

In writing this book, there have been many hands and minds at work, together. It could not have been produced without the talents and intellects of Jonathan Coad, Humfrey Hunter, Gary Ensor, Howie Safford, Alan Perlman, Árpád Burányi, Don Moorhouse, Dave and Cory Horgan and a very special thanks the very intelligent, Ian Ghanni for her keen insights and emotional support.

Finally, on that fateful day in London when I first met Jonathan Coad and this story took a turn for the better, after I was through showing him what I had collected for evidence to prove Dan Brown copied my book, Jonathan asked me to pray with him. I did this and he asked Jesus Christ – one of whose titles is 'the Truth' – to give us the strength to do His wishes and fight this battle in His name. In that this book is now in print, I have to assume that our prayers were answered.

Further, I am eternally grateful to Jonathan Coad, my co-writer and a legal genius, for his brilliant writing and evaluations of the legal principles that are the cornerstone of this book. It would not exist without his tireless work and his faith that in this world there is a distinguishing place for righteous behaviours. He is truly a man with superior morals and integrity and thinks and acts in a manner that should be emulated by all seekers of the truth on this earth and beyond.

Humfrey Hunter is much-admired for his own contributions to the production of this book and his unwavering courage in the face of what some would view as insurmountable odds. Like Jonathan Coad, he is an inspiration for me and for those others who demand that Justice everywhere, be served, not desecrated or destroyed.

To all of you – This is your true story too!

Jonathan Coad

I entirely attribute the pleasure of meeting Jack and Humfrey to God's grace, as I do the absolute delight of co-writing this book. The primary aim of my life is faithfully to serve Jesus Christ, one of whose names is the "Truth", which I believe this book to be, and one which the world should be told.

My profound thanks to Jack and Humfrey for according me the immense privilege of working with them on this wonderful project. I dedicate my part in writing this book to Charlotte, Emily and Benjy, all of whom I love dearly; and to Jesus Christ, to whom I owe everything.

The Authors

Jack Dunn is an international, award-winning author – 2008 USA IPPY Silver Medal for historical fiction. He has written 14 novels and 2 screenplays. His unique style of writing is a fact or fiction blending of historical events set in present day with fast-paced action and are thriller stories. His first book, *The Diary of General William Goffe* was released in 1982. It was syndicated in The New England region *Advocate* newspapers in weekly installments. It is estimated that from Vermont to New York City millions of readers read the story. *The Dance through the Maze* followed next in 1989. *The Vatican Boys* was first published and released in 1997. Then came *Holyoke, The Belle Skinner Legacy* in 2005 and *Dan's Big Idea* in 2007. The 2008 novel *Babylon's Tablet of Destiny* won Jack the prestigious national writing award presented in New York City in 2009. *Ark Evil* was published in 2010, *The Third Secret of Fatima – Spanish Atlantis* followed in 2012, *The Little Book of Copying* in 2013, *Dagon's Hat in 2013* and *Whorlland* in 2014. *The Brown Code* followed in 2014 and *The Durer Mystery* in 2015. Jack's most recent story, *Devils in the Country – The Jack Dunn Story* was released in 2016. Jack travels all over the world to find material for his stories, searching libraries, historical sites, remote places and secret histories that have long been forgotten. He lives in Western Massachusetts.

Jonathan Coad graduated from Jesus College Cambridge with an MA in law and pursued a successful career as a media lawyer. His practice areas are copyright, defamation and privacy. His media clients have included Disney, ITV, Sky, Viacom, MTV, Channel 4, Sony, *Huffington Post* and *Newsweek*. He has undertaken reputation management work for corporate clients such as Amazon, Procter & Gamble, Gucci, GlaxoSmithKline and Cambridge University. He has also acted for high-profile business moguls, senior politicians, music, TV, film and sports stars and members of the Royal Family. His book *Reputation Matters* is published early next year by Bloomsbury.

CPSIA information can be obtained
at www.ICGtesting.com
Printed in the USA
BVHW061955111121
621211BV00006B/900

9 781913 727116